LITERATURE AND SOCIETY

Literature and Society

Edited, with a Preface, by Edward W. Said

THE JOHNS HOPKINS UNIVERSITY PRESS
BALTIMORE AND LONDON

Originally published in 1980 as Selected Papers from
the English Institute, 1978, New Series, No. 3
Johns Hopkins Paperbacks edition, 1986

The Johns Hopkins University Press
701 West 40th Street
Baltimore, Maryland 21211
The Johns Hopkins Press Ltd., London

Library of Congress Cataloging in Publication Data

English Institute.
  Literature and society.

  (Selected papers from the English Institute; 1978,
new ser., no. 3)
    1. English literature—History and criticism—
Addresses, essays, lectures. 2. Literature and society
—Addresses, essays, lectures. I. Said, Edward W.
II. Title. III. Series: English Institute. Selected
papers from the English Institute; 1978, new ser.,
no. 3.
PR99.E67   1980   820'.9   79–17484
ISBN 0–8018–2294–7
ISBN 0–8018–3346–9 (pbk.)

Contents

Preface   vii
Edward W. Said

The Wages of Satire   1
Harry Levin

Chaucer's "New Men" and the Good of Literature
in the *Canterbury Tales*
Anne Middleton   15

Improvisation and Power
Stephen J. Greenblatt   57

"To Entrap the Wisest": A Reading of *The
Merchant of Venice*
René Girard   100

A Social History of Fact and Fiction: Authorial
Disavowal in the Early English Novel
Lennard J. Davis   120

Text, Ideology, Realism
Terry Eagleton   149

Ad/d Feminam: Women, Literature, and Society
Catharine R. Stimpson   174

Preface

With the exception of the essays by Terry Eagleton and Catharine Stimpson, which were specially commissioned for this occasion, all of the papers gathered together in this volume were read at the annual meeting of the English Institute in September 1978. Anne Middleton's paper on Chaucer was part of a panel on that poet; the remaining four made up a section entitled "Literature and Society."

Despite these differing circumstances all seven essays have, I think, a general common intention, and it is about this, and about the intellectual project of which it is a part, that I should like to make a series of observations.

Anyone who has attended the English Institute over the past decade will agree that an important intellectual shift took place during that period. Not every paper presented then exemplified the shift, but a significant, or at least a noticeable, number did. The simplest way of describing this change is to say that many people became interested in *criticism*, not as a kind of literate, discriminating gloss on a "primary" text, but as an activity that, in drawing on such disciplines as linguistics, psychoanalysis, anthropology, and philosophy, made much of itself as a highly specialized, often tendentious theoretical mode of discourse. One result is that the accepted reliance on the work of literature as coming before criticism not only in time but also in value was given up. A critic now seemed to draw many of his or her insights from another critic, and looked to other criticism rather than to poetry, say, for his or her best thought. Certainly this has often been the case with criticism since Coleridge, but rarely before has criticism seemed so self-sufficient. Naturally enough, this new fact of criticism emerged in many discussions during the Institute's meetings, sometimes even causing anger and a certain polarization within the Institute's normally amiable constituency.

I have little doubt that a good deal of the change can be explained by a few fairly obvious things. Any list of causes would have to include the extraordinary infusion into American (and more recently into English) critical discourse of European—especially French—criticism (*criticism* in the broadest definition of that word). Fifteen years ago few graduate students of English would have heard of Ferdinand de Saussure; today his *Cours générale* is as familiar and as potent-seeming as Freud's writings were forty years ago. Styles and critical strategies seem more commonly set in Paris than in New York or Chicago, and along with the ascendance in new authorities there has been a decline in older ones. For instance, English studies, or "english" as F. R. Leavis proselytized for it, seem no longer to stand at the very center of the literary curriculum. Allowing even for the perhaps modish and transient vogue of "interdisciplinary" studies that started off in the late sixties, we can say that on the whole there has been a serious, broadening attention paid to writing that hovers on the peripheries of strictly literary discourse—to myths, to the materials of popular culture, to sociological and psychological texts, to the work of philosophical and historical hybrids (Nietzsche, Rousseau, Bataille, and others). In a sense, then, there has been a reemergence of *comparative* literature, if by using that term we do not restrict the phenomenon either to philology or to the thematic study of works in their original languages. For, indeed, the new comparative style is metacritical, transnational, intertextual. Translations are used to establish affiliations and associations between genres, authors, national cultures, and traditions. And the net effect has been a new sense of freedom and speculation in the production of criticism.

But there have been drawbacks, and here we come to the putative mission of a volume like this one, none of whose authors can be considered *arrière* when it comes to using and understanding the most recent developments in the New New Criticism, as it has come to be called. My own estimate is that a paradoxical situation exists today. On the one hand there has never been so much attention to and debate about criticism; on the other hand, rarely has there been such a removal of criticism and critical attention from the ongoing production of society and history. (I would like to be understood here as speaking self-critically, since my own work and my own sympathies have always been engaged with the New New Criticism.) A mode of thought developed in the social, political, and cultural circumstances of Paris or Vienna or Berlin gets adopted in the American academy as a mode of thought, just that, and it has rapidly tended to become an orthodoxy mindlessly followed by a whole band of academic enthusiasts. To read an "advanced" critic today is often to read writing that is essentially a highly rarified jargon. The historical sense, the rudiments of scholarship and curiosity (which in the past have always characterized even the most abstract of serious theorists), seem no longer to have much to tell a new theorist. Above all, in much of the New New Criticism the issues debated do not involve values or social and cultural questions or urgent philosophical questions; they most often are about "texts" (so that one is made to feel that there are only texts), they deal in complex abstractions whose main reference is to other complex abstractions, their dense language belies a thin texture of ideas, experience, history.

Having said all this, I must not seem to be saying that I agree with many of the attacks on the New New Criticism now appearing in journals here and abroad. Most of those attacks are made from the rather empty standpoint of "humanistic" scholarship, which seems no less marginal, unworldly, and rarified than some of the theory being attacked. No: the New New Criticism has provided the current generation of literary and humanistic students with invaluable insights into cultural activity, and these must not be thrown out wholesale in the interests of a discredited conservative philosophy of gentlemanly refinement, or sensibility. Certainly the present volume takes no such backward-looking thesis for its point of departure. What it does concern itself with, however, is the situation of writing in history and in human society, and it attempts to deal with this complex subject from many viewpoints, all of which are informed but by no means emasculated by the latest trends in modern critical theory.

This was the mandate given our contributors by the English Institute Supervising Board. This and some generalities about how it was becoming increasingly untenable to maintain that everything in the world "was—or could be considered—a text." The gain for critical writing in the sheaf of papers that has ensued is considerable, and I need here only to indicate their range quickly.

Harry Levin's discussion of satire locates that perennial form in the world of politics, morality, and human desire, yet, touched by his customary learning and precision, each of Levin's references safeguards the satirist's circumstantial actuality. In Lennard Davis's essay on the emergence of the novel we have an original, erudite analysis of the form's paraliterary origins, not only in the newspapers of the late seventeenth century, but also in structures of law and power. Both Davis and Stephen Greenblatt, whose paper on Shakespeare is one of this volume's two unusual and brilliant examinations of that poet's dramatic practice, draw on Michel Foucault's analytic research into the "archeology" of authority and discourse; yet Greenblatt's discussion goes further than Foucault in tracing the precise "field," so to speak, of Shakespeare's invention, into what he calls "improvisation." The second Shakespearean essay, by the eminent Romance scholar René Girard, advances a socioanthropological thesis that draws for its force on Girard's famous studies of ritual violence, his theory of scapegoating, and his sense of a communal, almost guildlike band of initiates. Anne Middleton's impressively learned, detailed survey of Chaucer's "new men" combines, with singular grace, literary analysis with social commentary in the interests of sketching for us the outlines of Chaucer's literary "world." Finally, in the papers by Terry Eagleton and Catharine Stimpson, we have two canonically contemporary critical discourses—on the one hand Marxism and formalism, on the other, feminism— being made to yield unusually perspicacious lessons. Eagleton focuses severely on the question of realism, that central and persistent problem of aesthetics, and treats it in the ambience of ideology, an ideology encoded but by no means exhausted by linguistics, deconstructionism, and Lacanian analysis. For her part Catharine Stimpson puts forward an intelligent statement of the possibilities for feminist writing, and it is to her credit that she in no way reduces her subject to easy formulas. For her, "women's literature" produces discoveries and communities that are interwoven with the societies, the bodies, and the cultural formation of Vico's "world of nations": in her essay sexual differentiation is thus released from its bondage to what she calls "powerful, discriminatory ideologies."

In sum, this volume of essays from the English Institute demonstrates the vitality of the interchange in criticism between literature and society. No attempt has been made to have these essays make any monolithic affirmation (or definition) of either a literature or a society, though this is not to say that our critics pretend to value-free neutrality. At very least, then, this volume is a collective act of critical consciousness, as much to be regarded for critical knowledge as for social-historical engagement.

Edward W. Said

LITERATURE AND SOCIETY

Harry Levin

The Wages of Satire

> It is indeed acting but a poor part in life, to make a
> business of laughing at the follies of others. It is in-
> jurious to one's self; for there is a great deal more to
> be gained by soothing and praising what men do, than
> by finding fault with them. It may be said of satire,
> what was said of anger by some philosopher, it never
> pays the service it requires.

This epigraph comes tongue-in-cheek from Hugh Henry
Brackenridge's *Modern Chivalry*, that picaresque novel which—
rather more incisively than the mock-epic effusions of the so-
called Connecticut Wits—scrutinized the American republic in
its formative years. It may well happen that such endeavors fall on
infertile soil. Dickens's first visit higher led him to the impression
that "no satirist could breathe this air." Ambrose Bierce made
repeated attempts and embittered complaints before his ultimate
disappearance across the Mexican border. Mark Twain enacted the
paradigmatic role of the muffled satirical genius. Moss Hart laid
down a Broadway definition: "Satire is what closes on Saturday
night." Our talented neighbor, Robertson Davies, has drawn a suggestive inference from the somewhat more recent Canadian experience: "Countries that are not always sure of their own identity
are understandably suspicious of satirists." During the present
century we Americans have become pretty sure of our identity,
for better or for worse, and the attendant complacencies have
called forth the increasingly mordant critiques of H. L. Mencken,
Sinclair Lewis, John Dos Passos, Nathanael West, and the current
generation of black humorists. Ours must be among those times
and places, like Juvenal's, when it seems difficult not to write
satire. When such an impetus gets voiced in protest, there must be
at least a hope for some response.

Yet satirists have characteristically spoken of facing a hopeless as
well as a thankless task. Earnestly they have reaffirmed the jest of
Brackenridge: satire does not pay, it has seldom rewarded the

1

strenuous exertions that have gone into it. "Perhaps," so Dr. Johnson has attested, "neither Pope nor Boileau has made the world much better than he found it." And Swift, in a purported letter from Gulliver to his cousin and editor, Richard Sympson, confided impatiently: "I cannot learn that my book hath produced one single effect according to my intention." Political parties are still riven by factions; law courts are still teeming with abuses; men and women go on behaving like Yahoos, in spite of what they might have learned by reading *Gulliver's Travels* during the almost seven months since its publication. As for Voltaire, he rarely mentioned satire without deploring it, regarding it as unwarranted attack and himself as primarily a defender. When it was not "le poison de la littérature" it was "ce genre funeste, ce métier in-fâme"—colluding through that last adjective with everything he detested. His *Mémoire sur la satire* was a counterattack on his detractors. Anticipating Johnson, he asked himself what the satires of Boileau had accomplished, and answered that the results were nugatory even when they were not detrimental to both sides.

For unqualified belief in the power of satire, we should have to turn back—as Robert C. Elliott does in his interesting book of that name—to a primitive state of mind which believed as strongly in curses as in blessings. Seen within its own purview, malediction was a form of tribal magic, and Irish bards could exterminate rats by enunciating the appropriate rhymes. Satirists are like witches who stick pins in the effigies of their enemies. Professor Elliott likewise recalls Archilochus, their Greek prototype, whose aveng-ing iambics reportedly drove his fiancée and her promise-breaking father to suicide. But this was not a supernatural feat, since they had been shamed into acting upon their own volition. Their action did depend on communal standards of conformity and on the poet's effort to maintain them by scoffing publicly at deviations from them. Satire addresses its appeal to a sense of shame, accord-ing to Evelyn Waugh, among others. Hence, he would imply, it is devalued in a period as shameless as our own, when writers expose themselves. The most traditional function of poetry has been to dispense praise or blame, *laus et vituperatio*. At the higher level, hymns and dithyrambs celebrated the exemplary virtues of gods and heroes. On the lower plane, the object lessons were cautionary lampoons of meaner subjects. All that Aristotle had to say in the matter was to draw the foregoing distinction.

Sheer invective could be ceremonialized. The flyting, where insults were traded, was a game to be judged by the virtuosity of the rival name-callers. Carnivals, betrothals, and other rites of initiation featured licensed episodes of hazing, charivari, or pasquinade. Satire, as a literary genre, has never been easy to pin down. Though the Romans—through Quintilian—claimed it as their own, they could only define it as a mixed mode, with a Hellenic precedent in Menippus, whose lost medleys would ripen into the dialogues of Lucian and Erasmus. Insofar as it gives vent to denunciation and diatribe, satire has much in common with the prophet's jeremiad or the statesman's philippic. It often coincides with pamphleteering, as in Junius or Courier, not to mention Swift. Habitually stepping into controversy, its implicit war cries are "J'accuse!" and "I will be heard!" But it must be distinguished from such plaints as that of *Piers Plowman* or of Harriet Beecher Stowe by its closer dependence on comic techniques. Significantly, though the verb *to satirize* is of Latin origin, its synonym in Greek was κομωδειν: literally, *to comedize*. Yet Milton relates it to the tragic impulse and Brecht to the epic key. Comedy always has a satiric potential, usually balanced—and in Shakespeare's case overbalanced—by its purely festive or romantic element.

When comedy becomes more purposeful than playful, then it is satire. The most direct and powerful conjunction of the two has been the Old Comedy of Aristophanes, inasmuch as it held an institutional place in the city-state of Athens. This has frequently been compared to a municipal pillory, since it represented actual personages and subjected them to unsparing mockeries. Witness its recurrent target, Cleon, the war-mongering demagogue. Aristophanes, censured for one such allusion, forbidden to let his actor use an identifying mask, sarcastically mimicked a recognizable quirk of Cleon's speech in *The Knights*. But the Peloponnesian War continued nonetheless, meting out ironic retribution to the bellicose politician—now a general—by killing him off. Aristophanes could boast of having dared to oppose civic policy, but not of having affected it. Though the plays were popular, "the people were far from being guided by the same sentiments in the theater and in the elections," as the commentator Maurice Croiset remarked. It is a disquieting afterthought that Aristophanes may have exerted more impact when he ridiculed Socrates in *The Clouds*. That charlatanical figure was presented as the polar opposite of its living model. Whereas the original embodied the self-deprecating wisdom of the *eiron*, the caricature exhibited the specious pretensions to knowledge of an alazon.

Pedantry forever invites and merits derision, but scoffers are sometimes too ready to suspect it in the techniques of empirical science. Swift would burlesque the Royal Society, in his Academy of Lagado, with experiments as idiotic as those performed in Aristophanes' think tank, the Phrontisterion. Both satirists thereby lay themselves open to a possible charge of anti-intellectualism, and there is more than a tinge of the philistine in Aristophanes' campaign against the newfangled notions of Euripides. We are aware that the animus of *The Clouds* was not ad hominem; Aristophanes converses warmly with the real Socrates in that happiest of conversations, Plato's *Symposium*. The veritable target, dialectically dramatized in the agon between personifications of right and wrong, was the demoralizing influence of the Sophists; and Plato sets on record, in his *Protagoras*, a Socrates who is the sharpest critic of the Sophists' school of thought. Lessing has argued that the spectators recognized this difference when Socrates attended the performance and stood up, that Aristophanes—while portraying a "dangerous Sophist"—had merely misappropriated the proper name. The resulting confusion is like what happens with many a roman à clef, when the sins of a fictitious character are visited upon his human semblance. Aristophanes' strictures contributed to the danger that menaced Socrates, if not to his subsequent execution.

That was a Pyrrhic victory for satire. If the Aristophanic inquest proved ineffectual with the slippery Cleon, it succeeded in tainting the most virtuous of philosophers. Since the playwright was not an ideologue, his ideas were not especially consistent or systematic. Yet he had his positive values; he was an inveterate *laudator temporis acti*; and he reckoned with contemporary turbulence by the more peaceable criteria of the noble old Athenian democracy. Every satirist, negative though he may sound, must project his guided missiles from a launching pad of belief. Carlyle's nagging was grounded in his hero worship; Tacitus, denouncing the Roman emperors, idealized the Germanic chiefs. Dos Passos, testifying for himself and other realists who were disillusioned idealists, has written: "Maybe it is that the satirist is so full of the possibilities of humankind in general that he tends to draw a dark and garish picture when he tries to depict people as they are at any particular moment." In terms of Aristotelian logic, we must look for the enthymeme: the unexpressed principle, the unstated premise of an abridged syllogism, the affirmative conviction that lies behind the pejorative demonstration. To the extent that this can be taken for granted and shared with his public, it is an advantage for the satirist to speak from a conservative position, to be confirmed by a status quo.

Not that he is necessarily bound to become a spokesman for the Tories on any given issue. (Even Swift started out as a Whig, choosing panegyric as his earliest strain, and transposing it to satire after he had experienced worldly disappointments and ideological tergiversations.) But we do encounter a problem here which was formulated rather apologetically by Lionel Trilling in his well-known essay "The Liberal Imagination," with its large concessions to literary conservatism. We need not ignore the converse attitudes summed up by Van Wyck Brooks when he declared that the heart of the American writer was on the left. Yet the satirist must convince his audience that, when something is rotten or someone goes astray, there has been a departure from a certain ethos. It is simpler for him when the norms of that ethos have already been accepted by convention. Otherwise, it becomes a part of his job to inculcate those norms—in other words, to preach to the unconverted. He must be hortatory before he can wax sardonic, like Bernard Shaw in the prefaces to his plays. Satire is perceived as a radical force in the sense that it disturbs the peace, that it undermines the vested interests, which remain poised to resist and to strike back. It is not a question of politics but of human nature that we find it so much easier to reject novelties than we do to criticize traditions.

And, since not every change is an improvement, it serves little purpose to align our satirists along a spectrum extending from progressive to reactionary. All of them are iconoclasts in the most literal sense, in that they have dedicated themselves to the breaking of images. "The end of satire is reformation," affirmed Defoe. Yet reformation can look backward as well as forward. The satirist is an ipso facto moralist, promoting the good by excoriating the bad according to his lights. Albeit Shaw was more obviously an iconoclast or reformer, Aristophanes, as an avowed traditionalist, lamented the passing of a notably democratic regime. Faced with the new constraints, he underwent the straitening transition from Old to Middle Comedy in his last two surviving plays. He could draw upon his own rich vein of fantasy in avoiding the hazards of topical argument. But it was a crucial loss to omit the *parabasis*, that choric interlude which gave voice directly to the sociopolitical views of the dramatist. By the time of Menander, New Comedy had withdrawn its gaze from public to private life and had standardized its Dramatis Personae by using stock types instead of libeling extant personalities. Continuing through Plautus and Terence via the Commedia dell'Arte to an apogee in Molière, the comic stage concentrated more on general traits than on individual foibles.

Fielding would make the conventional disclaimer that fends off lawsuits based on noncoincidental resemblances: "I declare here once for all, I describe not men but manners, not an individual but a species." Molière's apologist, in his self-defense, had explained: "Son dessin est de peindre les moeurs sans vouloir toucher les personnes." At a highly serious moment, while defending *Tartuffe*, Molière added a moral emphasis: "Le devoir de la comédie est de corriger les hommes en les divertissant." Correction, as administered through schooling, involved castigation. *"Castigat ridendo mores"* was the Latin motto of the leading Franco-Italian Harlequin, one of Molière's theatrical rivals, and the schoolmaster's rod or scourge was the satirist's emblem. Swift retained his habitual doubts about its effectiveness: "Now, if I know anything of mankind, these gentlemen might very well spare their reproof and correction; for there is not, through all nature, another so callous and insensible a member as the world's posteriors, whether you apply to it the toe or the birch." Disclaiming "the satirical itch" in his preface to *A Tale of a Tub*, and arguing that panegyric is more invidious than satire, he points out that the Athenians could rail against their fellow citizens, whereas the English—though protected by libel laws—were free to level their "utmost rhetoric against mankind."

But he went on, in opening his preface to *The Battle of the Books*, to suggest that such rhetoric was lost upon the obtuse and impervious readers: "Satire is a sort of *glass*, wherein beholders do generally discover everybody's face but their own; which is the chief reason for that kind reception it meets in the world, and that so very few are offended with it." The metaphor of comedy as a mirror of human behavior (*"speculum consuetudinis"*) can be traced as far back as Cicero, and in the Middle Ages had been coupled with the moralistic hope that the viewer might be prompted to mend his reflected conduct. The fullest exposition of this idea is the Induction to Ben Jonson's *Every Man Out of His Humour*, the first of those three self-styled "comical satires" which unsuccessfully illustrated his critical and clinical theories. It is probable that Shakespeare was glancing obliquely at Jonson's saturnine spokesman when his melancholy Jaques offered to

"Cleanse the whole body of th'infected world,/If they will patiently receive my medicine." Here the image for the satirical process is not a scourge but a purge, not a punitive but a therapeutic occasion. The meaning is underscored by the vulgar pun between *Jaques* and *jakes* (the Elizabethan word for privy), which predicates a close and concrete equivalent for the catharsis of tragedy.

Pope would consider the punishment to be part of a treatment in ethical therapy. "Satire, . . ." for him, "heals with morals what it hurts with wit." For Samuel Johnson, on the other hand, such wounds found no cures. In his *Rambler* allegory on wit and learning, he opines: "Wit, cohabiting with Malice, had a son named Satyr, who followed him, carrying a quiver filled with poisoned arrows, which, where they once drew blood, could by no skill be extracted." By conflating satire with the Greek satyr play, through the usual false etymology, Johnson personified it as a sort of Cupid in reverse. Hence he tended to balk at it, as W. J. Bate has shown, despite his formidable powers as a moralist. Wits of the previous generation had been more ironically tough-minded in their prescriptions for social ills: Defoe in suggesting genocide as a remedy for dissent, Swift in proposing cannibalism as an antidote for famine. It is generally agreed that English satire enjoyed its heyday during the first half of the eighteenth century; it declined as, with the emergence of more sentimental and romantic touchstones, wit deserted malice and mellowed into humor. Addison's *Spectator* was a precursor here, anticipating Johnson with caveats against satire's poisonous darts. In the hands of Pope—who, for all his *Imitations of Horace*, took a sternly Juvenalian stance—it remained a "sacred weapon."

Far more professing to be a respecter of persons, he strove for their fullest exposure. When his interlocutor enjoins him to "spare the person and expose the vice," Pope completes the couplet by retorting: "How, sir? not damn the sharper but the dice?" Some of his victims deserve better from posterity than to have survived as mere footnotes to pungent epithets and virulent epigrams. (This is, incidentally, true of Shadwell, who wrote better comedies than Dryden, which have been disregarded because of *Mac-Flecknoe*.) But most of Pope's mothlike dunces were unworthy of the pains he took to break them upon his massive wheel (like the forgotten butts of Goethe's and Schiller's *Xenien*). As an ambitious monument to dullness, *The Dunciad* was ineluctably destined to display the attribute it celebrates. Moreover, a satiric undertaking which flails about so widely is subject to imputations that the author must be a disappointed and angry man seeking personal vengeance, wielding what Browning described in *Aristophanes' Apology* as "the comic weapon, . . . hate." Both Juvenal and Swift after him expressly acknowledged having been motivated by indignation, which can be either mean or exalted, depending upon the provocation. Swift discerned "two ends that men propose in writing satire": one, "private satisfaction"; the other, and more altruistic, "public spirit"—or, to rephrase, one revenge and the other reform.

The former may achieve its sublimation in the latter, when revenge is transposed into reform by a Swift. With a Wyndam Lewis, so manifestly begrudging the recognition accorded to some of his contemporaries, the satirist becomes a common scold whose competitive motives are suspect. With certain other temperaments, like that of Thomas Nashe, he engages in satire for its own sake, animated by sheer polemical exuberance. Its object, for an Aretino, is no more than blackmail. If poets are unacknowledged legislators, satirists may be self-appointed arbiters of morals. Often constrained to publish anonymously or under a pseudonym, they are adept and protean at establishing a persona, which may range from the urbane Horatian conversationalist to the impressionable Voltairean ingénu. They are likewise so prone to distort or exaggerate that their proffered mirror images go unrecognized by many of their beholders. When, if ever, can we be sure that the weapon has hit its mark, or—to put it more constructively—that the medicine has effected a cure? Joseph Hall, who proclaimed himself the first English satirist, divided his experimental productions into two categories: "toothless" and "biting satires." The first were by definition impotent, if not a contradiction in terms. The second constituted just enough of an irritant to get the biter bitten. In 1599, by a decree of the Anglican Church, all such works were banned and condemned to be burned.

The sacred weapon could turn out to be a boomerang. Satire runs a continual risk from the backlash of suppression. Furthermore, as Isaac D'Israeli noted, "Satirists, if they escape the scourge of the law, have reason to dread the cane of the satirized." Thus Dryden was beaten up by the hired thugs of the Earl of Rochester, as was Voltaire in his turn by those of the Chevalier de Rohan— and then, when the victim protested, he was victimized further by imprisonment in the Bastille. Juvenal had been exiled by the Emperor Domitian; so would Victor Hugo be under Louis Napoleon. Swift seems to have been denied a bishopric because Queen Anne was too literal-minded a reader to follow the religious parable in *A Tale of a Tub*. Defoe's heavily ironic pamphlet, *The Shortest Way with the Dissenters*, misfired with still more adverse consequences to the author, who was pilloried for seditious libel. Thereupon, cheered by the people who witnessed his official disgrace, he wrote an unregenerate "Hymn to the Pillory," along with a *Brief Explanation* of his intentions: "If any man take the pains seriously to reflect upon the contents, the nature of the thing, and the manner of the style, it seems impossible to imagine that it should pass for anything but an irony." Yet, taken at face value, it had been denounced by fellow Dissenters while being hailed by the Tory extremists whose bigotry it mocked.

Benjamin Franklin used a similar tactic in *An Edict of the King of Prussia*, where the ironic pretense was that Germany would exact the same demands from Britain that the British were exacting from the American colonies. Resident in England when it appeared, Franklin was amused to watch English friends being all but taken in by the hoax before recognizing its critical thrust. Irony is so ambiguous a device—not to say two-edged—that it is more than ordinarily susceptible to miscarriage, since it aims at levels of perception beyond the ironist's control. Socrates was both its incarnation and its martyr. Lord Northcliffe is reported to have forbidden its use in his newspapers on the grounds that it misled too many readers and that it was resented by most of those who understood. Shaftesbury, who had more confidence in the reading public of his day, had been willing to let it judge for itself. Satire was a corrective for him, "a remedy against vice" and a vehicle of poetic justice. From the postulate, "Nothing is ridiculous except what is deformed," he reasoned that "a subject which could not bear raillery was suspicious," and came to the reverberating conclusion that ridicule was the test of truth, "which may bear all lights." This accords with President Truman's assertion that a demagogue cannot stand laughter (evidently he was not thinking of Cleon). But it does not fit in well with the libelous put-down of the truthseeker, Socrates.

Tested in the light of history, the Shaftesbury-Truman doctrine seems to have been overoptimistic. Hitler's demagogy was incomparably worse than Cleon's; and it evoked a folklore of underground humor among his victims; but that could hardly have resulted in dismissing him as a laughingstock. Conversely, the grotesque cartoons in Nazi publications like *Der Stürmer* made effective propaganda for Antisemitism. Gibes could hurt the underdog if not the top dog, who was insulated from the stings of defamation. Today, on the other side of the Iron Curtain, jokes against the government abound. One of the oldest and most familar might be reiterated as an archetype. A comrade asks, "What is the difference between capitalism and socialism?" To which his more sophisticated comrade replies: "Capitalism is the exploitation of man by man, and socialism is the reverse." This not only neutralizes the purport of the basic Marxian antithesis; it parodies the doctrinaire tone of a communist catechism. It could not be more subversive, yet it has propagated, and seems to have had no practical effect. Perhaps it may have functioned, like *samizdat*, to register alternative possibilities under repressive conditions. But such muted disgruntlement might also have acted as a safety valve to let off steam from a dissidence which could otherwise have exploded. A joke, by Freud's account, is a way of sublimating hostility.

Under these clandestine circumstances, the fight is for survival rather than conquest; the commitment is to keep an ethic of humanity alive against monstrous odds. Since totalitarian regimes have trouble in living up to their own propaganda, they offer a standing incitement to satire, which of course they can ill afford. It broke out in Soviet Russia, while permitted, through such ironists as Bulgakov, Kataev, and Ilf-and-Petrov; and, though now suppressed in the mother country, is exported by Siniavsky and Voinovich. Yet their major theme, the bunglings of the bureaucracy, had deep roots in the Tsarist tradition, and could hark back to Gogol as its past master. Curiously enough, the work of literature that influenced the course of Russian empire most decisively was composed by the least didactic of its great novelists, Turgenev's *Sketches of a Sportsman*. This has been credited with playing a part in the demise of serfdom, mutatis mutandis, comparable to that of the heavier-handed *Uncle Tom's Cabin* in the abolition of slavery. Doubtless neither could have been more than a contributing factor, publicizing a historical movement which battled on many different fronts. Dickens, as Humphrey House has demonstrated, was not so much a social reformer as he was a humanitarian publicist. Did Cervantes smile Spain's chivalry away, as Byron regretted, or did he smile to see it crumble away?

Questions regarding the efficacy of satire as a means of signalizing and attaining definite objectives are more readily met when they involve particular cases rather than widespread causes. Voltaire's crowded and prolonged career was a sequence of crusades against the despotic and superstitious adversaries that he lumped together under his militant slogan *"Ecrasez l'infâme!"* His successes could be measured by the campaigns he waged and won on behalf of those condemned to death for heresy: the rehabilitation of Calas (unhappily posthumous), the actual deliverance of Sirven. He could not have done this without recourse to "public opinion"–a concept he was early in formulating. Gibbon would introduce it into English not long afterward, and Jefferson would duly apply it in an American context. Voltaire's strategy was posited upon the growth of a literate middle-class audience, and consequently a greater concern for its sympathies and potential support. Swift, among his devastating Houynhnhyms, had disparaged relativistic opinion in favor of absolute reason; but that was not held up to men as an attainable ideal. He had previously triumphed as a pamphleteer, fabricating his Bickerstaff predictions to confound the quack almanacs of John Partridge. "The Dean did by his pen defeat/An infamous destructive cheat," Swift was entitled to crow in self-eulogy after his *Drapier's Letters* had deflated the monopolistic coinage of William Wood.

Facetiously, a year before he published *Gulliver's Travels*, Swift told a friend that it would "mend the world." He was speaking more seriously in a better-known letter to Pope, when he announced a countervailing intention "to vex the world rather than divert it." There too he disclosed the "great foundation of misanthropy" on which he was constructing his masterpiece: "I have ever hated all nations, professions, and communities, and all my love is toward individuals. . . . But principally I detest that animal called man, although I heartily love John, Peter, Thomas, and so forth." Satire at that stage moves beyond revenges and reforms, well beyond individuals or institutions, toward a sweeping overview of the human condition. Nothing is so broadening for our perspectives as travel, and it is no accident that so many satires—from Lucian's *True History* onward—are *voyages imaginaires*. These detach us from our culture-bound scales of measurement, whether by diminution in Lilliput (whose inhabitants are one-twelfth the size of man) or by magnification in Brobdingnag (where the natives are twelve times larger than ordinary humans). Voltaire's interplanetary science fiction, with *Micromégas*, comprises both extremes in the very name. Whether a giant is less absurd than a dwarf hinges upon the observer's height. Swift was even-handed in discerning the frailties or blemishes of each—unlike Rabelais, whose gigantism was much more high-spirited.

Reduction is the more habitual method of imposing absurdity. George Orwell reduces society to the rusticity of a beast-fable in *Animal Farm*, and to the regimentation of a dystopia in *1984*. Yet belittlement can scarcely be envisioned without a corresponding enlargement in the point of view. This might be termed—in the wake of Brecht—a *Verfremdungseffekt*, a deliberate alienation or psychic distancing. Though satirists can all too easily get enmeshed in petty immediacies, the greatest satires are those that take the longest views: *Gulliver's Travels*, preeminently, along with the closely affiliated *contes philosophiques* of Voltaire. The Frenchman, in spite of contemporaneous prestige as a philosopher, poet, and dramatist, survives for us largely because of these bagatelles. Though they rapidly and cynically venture across the world and into outer space, they return to the darkest and deepest problems of mankind, not to solve them but to sustain the episodic inquiry. *Candide*, which so rigorously tests and so critically undermines the philosophy of its subtitle, *L'Optimisme*, is concerned with nothing less than theodicy: cosmic justice, the nature of evil, the preoccupation of *King Lear*. *Zadig* arrives at a conventional happy ending after an extremely gloomy chapter in which a hermit, who turns into an angel, urges the hero to accept a grossly malfunctioning universe. The hero's last word, interrupted by the flight of the angel, is "*Mais*—." The satirist's vocation might be succinctly epitomized in that suspended monosyllable: "But—."

 *Anne Middleton*

Chaucer's "New Men" and the Good of Literature in the *Canterbury Tales*

The good of literature for Chaucer resides in its worldliness and its moral function. Chaucer had explored various ways of making and understanding this claim in every long poem of his career, but he presents it in its most complex and indirect form in the *Canterbury Tales*. He examines its meaning through the professed literary tastes and aspirations of a small group of especially self-conscious literary performers among the pilgrims—a heterogeneous and somewhat arbitrarily selected group that I have, perhaps still more arbitrarily, chosen to call Chaucer's "new men."

There is some warrant in recent studies of Chaucer's audience for applying the term "new men" to fourteenth-century figures,[1] but it is perhaps more familiarly used in Tudor social and literary history, where it refers to those lower gentry and civil and legal professionals who attained office and privilege in significant numbers under the Tudors; by extension, it connotes as well a characteristic set of educational, literary, social, and civil ideals that seems to have attained cultural prominence with them. In borrowing the term, however, I am chiefly interested in its extended sense, rather than in its primary reference to the career patterns or typical ambitions of members of certain social estates.

Chaucer's new men do not all belong to ascendant classes, groups, or estates: some quite the reverse. Considered from the perspective of the social historian, they are an oddly mixed group: two ambitious laymen, predictably enough--the Franklin and the Man of Law—but also two clerics, the Monk and the Clerk; and the Squire, a member of the gentry.[2] But as Canterbury

15

performers, these men share a common kind of self-consciousness: they preface and interlace their tales with profuse instructions on how to take them, and in doing so present some shared assumptions about the place of literature in the world, and the means by which it achieves its good effects. In brief, they agree that the pleasure and the use of literature are one thing, and are realized in worldly performance. The good of a story lies not only in the exemplary virtues it depicts, the kernel of content, but in the virtues required to derive pleasure from it: the capacity for wonder, sympathy, and thoughtful speculation—in short, in sensitivity to style and its expressive values. Their views represent literary theories and ideals that had had little coherent vernacular expression in England before Chaucer, but closely resemble central ideals of early Renaissance literary culture. In these figures, Chaucer presents not only satiric portraits of social types as they act in the common world, but speculative portraits, the most complex of his career, of the literary values of his most devoted audience.

If justification is needed for my kidnapping of the term "new men" for a group I define chiefly through literary conduct rather than objective social status, I derive mine from one of their own most cherished and distinctive practices: they "kidnap" terms, genres, and modes of idealization that traditionally support cultic values, whether those of a class or of a professed religion, into idealizing fictions of their own that shift the traditional uses for these terms and cultic objects.[3] "Gentilesse," "chivalry," "suffraunce," "patience," for example, are stretched and recombined in fictions whose most characteristic effect is to call our attention to the process of fictional idealization itself, and the process of telling, reading, or hearing a story so as to sustain its practical life in the world. In a similar spirit, I use the term new men as freely and advisedly as the new men used their kidnapped fictions: as an instrument of speculation rather than exclusion. By examining the literary conduct and assumptions of a group of pilgrims who, taken together, closely reflect Chaucer's principal "point of attachment" to an actual audience,[4] I hope to define an ideal of vernacular eloquence common to them, which may have been close to Chaucer's own.

The Man of Law and the Franklin might seem like the most obvious examples of new men on the pilgrimage. Their evident ambition, as individuals perhaps typifying ascendant groups, and their consequent efforts to appear worthy in public, have been remarked in their tales by much modern criticism.[5] In these two figures, manifest social identity and literary performance have seemed to be somehow complementary, though there is widespread disagreement as to how the tale reveals the social or moral identity of the teller, or how an understanding of the teller's position enhances an understanding of the form or rhetoric of a tale. This relationship is generally—and, I think, by design—problematic in the *Canterbury Tales*, but perhaps especially so in such instances as these. The most effective and consistent expression of values in men whose social prospects are charged with possibility will not, for this very reason, be openly argumentative or assertive in rhetorical form. The newness of a new man's ethos will be disguised and diffuse in his story, characteristically—and paradoxically—appearing as an earnest and insistent honoring of old ways and the received high culture, for it is these to which he wishes to show himself accustomed and entitled. He will surround crucial terms and forms for expressing these traditional values in narrative with special conditions, attributing their operation in his story to an exceptional infusion of unaccustomed grace, not readily found or capable of being imitated under modern conditions. The Franklin's tale, for example, shows a far more acute consciousness than the Knight's of the unique and precarious conditions that circumscribe the operation of the "gentil" deeds in his story: for him, chivalric manners and mores not only provide a vocabulary for idealization, but in addition belong to "olde dayes" and are themselves, as terms, problematic, subject to change, decay, transformation. What in "olde dayes" was magic is in our day "supersticious cursednesse." For the Franklin, the "gentillesse" of chivalry is an idyll, as well as an ideal. Yet it is the Franklin's diffuse altruism and geniality, his light touch in recommending this conduct to his audience's wonderment, rather than the Wife's combativeness in recommending her "doctrine" for emulation, that best characterizes a new man's rhetorical strategy as narrator in acknowledging the complex ethical relations between the "then" of his story and the "now" of this world. There is thus nothing inevitably direct or easily interpretable about the way a member of a socially emergent group will express emergent ideals in literature or about literature, precisely because of the complex and necessarily disguised part that literary performance may play in social ascent.[6] For the Franklin and the Man of Law, a literary performance is a social performance; what links these two to the other new men for the present purpose, however, is their diffuse ethical interest in old stories, not as the repository of doctrine or cultic example, but as the locus for narrative of general ethical idealization, meant for modern worthies to admire, and thereby to display the virtues of the civilized man.

If these two ambitious laymen seem obvious instances of new men in both senses, the other three do not: they do not belong to clearly ascendant groups or vocations. Two, the Clerk and the Monk, are clerics, neither of them in secular positions; the other, the Squire, insofar as he belongs historically to the military-feudal social order, has seemed to many readers to represent the opposite phenomenon in social and literary history, the "waning of the middle ages," and to embody, despite his youth, a dying rather than a new order and ideal.[7] His eager love-service, and his purely decorative chivalry—like the Monk's unexpected fund of Boethian tragedies instead of the robust manly fare Harry Bailly anticipates from a religious who has so emphatically professed his modernity and worldliness—would seem, like the very categories under which they are introduced, to portray 'obsolescent' rather than 'emergent' figures. Like many of the Canterbury pilgrims, however, these two display traits and hopes of both kinds. What marks them as new men for our purposes, however, is their high self-consciousness about precisely this aspect of themselves, and their prominent inclusion of it in their performances. Both the Monk and the Squire, like the other three, are preoccupied with the proper style and rhetorical means for recommending a 'noble' story to modern and high-minded lay listeners. Their performances emphasize the wonder and pathos of the events they narrate, not their kernel of doctrinal significance.

One might also take exception on the basis of his social location to the Clerk as a new man. This lean and ascetic figure does not look much like a portrait of either ambition or modernity, and he is often regarded by modern clerks as an ideal portrayal of the self-less man of learning. He is not "so worldly for to have office," and has "unto logyk longe ygo"—a discipline that scarcely fits one for anything but further university study, and was, of all the *artes* in the medieval curriculum, to be the chief target of humanist scorn for its remoteness from the arts of civil life.[8] The relation of the Clerk's loves and aims to this "studye" are obscure; he would gladly learn and teach, but we do not know what he professes. The study that shows its imprint most clearly to his fellow-pilgrims is not logic but eloquence: his speech is "sownynge in moral vertu." This odd phrase may refer to either the subject or the manner of his discourse (see *Oxford English Dictionary*, s. v. *sound*, v.[1], 1.5, 6), but it is his manner of speaking that receives the narrator's fullest praise: whatever he said was spoken

> in forme and reverence,
> And short and quyk and ful of hy sentence.[9]

While the Clerk has evidently, like Faustus, longed to "live and die in Aristotle's works," he presents himself among the pilgrims as a professed devotee of Petrarch's "wordes and werk." It is the character of that devotion, as well as its subject—paradoxically a very modern way of loving what is to be found in old books—that marks him as a new man, though he lives his life in an austerely medieval calling, and is to Harry Bailly an old and familiar type, the impoverished perpetual student. His "hy sentence," however, like that of all the new men, does not work directly to recommend exemplary conduct or belief to his contemporaries. His performance, in fact, foils utterly and thereby satirizes the audience's implicit demand that a story provide useful exempla. For him, as for all of them, sententiousness is a feature of style that sustains an interesting distinction between "then" and "now," and makes the thoughtful understanding of that distinction a virtue in the performer and hearer.

It is a common array of narrative and rhetorical strategies, and a set of ethical assumptions about literature these imply, that unites this group and defines their modernity. Of all the pilgrims, they have the most to say about style and manner: it seems to be where they locate the human use and value, as well as the pleasure, of their stories. For these men, to perform well as a teller or hearer of a story is to *display* as well as to inculcate virtue: the ethical claims of literature are for them inseparable from its status as a mode of social performance. In what follows, I shall trace this conception of the social place and 'good' of literature in Chaucer's earlier work and literary milieu, in order to show how he uses these men to exemplify one way of understanding the *Canterbury Tales* as a structure.

Chaucer makes his pilgrims appear before us, not moving among the "labors of their bodies and the works of their hands" in whatever daily lives we attribute to them, but acting, playing for each other in a play version of worldly striving. True, they are travelers, but the journey is not the burden of their speech, and speech is what they are made of. The action they perform before us, and the social context in which they act, is the wholly gratuitous common enterprise they have agreed upon, the contest that will discover and honor ("at oure aller coste") the story "of best sentence and moost solaas." The game, insofar as it is a search for the best story, as well as a contest to determine a winner, is a playful vernacular form of the philosopher's quest, the search for the good and the beautiful. The new men act into this aspect of the situation with particular force and clarity; they explicitly play the game as quest rather than contest. They are eager to tell, and to be seen in the company of, good and high-minded literature, not just diverting stories: they want to show who they are chiefly through their relation to the high forms of literary entertainment. They do not announce the "matere" of their stories, but specify instead what sort of ethical atmosphere they wish to create. In this they are pointedly contrasted with several other kinds of narrators on the pilgrimage.

Fabliau narrators are content to make strong, punctual impressions on us by their performances. Each announces that his tale is "of" or "about" a certain person, whom he identifies with respect to his worldly occupation ("a carpenter"), and the concrete action the story will report ("how that a clerk hath set the wrightes cappe"). For the fabliau storytellers, the narrative subject is not a theme or virtue ("gentillesse," "patience"), but a brief and circumscribed act, and they imply that the act of telling the tale is its verbal counterpart, the equivalent of a rude and playful buffet, which has little persuasive design upon the reader or hearer. True, such a blow—like such a story and the kind of event it presents—is sometimes colloquially said to "teach him a lesson," but that lesson has no paraphraseable content or general wisdom to offer. The performance character of the fabliau is that of an interlude—an irruption or interposition into some other process. In the literal rather than pejorative sense they *divert* rather than *entertain*—a subject, a theme, or the constant idea of a hearer. In contrast to these players of the Canterbury game, the new men tell stories that entertain by calling a good deal of conscious attention to the rhetorical process itself as it sustains its theme; in this aspect, they imply, lies the good of their stories.

The new men are distinguished on the other hand from explicitly didactic or confessional narrators, whose stories strive to offer axioms for conduct or belief that are referred directly to the audience's moral life, or to the speaker's own "secte": the Parson furnishes an instance of the one, the Wife of Bath the other. Unlike these, the new men do not insist that their themes generate a distinct, sententious kernel of general moral truth, a "message" that the story is to prove or convey. Their narrations are full of sententiousness, but it is largely free-floating, tending to give the whole story a general air of significance, the sense that "more is meant than meets the ear." For them, "sentence" is a feature of style, not an assertion of doctrine. This diffusion of argument and assertion in their stories contrasts their performances with those of the two pilgrims modeled in part upon Jean de Meun's confessional figures in the *Roman de la Rose*—the Wife and the Pardoner—and a similar figure drawn from Deschamps, the Merchant. Those pilgrims' stories, too, are pervasively sententious, but there the rhetorical appeal of the story is blended in almost indeterminable proportions with what seems like an appeal for vindication by the narrator directly to the hearer, across the story, as it were. The animus raised by those three speakers' narrative rhetoric seems to be enlisted to some degree on behalf of the teller as well as his theme. The new men's sententiousness, however, is generally in the service of speculation and admiration, not "pref." While they, too, may be seen as displaying facets of their public identities in their performances—and in ways that I have no space to describe here they all do—they are not confessing their opinions or personal dilemmas, or professing doctrine. They offer themes for consideration, human qualities examined in more altruistic and idealized forms than the confessional characters use. Whatever argument lurks in their stories is largely invested in the style itself, in a generally convincing accession to the social spirit of edifying recreation.

It is this willing accession to the enterprise of high play that most pervasively characterizes what being men of consequence means to them. They all explicitly make this accession aloud: they are eager to be seen as magnanimously free from immediate ego-centric pressures and specialist or sectarian attributes—to set aside necessity, care, and "possessioun," and *be entertaining.* Their tales, too, all of them drawn from the rich late-medieval fund of secular ideal romantic story, display the wonderful changes brought about in worldly relations generally by a striking display of individual nature or feeling, of *virtù*. These tales, like the obliging gestures with which their narrators offer them, celebrate the generative power of a free act. The new men both live and tell myths about *virtuosity.*[10]

Festivity, the capacity to play, is an apparently gratuitous facet of human culture; it seems to have no obvious or direct relation to biological or economic survival. Whatever benefits play and plea-sure confer on civilization evidently lie precisely in their being ex-perienced as *unnecessary*, as free activity. For that reason, a willingness to entertain—like hospitality, personal ornament, the giving of gifts, the support of the performing arts, and philosophi-cal speculation—is, and historically has always been, a recognized way of asserting one's free condition in the world. In this respect, the new men's agreement to be entertaining may be seen as a self-serving social gesture. But what this self-reference says about the social ambitions of fourteenth-century people is not finally the point; what Chaucer does by showing it to us is. In these figures, he shows a desire to expand the significant of this traditional social gesture. All of these men recognize what the chief high-secular subjects are: they are all one form or another of chivalric love and the suffering that attends it. All of them strive in their performance to alter the decorous and ethical limitations of that "matere" and its social uses as they are currently understood. In doing so, they offer several versions of Chaucer, who has been doing just that for his entire career.

Chaucer assigns to his new men much of the same genial deference and willingness to obey a request to be entertaining, as well as many of the same speculations about the vernacular poet's enterprise and ideal mode of address, he had associated with himself as speaker and actor in his earlier work. Through these figures, Chaucer opens for us again, in the most precisely differentiated terms of his career, a matter he had considered explicitly in his poems from the first: the vernacular poet's place, and the nature of what he does, in the human community—the 'good' of literature. The pilgrims are all within their "pley" both performers and critics; through the most acutely self-conscious of these players, Chaucer presents a "theory of poetry," in Curtius's sense of the term,[11] and describes the ideal of vernacular eloquence that seems to correspond to its conditions.

Briefly, that mode of eloquence was what Chaucer called "enditing." It is a term Chaucer uses in the *Canterbury Tales* chiefly in association with these performers; he seems to mean by it an art of celebrating the human world as if it mattered, and as if the act of celebration were itself virtuous. And by the world, he meant the common world of appearance, in which people now alive appear to each other in their deeds.[12] "Enditing" in Chaucer's sense is an ideal secular high rhetoric. Its angle of vision on the world is always from a point of reference within it (as a courtly maker's rhetorical perspective, though it may include many moods, is always that of a member of courtly society). The Boethian perspective of world transcendence yields nothing Chaucer calls literature or "enditing"; insofar as there is "enditing" in the *Consolation* it is that which momentarily celebrates the "ravysshyng swegh" of some humanly comprehensible beauty as it touches mortal minds.[13]

For Chaucer, the idea of "enditing" was one that reconciled two contrasted aspects of literature and the writer's role he had considered repeatedly in his earlier work: on the one hand, the mode of existence of the "maker" as participant-entertainer and celebrant of the cult values of love,[14] and, on the other, that of the "poete," who was absent in his own person from the world of the living, but endured as it were in petrified form, through books.[15] The problematic absence of those he called "poetes" from the world of social performance and public action troubled him repeatedly, as his most notable metaphors for their status suggest. They are the soil of "olde feldes," the pillars that bear up chivalry; their substance is the icy rock on which Fame has built: the implicit challenge these figures present to the living seems to be to *work* these intractable substances, in order to shape or "make" something of present human use and fruitfulness. To be "in bokes," either in the sense that Vergil was for Chaucer, or is to us—or as Chaucer is himself "in bokes" while reading Vergil, and therefore for the duration not present among "loves folk"—seemed to be somehow to lose the name of action.[16] To understand the life of "poetrie" in the world of the living was a major preoccupation of both *Troilus* and the *Canterbury Tales*.

In reconciling "making" and "poetry," "enditing" offered a middle way through which vernacular writing could attain both high style and broad public rather than coterie standing. Both the form of the problem as Chaucer conceives it, and his solution, closely parallel those achieved, though with simpler formal means, by his two London contemporaries, Gower and Langland.[17] And that it is for him an ideal of eloquence—an organizing principle of artistic thought, rather than a peripheral feature of a highly sophisticated literary vocabulary—is shown by the precision and consistency with which "enditing" is defined in use, and by the honorific purposes to which the term is put by those many speakers in the poetry who use it to locate themselves ethically and socially and stylistically in the world. The users of the word in the *Canterbury Tales* include the same group who, in their performances, manifest a high emphasis on style in their presentation of worldly *virtù*. It is around the extended group of new men that we hear most about "enditing" and the proprieties of the high style. They act as several different hypothetical versions of the literary performer, through which Chaucer considers the pleasure of art, and its use.

Chaucer had already raised the issue of vulgar eloquence repeatedly in his earlier long poems. In order to see how he arrived at an idea of "enditing," it is instructive to notice the form in which this matter first presented itself to thought. Twice he made the search for the ideal matter and manner of vernacular poetry the explicit subject that generates debate: it is what the voices talk about in the *Hous of Fame* and again in the *Legend of Good Women*. In both of these poems "Geffrey" is called to account for some aspects of his devotion to literature. In the earlier poem it is primarily as a reader of "olde bokes," and a sometime maker of love poetry, that he is confronted and urged to "newe thynges" by the Eagle, an instructor who considers himself well qualified by his plainness of speech for the task of directing Chaucer's attention to "ought elles that God made." In the *Legend*, Chaucer is challenged as a writer. As he disports himself amid familiar scenes of courtly pleasure, professing to be no partisan in the poetic game of the flower and the leaf, but merely a grateful gleaner in the fields of its rhetoric, he meets the God of Love, who is not amused. He charges Chaucer with having ventured too far beyond the bounds of courtly making, and thereby strayed into "heresy," violating the cult's most honored subject, the praise of worthy ladies.[18] Chaucer's assigned penance is to "make" a legend of Cupid's saints, in the execution of which the narrator is, in fact, always pointedly reining in his theme to preserve his orthodoxy. As he tells his short tales of wronged women, Chaucer again and again curtails their embarrassing tendency to interest us, and him, in the greater action of which they are a part (for example, the story of Troy and Rome as the context of Dido's woe), or in the general ethical themes they present (Pyramus' truth in love is equal to Thisbe's; Tereus' and Tarquin's crimes are hardly those of faithless lovers; Hypermnestra is more gravely betrayed by her father than by her husband; and so on). Yet while he circumscribes the narrative expansion of his assigned "matere," he also avoids emotional intensification. While there are moments of pathos in speech and gesture (Dido's unavailing plea to Aeneas, for example), these remain isolated, and are not successfully incorporated into the narrator's single large gesture that defines the shape and common purpose of these stories, namely, to reinstate himself in the graces of the God of Love by telling them. He muffles the traditional climax of this kind of narrative, the aria of complaint by the abandoned lady herself, the display piece of pathetic rhetoric for which the brief story of betrayal usually only provides the occasion and stage. For this kind of poetic pleasure, Chaucer sends us elsewhere—to Ovid, who can "wel endyte in vers."

Chaucer's subdued and tonally uncertain treatment of these arias is a consequence of their dual rhetorical purpose. Ovid's heroines must complain to their lovers so as to enlist our sympathies, and convince us of the human justice of their cause against their cruel lovers. That we know they did not succeed in so moving the men to whom their "epistles" are nominally addressed only intensifies their pathetic appeal to us. The speech of Chaucer's ladies, however, bears a second burden of decorum. Within the frame story, his heroines are love's martyrs, and it is the quality and intensity of love service, not their articulateness in appealing their rightful sense of loss and betrayal, that constitutes their virtue as saintly sisters.[19] The difference is that between Anelida and St. Cecilia: since saintly torments are validating triumphs of the faith, not pathetic worldly pain pleading for remedy where there is none, the speech of a martyr of love ought to consist of ecstasy and rejoicing rather than complaint. The martyr-heroine's suffering must therefore be "endited" by someone other than herself: the second, cultic, context of these legends requires, as Ovid's do not, a mediating narrative voice to interpret this pathetic "matere" to us, to celebrate to the faithful the cultic significance of this passion.[20] This task would seem to demand high rhetoric of Chaucer himself, to praise the lady's constancy in her devout service and condemn the wicked callousness of the faithless lover. The problem here, however, was not the figure of the saint but that of the infidel. A hagiographer can authoritatively heap scorn on the pagan oppressor: his audience knows the saint's tormentor will be damned in the life to come. But what of the infidels of love, many of whom in the *Legends* are also the heroes of epic and historical narrative—Jason, Theseus, Aeneas? To condemn these at length would require Chaucer to betray the "matere" of long narrative for the sake of making an act of devotion. And what of outright moral monsters like Tereus? To make Philomela a secular saint required Chaucer to make her a martyr for "hire sustres love"—hardly the kind of service the God of Love had in mind in the Prologue.

Besides providing serious structural obstacles to narrative, the assigned rhetorical task of cultic service imposed a tonal restriction. The humility and modesty proper to the manner of a penitential act, and proper, as well, to an ingratiating "ladies' friend" (*Legend of Good Women* 2561) who contrasts himself with the false lovers he condemns, evidently forbade a strongly assertive interpreting and celebrating voice in the narrator. The hagiographer's rhetorical authority is not available to Chaucer as speaker here, for his lord is not "a god whose temper-tantrums are moral." The God of Love's will is seen as arbitrary and capricious, his gifts and exactions in no way concerned with "intente."

The complexities of Chaucer's position as performer in the *Legend* call attention to some fundamental conflicts within his conception of his enterprise. The God of Love, it seems, keeps his devoted servants on a rather short tether: placating him requires the writer to renounce epic subjects and their complex narrative sweep, and the broadly human rather than cultic ethical questions that attend them. It also entails suppressing the full use of the rhetoric of complaint, a traditional form whose forensic qualities Chaucer had tended in his lyrics to heighten, and extend to general philosophic speculation, largely free of specific occasion.

Without free access to such themes, modes, and manners of poetry as these, "Chaucer" in the *Legend* is confined to being merely chivalrous on behalf of his heroines, making small skirmishes rather than a "gret emprise" in the service of love. The only thing he can do for his ladies as a writer is to trounce the offending gentlemen into oblivion with a pen: "Have at thee, Jason!" he bravely exclaims. In this game of poetic soldiering for love, the poet's speech is a weapon of gallantry, and his enterprise a form of honoring one subject by forcibly making another one disappear.

It is this "gallant" Chaucer that the Man of Law grudgingly praises in the Prologue to his own tale. For him, Chaucer is the poet of the *Legend*, a harmless and undeniably industrious "maker" of tales of lovers, whose chief merit (since "he kan but lewedly/ On metres and on rymyng craftily") is that they do not offend morally. Though the Man of Law is here chiefly flourishing the currency of his literary cultivation, rather than, like the God of Love, indicting Chaucer for his errors, his critical terms and values complement those of the *Legend* to round out a working definition of the "maker" and his literary setting as Chaucer understood it. A few points of agreement with the God of Love are striking, and essential to the definition. For one thing, he, too, judges Chaucer on the moral acceptability of the content of the story—the behavior depicted in it, not its rhetorical "intente"— though the two critics differ about which morality he ought to display, and between them leave him almost no acceptable narrative matter at all. The God of Love would have Chaucer affirm the moral imperatives of his cult; the Man of Law insists on general standards of social irreproachability: one should not murder children or commit incest, and therefore should not present those acts in stories.[21] But though they each have a different notion of the community whose 'community standards' Chaucer ought not to offend, neither doubts that his "making"—an enterprise that, we should notice, seems to include in a single activity the composing and circulating of his work—is a social performance; the scene into which the maker acts is contemporary, stylish, and polite. Second, telling these stories is efficacious chiefly for the teller rather than the hearer. It is a way of reaffirming one's possession of the tastes and qualities that assure one's membership in polite society; their force is therefore simply cumulative. For the God of Love, they are like the recitation of a long litany, a renewed profession of faith; for the Man of Law, they work like one's familiarity with legal precedent, and Chaucer has simply run through all the variant cases of that particular principle:

> And if he have noght seyd hem, leve brother,
> In o book, he hath seyd hem in another. . . .
> What sholde I tellen hem, syn they ben tolde?

$$(\text{B}^1\ 51\text{-}56)$$

The power of these tales to generate fresh 'makings' evidently does not extend far beyond Cupid's court; the Man of Law turns away from the games and rituals of that court; he finds among merchants, those "fadres of tidynges and tales," plainer fare befitting his busy public self.

Finally, and perhaps most significant, the God of Love and the Man of Law are virtually our only witnesses in Chaucer's work for this specialized poetic use of the term *to make*. Though Chaucer shares some genres and lyric forms with the French *faiseur*, and refers occasionally to himself and some contemporary writers as "makers," he rarely uses the verb *to make* without specifying an object, metonymically to mean "to compose verse." He often uses the verb for literary activity, but specifies the product: "balade," "lay," "song," "vers," "mistralcies," and the like. His praise of his contemporary, "Graunson, flour of hem that make in Fraunce," in the *Complaint of Venus* is one of very few occurrences in his work of the French metonymic usage. Nearly all the rest cluster around the Man of Law and the God of Love. The Man of Law begins his capsule critical survey "in youthe he made of Ceys and Alcione"; the God of Love is even more insistent and belittling. He uses the verb several times in listing Chaucer's earlier compositions, both with an object ("boke," "lyf," "lay," even, ignominiously, "thyng," an idiom used elsewhere in Chaucer only for the Man of Law's "writyng"[22]) and without: "He shal maken as ye wol devise," "Suffiseth me thou make in this manere."[23] Chaucer the dreamer also uses the term metonymically in the *Legend*, but not for his own work: he refers to "Ye loveris that kan make of sentement," but he declines to compete with them in their game. Queen Alceste, however, Chaucer's advocate, diverges from these terms in her defense of him: she refers to his heretical works as "enditing," shifting the ground of appeal from "matere" to intent.

> Or elles, sire, for that this man is nyce,
> He may translate a thyng in no malyce,
> But for he useth bokes for to make,
> And taketh non hed of what metere he take,
> Therfore he wrot the Rose and ek Crisseyde
> Of innocence, and nyste what he seyde.
> Or hym was boden make thilke tweye
> Of som persone, and durste it not withseye;
> For he hath write many a bok er this.
> He ne hath not don so grevously amys
> To translate that olde clerkes wryte,
> As thogh that he of maleys wolde endyte
> Despit of love, and hadde hymself ywrought.

(*Legend*, G 340–52)

"Making" in this passage implies an exercise of craftsmanship for the social pleasure and refreshment of others; "enditing" suggests the infusion of "matere" with an intention, a meaning and design upon the audience for which the "enditer" assumes some responsibility and authority.

The range of usage for "making" implied by the Man of Law and the God of Love, along with references in the shorter poems and earlier work to "balades" and "minstralcies" as "made," establish the connotations and social environment of the term, and reveal an idea of the means, purpose, and domain of literature implicit in it. The testimony of the two dream visions we have considered suggests that the "courtly maker" conception of the poet's enterprise does not enable a writer to sustain a long poem, only a long series of short ones. Chaucer's two invented critics further emphasize the socially or cultically reaffirmative function of "making," and show that it is conceived as a performance in the current scene of polite amusement and secular ritual. And that he uses the verb metonymically almost entirely in contexts that imply a dismissal of the seriousness of intent in a writer's practice, or a constriction on his freedom of invention, is particularly telling.

When Chaucer treats the question of the poet's enterprise as the explicitly debated subject of a poem, it seems he has no way to end it. If decorous "luf-talkyng" no longer securely defines the writer's "matere," then the occasion that dictates the form and social function of composition is absent, and no other context supplants it; the *Hous of Fame* and the *Legend* are the two notoriously disputed unfinished works of his career. But he found another way to take up the matter within a poem: formally rather than referentially. In two of his other long poems, the *Parlement of Foules* and the *Troilus*, Chaucer builds his ideas of the role of the verbal artist into the fictive structure and rhetorical process of the work. This enables him to project imaginatively a place for the writer's work beyond its performance value, to conceive of its function in a broader arena of action than that of contemporary cultic expectations. In these two poems he describes writing as potentially belonging to the world at large, enduring in historical time largely through the medium of books, and tries to conceive of how the world that "neweth everi dai" can use this literary inheritance, and in what form it becomes active again among the living. The enduring mode of existence for the writer he calls "poetrie."

Both the *Parlement* and the *Troilus* avoid the formal problems of poetic closure, and the constraints on the speaker's rhetorical posture, that beset the other two we have considered, largely by keeping making and poetry out of dramatized confrontation. By

scenically and dramatically separating these two notions of literature within the poems, Chaucer can both define "poetrie" and suggest his reasons for never calling himself a "poete." Poetry is for
him at once the highest and most austere achievement of the
writer, and disturbingly, intractably, noncontemporary. It endures,
but it does not live; it is silent with respect to the present. It is a
lasting treasury, but not a living voice. Chaucer seems, somewhat
wistfully, to speak of it much as Socrates in the *Phaedrus* characterized philosophy recorded in writing: it is dead to the world of
action, and can have no real designs upon the world.[24] Its beauty
declares only itself, but not its paternity, or its "intente." It confers no certain good on the living human community as a whole,
and purchases for its devotees at best the questionable immortal-
ity of a pagan heaven.

The *Parlement* separates the two domains of literature scenically
and spatially. It announces its dual theme by a witty play on the
commonplace *ars longa vita brevis*, which counterpoises the poetry
that arises from, and celebrates, "love in dede," with the poetry
and philosophy celebrating love "in bokes"—the love of common
profit, expressed not in courtship but in wise governance. The
tutelary figures of the one are Venus and Nature, of the other
Scipio Africanus; and the meaning of the relation between the two
scenes over which they preside has been the chief problem in
interpreting the poem. For our purposes, though, it is less important to specify that meaning than to notice the complete tonal
assurance with which each scene is realized—and the utter forget-
tability and tonal obscurity of the passagework between them, the
hundred or so lines describing the contents of the walled garden,
which Chaucer derived from Boccaccio's *Teseide*. What is there is
visually clear enough; what is obscure is the auspices under which
we (and Chaucer) are there, and hence the rhetorical purpose of
this venture. Chaucer presents in the *Parlement* the assured voices
of two excellent writers, but provides no common theme over
which they can meet. One is a gracious performer who can end a

scene of courtship debate in a purely musically satisfying way, as one might end a banquet entertainment, with a charming song. The other is a man of letters, who is looking for the "good" as well as the charm in the literary life, and is willing to stay for the answer. In the plot of the *Parlement*, the dreamer's literary exertion and its reward are oddly incommensurate: for his devotion to Scipio's book, Chaucer is repaid with yet another visit to a love garden—perhaps in the hope that under Ciceronian auspices the scene will resolve into a higher kind of sense. The structure of the poem, however, is designed not to harmonize the writer's two roles, but to keep their incommensurability at bay: the garden scene ends without decision or agreement, but rather with postponement and a chorus. The two poetic places are never brought within one frame of reference, and the two episodes, one embedded within the other, are given separate closure. The song ends the "making," whereupon the speaker closes the original thematic scene with the hope (rather than the confidence) that if he continues reading, "I shal mete som thyng for to fare the bet." It is easier, it seems, to end an entertainment than to draw a useful conclusion to—or from—a book. For the end of song as he conceives it is immediate social pleasure; the end of books is said by those who care about them to be to change your life—they have an authority that 'making' does not. Chaucer presents himself in this poem as willing to take that claim for "poetrie" seriously, and at the end we leave him cheerfully awaiting his great transformation.

Chaucer ends the *Troilus* with a more complex form of the same multiple closure, keeping the two aspects of literature in indefinite relation to each other. Throughout *Troilus*, he separates "making" and "poetry," performance and book, rhetorically—as dramatic roles—rather than spatially. Chaucer shifts fluently between them as he simultaneously retells the old story he cannot change and conducts a service of love, ultimately to the virtual undoing of its cult value. At the end, however, he calls the whole cast of appearances out to take their leave. This final serial display of several distinct literary actions is his fullest survey before the *Canterbury Tales* of the competing notions of the good of literature within which he conceived his work.

First he must end the "storie," insofar as it is "of Troilus." In doing so Chaucer reminds us that it has been all along two stories, only one of which he has amplified, namely, the tragic story of Troilus' love, just concluded. The other, not yet ended, is that of his "dedes" in the war: it remains vestigial, a stillborn twin of the first. For the latter, he refers us to Dares; but before going on to end Troilus' life, and sending him to the comic transcendence of worldly deeds and passions alike, Chaucer pauses to commend the book he has just written, the love tragedy, to the world at large.

> Go litel book, go, litel myn tragedye,
> Ther God thi makere yet, er that he dye,
> So sende myght to make in som comedye!
> But litel book, no makyng thow n'envie,
> But subgit be to all poesye;
> And kis the steppes, where as thow seest pace
> Virgile, Ovide, Omer, Lucan, and Stace.

(V. 1786–92)

It has been noticed that Chaucer distinguishes tragedy from comedy here at exactly the point in the narrative at which he turns one to the other: as he has concluded the love story and is about to kindle the vestigial life of worldly glory into a moment of visibility in our minds just as it is extinguished and repudiated.[25] It is possible to see the stanza as turning in the same way on another pair of counterpoised terms, "making" and "poetry," and about these it is still more equivocal. Where the turn from the one to the other appears in the performance is crucial to the meaning of the equivocation.

The stanza seems to urge the book forth on a journey, out of the envious company of other "makyng," and into reverent discipleship to the "poets," to make a clear distinction between the two places where literature lives: at court and now,[26] on the one hand, and, on the other, in the temple of art, an "eternal image of antiquitie." Yet the terms and structure of the passage are framed so as to obscure the threshold the book is asked to cross, and the differences between the two realms it provisionally occupies. The stanza turns on three words formed on the root verb *make*, whose uses do not reinforce each other, but create conflicting understandings of the verb that generate ghosts of interfering readings of the stanza.[27] The adjustment in understanding these *make*-words each time calls a great deal of attention to the general possibility of misconstruing the "intente" of the gesture, or of the whole work—a possibility that becomes the explicit subject of the succeeding stanza. The act of commending the book, like the act of interpreting the gesture, is designed to feel as precarious as it is tentative, to sustain a confusion in the very act of making distinctions.

Insofar as this work is of love, and its rhetorical fiction is that it is conducted in the presence and faithful cultic service of love's devout, it is a "makyng," a contemporary performance. Insofar as it has in many respects the "forme of olde clerkis speche," the emotional seriousness, amplitude, and decorum of a "poet's" story—in short, all the features Chaucer was pointedly to jettison in chastened conformity to the God of Love's religion—it seems tentatively to emulate "poesye" as practiced by "Virgile, Ovide, Omer, Lucan, and Stace." Chaucer does not, however, as Dante boldly does, make himself "a sixth among those high intelligences" (*Inferno* IV.100–102); he is content to lay his "litel book" reverently at the feet of tradition, the society of the mighty dead, without inserting himself, and the uncertain status of his enterprise, into such august company. The stanza ends with an imagined silent act of homage, a pageant; Chaucer no longer tries to imagine direct conversation with these ancients. By placing the passage after what seems to constitute the "making," the love story, is ended, but before the end of what for most of the ancient poets would have constituted the real, publicly significant story, Troilus' worldly "dedes," Chaucer calls the greatest possible attention to the complexities of the literary dual allegiance of this poem, and its urgency as a problem confronting the vernacular writer generally.

The kind, as well as the realm of literature, to which *Troilus* finally belongs remain ambiguous. As the contrast between the kinds "tragedye" and "comedye"—whatever actual works they may refer to—is collapsed by the more comprehensive gesture that directs this "litel bok" out of the bosom of its family toward "poesye" where its masters dwell, a realm that evidently includes both kinds; so the difference between "makyng" and "poesye" is subsumed in the motion and aspiration of the one toward the other. The tone is fond, paternal, and modest, and the figure of speech suggests that the relation between these two modes is that of youth to maturation. The author, it seems, is not urging a wholly new definition of his enterprise at the eleventh hour, but rather suggesting what aspects of this child of his pen show promise, how the concerns of "making" "up groweth with youre age" to become the concerns of poetry. Though the stanza does not decide whether this "litel bok" is "making" or "poetry," it suggests what is at stake for a practicing writer suspended between them.

The important question raised by this pivotal stanza and its location in the work is not simply a problem of genre, or level of style, a matter of what kind of subject—singular passion or public deeds —is properly celebrated in "high art," but *what kind of function does one honor by considering any art "high"?* It is more fundamentally a question of how each of these arts, "making" and "poetry," is conceived to act in the world—and here, at this point in Chaucer's career, it is the "poesye" of the ancients, not the (to a modern, or at least humanist, view) slighter, more minor art of the "maker," that seems to have the less certain footing. "Poetry" remains for him an enterprise that can only be thought of in the perfect tense.

As if to confirm this point—that the relevant conflict between the two modes is their life in the world—Chaucer now turns from ending the twofold *story* of Troilus, to conclude the *work*, again in two separate aspects. He bids farewell first to the present auditors of the work as performance, the "yonge, fresshe folkes," speaking finally, as at first, as a sober priest, bringing a service of love to an end. He then concludes the work as a book, commending it as a finished piece to "moral Gower" and "philosophical Strode," transferring corrective authority over the work from the provisional judgment of lovers that have "felynge in loves art," invoked several times during the performance, to the final judgment of his intellectual peers, fellow readers in moral and philosophic books. But in each of these leave-takings the speaker in turn invites the audience to take its leave of what in each case comprises the central good or value of the literary mode in which each has been addressed. The young lovers are urged to recognize that the cult in whose service they worship through such rituals as these is a cult of vanity; the readers of "poetry" are likewise reminded that the "forme of olde clerkis speche" celebrates a worldly "travaille," the pursuit of honor and virtue, which is equally vain from the perspective of eternity. As Troilus rises above both versions of his story, the author now transcends both versions of his work. The final stanza of the poem then unites the two audiences, the author, and all possible hearers as "us" in a prayer for mercy.

Neither literary enterprise, any more than any other worldly work, however charitably intended or lovingly executed, and with however lofty a style, will survive the world itself, nor can either contribute intentionally in any way to the soul's salvation. At the end of the *Troilus*, as at the end of the *Canterbury Tales*, Chaucer is quite clear about this: no work of literature can, by its very nature, have *as a deed* the kind of efficacy that the smallest prayer has.[28] To acknowledge this, however, is for Chaucer not the end of the matter, but the ground for a more precise speculation.

It remained to be seen whether a writer who acceded, as Chaucer seems to have done, to the contemporary emphasis on the performance value of high vernacular literature was thereby committed to the Man of Law's or the God of Love's restricted conception of the "commune" itself within which it was enacted, and the kinds of affirmation it was to perform.

What was it that the mighty dead had been doing, whose finished products we now admire as "poetrie"? There is no present-tense verb form in Chaucer's vocabulary, corresponding to "making" for what the "maker" does, that refers to what the poet does as a present activity rather than a past achievement. There is poetry but not "poeting," and "making" apparently does not cover the intentional as well as craftsmanlike excellences of ancient "poesye." The answer, and the corresponding term in the system, seems to have been "enditing," the celebration not of the court to the court, but of the human world and condition to the whole commonwealth. "Enditing" is the one literary enterprise Chaucer attributes both to the ancients, conceived as they acted into their own time, and those now living. The anomalous standing of Chaucer's own writing—as both "making" and aspirant to the status of "poetrie"—could be indefinitely sustained as long as Chaucer in his own person did not have to call it one thing or another.

In the *Canterbury Tales*, Chaucer solves both problems that had always attended his taking up the good of literature and its worldly status within a poem. This time the question was to appear both referentially, in the pilgrims' critical debate, and formally, as the generically identifiable voices within a tale, and the several stylistic means of self-revelation in "compaignye." The pilgrim-storytellers—as beings entitled, by the occasion on which they are gathered into a company, to be philosophical, to wonder about and seek the good of that very enterprise—provided several voices, several worldly angles of vision, several modes of social and literary performance, from which to reason on this matter. Any one of them could serve for Chaucer a speculative as well as satirical purpose: they could be an array of possible selves, playing the socially reconstitutive game of "making" in the company of the other players.

The best way to deal with the charges of the God of Love and the Man of Law, Chaucer found, was to move the whole matter in both senses *out of court*. This simple transference out of a courtly scene of a kind of entertainment that traditionally belongs to it—with the result that the unity of the reigning literary ethos is irretrievably broken by the movers—is one of the most deeply comic and fertile premises of the work. To think of the courtly milieu of "luf-talkyng" as a structural substratum of the *Canterbury Tales* is to find unexpected hilarities among its surface features. Consider the Wife of Bath, for instance, as a voluble respondent to that traditional demand of the "maker" to praise virtuous ladies; or the Pardoner as a performer—and one proud of his virtuosity at it—in a context whose original strictures require one to adopt the pose of being an ardent lover, and to claim that the inspiration kindling such eloquence as this emanates from the love of one special hearer in the company. It is the new men, however, who seem most conscious that the shattering move has taken place: they seem to know that this is a transferred "gentle" game, and they play thoughtfully with this aspect of it, as if they recognize that any request to tell a good story means, in high circles, to "sey somwhat of love."[29] They find themselves in the dual role of the author of *Troilus*, suspended between amusement for the court and wise counsel for the world. They all acknowledge, or are pointedly reminded of, the customary gentle modes of entertainment, yet, chiefly by measuring aloud the distance between their own performances and the "high style," invite our attention specifically to how the manner of acceding to the rules of the game expands our apprehension of its matter, its purpose, and its now-enlarged social function.

In marking the distance between the two—as in telling what

time it is, and where on the road to Canterbury we are—Harry Bailly as master of ceremonies plays a critical part: you can set your watch, or your style, by him. No one in the group more steadfastly exemplifies the current received standard usage in literary matters. "Sey somwhat of love" is his request of the Squire, the only pilgrim who looks as if this literary fashion is basic to his way of life. Harry shows a similar inclination to literary type-casting in all of his invitations to "pley." From the worldly Monk, he hopes for robust, but distinctly high-class, masculine fare: something of hunting—or perhaps, he implies, the more extended sense of "venerye." On the other hand, Harry warns the unworldly Oxford Clerk to set aside any moralistic clerkly designs on us to change our lives, and he is even more firmly insistent on the proper manner of his play: he should by no means "endite heigh stile"; that is for addressing kings, and the present company and game require plain intelligibility. All of these figures respond with manifest geniality to this assignment of parts, but in each case the whole performance is significantly out of frame with the imposed expectations. In this way each of them shows a different aspect of the possible literary eloquence to which a newly conceived social context gives place.

The Squire's Tale is unfinished—indeed, according to this ambitious prospectus it is scarcely begun—and proceeds with an amiable dilatoriness that many have seen as an inept version of his father the Knight's measured rhetoric of noble amplification.[30] Some of the same tropes and gestures are there, to be sure, but in the service of a wholly different effect. His performance exemplifies the effort to convert the ardent rhetoric of 'making' into the more general worldly celebration of 'enditing'; Chaucer praises him for both (*General Prologue* A 95). His rhetorical amplifications are not devoted to material splendor, or to visible symbols of a changeless universal order, but to the subjective effect on the human perceiver of splendors and marvels whose objective beauty he does not describe. This kind of dilation supports a different meaning from the Knight's: for the Squire, nobility of mind is the capacity for wonder and ready sympathy; the roots of human greatness lie not in prowess, or in the high-minded resignation of his father's Stoicism, but in human curiosity, and strong empathy with what the soul recognizes. "Pitee renneth soone in gentil herte" is not for the Squire, as it is for the Knight, a maxim dictating the tempering of the ruler's justice with mercy, but a definition of the gentle heart's chief virtue, namely, its "sentement," a generalized version of the noble love that characterized the "gentil herte" for Dante.

We never learn the size or visual details of the steed of brass, or see its entrance into the hall—all things the Gawain-poet or the Knight would have told us—but we do follow the wondering of the beholders as the mind moves out of itself and its sense of the immediate dramatic situation to recall similar marvels in "olde poetries," and finally to human crafts and natural phenomena, which, considered curiously in a mood of heightened suggestivity, become as wonderful as the King of Araby's magical gifts. The rhetorical process of unfolding these marvels is as lively and mercurial as St. Augustine's exclamatory catalogue of worldly wonders (*City of God* XXI), and it ultimately produces a similar effect: an implicit argument that miracles are still and always possible, that remembered images can leap into new meaning in a sudden encounter, and that only custom and habit obscure these marvels and their uses from us: the world is meant to be read. The Squire's rhetoric celebrates not stability but change, the swift and generative motions of the "corage" as it apprehends the worldly scene and responds to it. This "felyng" mind enriches the present moment by averting the immediate assimilation of new wonders to the familiar and present, by keeping them slightly alien and surrounding them with likenesses to the storied past. By such means, it is not the far-off exotic "then" of the story, but the "now" of seeing, hearing, and feeling that is made into art. Where the Knight's orderly pageant of chivalry is ultimately a celebration of the unmoved First Mover, around whom man's whirling fortunes turn, the Squire's more disorderly spectacle honors the magical possibility in the world that "neweth everi dai."

This breathless performance was evidently heading toward becoming a vast and exotic family romance, with its roots in Byzantine and Arabic story material,[31] in which Christian and Saracen enmity is overcome through the mutual recognition of chivalric virtue, and the two warring faiths are brought to make peace through an ideal marriage of Christian princess and Muslim hero—a wishful hope for reconciliation quite divergent from the chivalric rhetoric of the Crusades. But the story need not have gone any further for the mode of performance to make its point. The Squire's rhetoric depicts mind in motion; it is for this reason not the least bit surprising that this tale particularly charmed Spenser: the nobility it honors is that of the ethically responsive mind, manifested in ready feeling and eloquence.

The Franklin goes to the heart of the matter in praising the Squire for "spekyng feelyngly," and his tale, too, invites us to admire the capacity of human beings to rise feelingly to new occasions. His rhetoric, however, includes a caveat about the making of material appearances and, what for him amounts to the same thing, dwelling on speculative puzzles that take the mind away from what concerns the human condition, such as Dorigen's wondering on God's purpose in making the rocks.[32] The Franklin's profession of "pleyn" style and his professed avoidance of the "colours of rethoryk" introduces into his performance a countercurrent that uneasily recalls that making an appearance in the world is always at the same time making a semblance. He is often faulted in Chaucer criticism for a sentimental sanguinity that confuses reality and appearance; his fable, however, argues that practically speaking they are the same thing.

His story speculates on the way a care for the making of worldly appearances, not only by magic, but by the gestures that smooth the social fabric and the will to make life artful, generates eruptions through that fabric of "monsters and mervailles" that present real worldly dilemmas. The remedy for them offered by the story provides no acts that can serve an audience's moral emulation; they are acts of virtuosity, incapable of use or replication in any world other than that in which they happened to succeed. The Franklin's uneasiness with the "supersticious cursednesse" of magic, like his disavowal of rhetorical colors, argues some recognition on his creator's part of the inevitable consequences of the position that all art is worldly: each story becomes a "world" whose relation to the common world is problematic. The Franklin seeks to establish that relation with a question he invites his audience to debate: "Which was the mooste fre, as thinketh yow?" The practical virtue of the tale is in its providing of a feast for the living mind's appetite. The Franklin, for all his professed plainness, is also an accomplished host, a "worthy vavasour."[33] For him, stories do not provide exempla, static images of model behavior one can transport out of the stories; they offer no lives we can imitate, but rather lives we can examine. Stories are social parables whose power lies in the quality of talk they create. Like a good host's leading questions, they invite us to put examined, conscious human bonds in place of unexamined ritual. The courtly game of ideal talk has not for him lost its reaffirmative function, but he has, with his performance, expanded the social significance of that reaffirmation.

The Monk, too, eludes Harry Bailly's grasp, declining to perform entirely into the prescribed scene. His Boethian tragedies, whose nominal rhetorical thrust is an argument for world transcendence, become in his hands laments for the passing of human greatness. The Boethian perspective goes out of focus, the more so the closer the subjects are to the modern world and the bearers-up of chivalry. The Monk "endites" false Fortune for destroying "corage of heigh emprise," and "biwailles" with the highest powers of his rhetorical art not human blindness or worldly vanity, but "the deeth of gentilesse and of fraunchise." "Enditing," it seems, can celebrate the chivalric virtues, but no longer as they are part of a class ideal of inward individuation, the secret flowering of individual identity in the soul, but rather as these qualities were to be celebrated by fifteenth-century rhetors in encomiastic chronicles and triumphs: as the virtues that were to be definitive of public character in the great national monarchies.[34] The chivalry honored here is closer to that of Spenser than that of Chrétien.

Finally, the Clerk, too, frees himself from the ground rules Harry has imposed on his performance, both by obeying them to the letter—much as his Griselda shatters Walter's imposition of his will by infinite and impassive accession to it—and then by collapsing his sad and serious tale back into a playful performance, pretending to deny its present moral application in an envoy that is certainly Chaucer's virtuoso performance in a courtly lyric form. The unworldly Clerk is Chaucer's last and most complex exploration of "poetry's" absence from the world; at the same time, and with some of the same means, the performance becomes a comic testing in extremis of the proposition that pure play, and pure beauty, have no moral designs upon, and no reference to, the world of action.

As a character, the Clerk is a study of the Petrarchan man of letters, leading a life wholly "in bokes" and in "poetrie." He professes a stylish and grave, but wholly secular, *contemptus mundi*, which means in his case only and exactly what it says: a distaste for present worldly life, and a corresponding sense of companionship with the mighty dead in books.[35] It entails neither the desire for God on the one hand, nor, on the other, a devotion to virtuous action. His desires, like his physical substance, are barely there, or pallidly optative: he is lean, like his horse; he possesses almost nothing. Not even the "twenty bokes" we always attribute to him in memory necessarily belong to him, according to the grammar of the sentence. We only know he *would rather* have them than "riche robes"—a characteristically extreme contrast to the threadbare cloak he does have—or "fithele or gay sautrie"; it is axiomatic

with such as the Clerk that melodies unheard are sweeter. If he is
an ideal, as many critics have thought, it is an ideal of style, not of
moral action or "intente," as, for example, the Parson is, about
whose self-presentation we learn little, while we hear much about
his regular activities, which wholly define and absorb him, and
place him vividly in our minds as an actor in some other scene
than this company. The Clerk, however, declines to be present in
any worldly scene. Every unit of language of which Chaucer composed him tells the same story: from the minutest details of syntax in the portrait (which tell us what he *does not have*, what he
does not yet do, what he would *rather do*, what he *does not say*,
and *the style he does not use to say it*); to his opening remarks as
a storyteller (in which he tells us about the proem he is leaving out
for the sake of simplicity, and reminds us that, like the author of
this tale "now deed and nayled in his cheste" we, too, shall all
die); to his final witty denial that his tale has been about any ideal
of human relations; to his envoy, rescinding the symbolic meaning
he has offered instead, and ironically lamenting the departure of
virtuous models of conduct from the company of the living forever. Chaucer presents the Clerk's unworldliness as in every respect
not that of a man of spiritual vocation, but that of a man who
quite simply will not appear in this world: his only acts are vanishing acts. Minimalism is not only Chaucer's technique in presenting
him, it is also the Clerk's way of existing in the world. His manner
of address is infinitely weighty and infinitely brief, a very vanishing
point for art, which presents to the world nothing but itself.

As a performer he is perhaps the most outrageous player of the
Canterbury game. His rime royal and his envoy are the most ele-
gantly turned Chaucer ever made, but they playfully refuse to turn
the good of the story outward toward an audience. He declines to
translate his story's "then" into this audience's "now," insisting
that it cannot be done; instead he ends his "ernestful matere" and
offers to add "a song to glade yow" as his contribution to the
spirit of "myrie" play. Unlike the other new men, he does not

comment on the relation of the translated story, "endited" in "heigh stile" by Petrarch the "lauriat poete," to the current demand for entertainment. Like Chaucer in the *Parlement* and *Troilus*, he leaves "making" and "poetry" tantalizingly juxtaposed.

The "intente" of the Clerk's final gesture is baffling. It may be seen as an effort to defend and preserve the purity of Griselda's example by isolating it, refusing to put its pure gold to the vulgar "assayes" of practical use "now-a-dayes," a purpose consonant with the Clerk's own avoidance of worldly "office." It may also be read as yet one more profession of obedience to Harry's request that he avoid making moral claims upon us in his "pley"—an assent whose patent irony requires the hearer to affirm the opposite: that this "ernestful matere" is both useful to hear and not "impertinent" to play and pleasure. Whatever the intent of the gesture, its curious similarity to earlier Chaucerian multiple closures is clear, and suggests an interpretation.

With this tale, the Clerk challenges an audience as Griselda's impassive patience challenges Walter. He offers a tale so beautifully made, with such art-concealing purity of line, that we must ourselves insist on its value, across the narrator's denial that this value can be made useful or explained. He insists that he has obeyed our pleasure in all things, utterly fulfilling our implicit demand that he make an object of pleasure rather than one of moral use: his envoy, however, catches his audience in the act of trying to find a relation between the two, retrospectively searching the perfect serenity of its style for clues to what it means.

In this way of posing the relation between "making" and "poetry," however he is yet another—and the most extreme and comic—version of the perpetually ingratiating entertainer Chaucer. Like Chaucer he rides meek and still and must be coaxed into performing; like Chaucer, he is treated as infinitely pliant to detailed requests to be purely amusing and to avoid bookishness. And like Chaucer, he must somehow fulfill an utterly self-contradictory demand: he must make us feel improved and vindicated, as well as entertained, without manifesting any persuasive designs upon us. The Clerk's reply is comically radical: his ironic retraction of his story's practical moral or allegorical use implies that "poetrie" has no life for practice or the present. His final gesture fulfills instead the customary expectations of the "maker": that he act into the social situation obligingly and freely, and that his "making" be purely stylish and recreative, and affirm us in the feelings we came with; yet it also announces that this is done at the cost of keeping "enditing" the form in which "poetry" comes into current worldly use, "in stoor," perhaps awaiting a more rarefied and princely taste than that of this company to recognize the goodness in its simple beauty. If the Clerk is an ideal, it is as his Griselda is —as one without a present world in which to live. Like her impassive face, "ay constant as a wal," his perfect stylistic edifice is his only worldly resource.

This is perhaps a perverse, and certainly too condensed, reading of the Clerk's performance. It is intended, however, to suggest some possible implications of the intellectual genesis of the *Canterbury Tales* I have described. When a courtier's amusement becomes the pilgrims' game, "making" becomes "enditing," and its emotional and ethical vocabulary become problematic, fertile ground for speculation, by being assigned to unlikely players and placed in narrative situations that generate questions not easily referred to cultic values. When "making" becomes "enditing," its court of appeal becomes the world.

Even in its transferred form, this theory of poetry and ideal of eloquence retains signs of its origin. The end of "enditing," like that of "making," is worldly pleasure and mutual understanding, not the inculcation of any transcendent truth; and as "making" was a way of affirming and celebrating the graces requisite to courtly society, "enditing" was a way of honoring and exercising the virtues conducive to worldly peace and secular felicity: in a heterogeneous society, these will be the virtuosities that assure "the sufficient life."

The young people of the *Decameron* choose for their last day's storytelling a subject that seems especially well-suited for preparing them to reenter their plague-devastated city: "those who have performed liberal or munificent deeds, whether in the cause of love or otherwise." And whether in the cause of love or otherwise, the stylistically self-conscious and high-minded Canterbury pilgrims tell some of the same stories; one feel it is with the same implicit sense of worldly and public purpose: "And thus our lives, which cannot be other than brief in these our mortal bodies, will be preserved by the fame of our achievements."[36] The examination of virtue through stories has itself become a virtuous act, and tale-telling a heroic pilgrimage to truth.

The fifteenth century was well justified in considering Chaucer its primary English model of the "rhetorical poete." He not only provided a tonally varied high vernacular eloquence as a model, but reasoned deeply and fruitfully in his own fiction on the social environment and philosophical purposes for which it was to thrive.

NOTES

1. See Paul Strohm, "Chaucer's Audience," *Literature and History* 5 (1977): 26–41. Strohm notes (p. 40) that the phrase was originated by Orderic Vitalis to describe men brought into positions of authority by Henry I. On Chaucer as a "new man," see D. S. Brewer, "Class Distinction in Chaucer," *Speculum* 43 (1968): 290–305; Donald Howard, "Chaucer the Man," *PMLA* 80 (1965): 337–43, reprinted in *Chaucer's Mind and Art*, ed. A. C. Cawley (London: Oliver and Boyd, 1969), pp. 31–45. For an opposing view, see D. W. Robertson, Jr., "Some Disputed Chaucerian Terminology," *Speculum* 52 (1977): 571–81.

2. On the political and social fortunes of the lower gentry in the fourteenth century, see Strohm, "Chaucer's Audience," p. 28; also N. Denholm-Young, *The Country Gentry in the Fourteenth Century* (Oxford: Clarendon Press, 1969); F. W. Maitland, *The Constitutional History of England* (1908; reprint ed., Cambridge: At the University Press, 1955), pp. 23–39; K. B. McFarlane, *The Nobility of Later Medieval England* (Oxford: Clarendon Press, 1973), pp. 8–15.

3. See Northrop Frye, *The Secular Scripture* (Cambridge: Harvard University Press, 1976), chap. 1, esp. p. 29. On the cultic value of a work of art in an established tradition, see Walter Benjamin, "The Work of Art in the Age of Mechanical Reproduction," in *Illuminations*, tr. Harry Zohn, ed. Hannah Arendt (New York: Schocken, 1969), pp. 220–24.

4. See Strohm, "Chaucer's Audience," pp. 30–34; Arnold Hauser, *Philosophy of Art History* (1958; reprint ed., New York: Meridian Books, 1963), p. 230.

5. See, for example, D. W. Robertson, Jr., "Chaucer's Franklin and His Tale," *Costerus*

1 (1974): 1-26; Roy J. Pearcy, "Chaucer's Franklin and the Literary Vavasour," *Chaucer Review* 8 (1973): 33-59; Alan Gaylord, "The Promises in the Franklin's Tale," *ELH* 31 (1964): 331-65; R. M. Lumiansky, "The Character and Performance of Chaucer's Franklin," *University of Toronto Quarterly* 20 (1951): 344-56; for a recent analysis of the criticism, see Gertrude M. White, "The Franklin's Tale: Chaucer and the Critics," *PMLA* 89 (1974): 454-62. On the Man of Law, see Alfred David, "The Man of Law vs. Chaucer: A Case of Poetics," *PMLA* 82 (1967): 217-25; Marie P. Hamilton, "The Dramatic Suitability of the Man of Law's Tale," in *Studies in Language and Literature in Honour of Margaret Schlauch*, ed. M. Brahmer, S. Helsztynski, and J. Krzyzanowski (Warsaw: Państwowe Wydawnictwo Naukowe, 1966), pp. 153-63.

6. For an interesting parallel to this nonassertive and flexible rhetorical strategy in studies of the evolution of "altruistic" behavior patterns in animal societies, see John Maynard Smith, "The Evolution of Behavior," *Scientific American*, September 1978, pp. 176-92. Smith applies the term *bourgeois strategy* to the tactics that serve to "settle real contests conventionally," noting that this is "the only evolutionarily stable strategy for the game" (p. 189).

7. It should be remembered that a class ideal or ethos may be seen as "in decline" while—and perhaps because—certain individuals or groups professing it, or believing they exemplify it, are socially in the ascendant. It is their ascent under that banner that changes the content of the older terms. See Michael Stroud, "Chivalric Terminology in Late Medieval Literature," *Journal of the History of Ideas* 37 (1976): 323-34. On the Squire's military service, see Alan Gaylord, "Chaucer's Squire and the Glorious Campaign," *Publications of the Michigan Academy of Science, Arts, and Letters* 45 (1960): 341-61. On the "obsolescence" of the cultural traditions espoused by both Squire and Franklin, see Pearcy, "Chaucer's Franklin and the Literary Vavasour," pp. 50-51.

8. See, for example, Petrarch, "On Dialectic," tr. Hans Nachod, in *The Renaissance Philosophy of Man*, ed. E. Cassirer, P. O. Kristeller, and J. H. Randall, Jr. (Chicago: University of Chicago Press, 1948), pp. 134-39. On the general humanist reorientation of study from the service of contemplation and abstract reasoning to that of action and facility, with a downgrading of logic to a "serving science" attendant upon eloquence, see G. K. Hunter, "Humanism and Courtship," in *Elizabethan Poetry: Modern Essays in Criticism*, ed. Paul J. Alpers (New York: Oxford University Press, 1967), pp. 3-40.

9. *General Prologue* 305-306. All citations of Chaucer are to *The Works of Geoffrey Chaucer*, ed. F. N. Robinson, 2nd ed. (Boston: Houghton Mifflin, 1957).

10. See Hannah Arendt, *Between Past and Future* (New York: Viking, 1968), pp. 153-54; and idem, *The Human Condition* (Chicago: University of Chicago Press, 1958), pp. 175-99.

11. Ernst R. Curtius, *European Literature in the Latin Middle Ages*, tr. Willard R. Trask (New York: Pantheon, 1953), pp. 468-75.

12. "Reality, humanly and politically speaking, is the same as appearance" (Arendt, *Human Condition*, p. 199). She includes a related suggestion, which I cannot pursue here, that complements these remarks, that "the human condition of work is worldliness" (p. 7). That the multiplicity of perspectives on the common world afforded by work-life is a structural principle of the *Canterbury Tales* has been argued by Jill Mann, *Chaucer and Medieval Estates Satire* (Cambridge: At the University Press, 1973).

13. *Endite* (indite) in all its forms means in its most basic sense "to compose"; it

renders L. *dictare*, "to dictate for writing" and, by extension, "to compose in writing" (Lewis and Short, *A Latin Dictionary* [Oxford: Clarendon Press, 1879], s.v. *dictare*, II). In most of Chaucer's uses of the term, however, it seems to connote rhetorical composition, usually in a serious manner or elevated style, and often has slightly honorific overtones. It can be rendered accurately most often in Modern English by "compose rhetorically," "declaim," "declare," or even "celebrate." It implies in Chaucer's usage not only composition in writing, but an intensified and augmented form of that activity.

It is distinguished from the physical act of writing, and from writing as record or simple communication, in several instances:

> She (Philomela) coude eek rede, and wel ynow endyte,
> But with a penne coude she nat wryte.
>
> > (*Legend of Good Women* 2356-57)
>
> "For trewely I nyl no lettre write."
> "No? than wol I," quod he, "so ye endite."
>
> > (*Troilus* II. 1161-62)
>
> I dar nat, ther I am, wel lettres make,
> Ne nevere yet ne koude I wel endite.
>
> > (*Troilus* V. 1627-28)
>
> Towchyng thi lettre, thou art wys ynough.
> I woot thow nylt it dygneliche endite,
> As make it with thise argumentes tough;
> Ne scryvenyssh or craftily thow it write.
>
> > (*Troilus* II. 1023-26)
>
> And if thow haddest connyng for t'endite,
> I shall the shewe mater of to wryte.
>
> > (*Parlement of Foules* 167-68)

Enditing in these examples seems to mean that aspect of composing concerned with its propriety of expression, its adequacy both to the subject and the tone of the occasion. It is distinct from the finding of "matere," and from the simple telling or conveying of it. It denotes the activity of realizing the expressive rather than the communicative power of the "matere": hence it constitutes the gift of the Muses to the writer. They help the writer achieve a propriety of manner sustaining the meaning in an act of narration, conferring on it its power to move.

> For lo! rendying Muses of poetes enditen to me thynges to ben writen.
> (*Ecce mihi lacerae dictant scribenda Camenae*)
>
> > (*Boece* I. m.1, 4-5)
>
> And ye me to endite and ryme
> Helpeth, that on Parnaso duelle.
>
> > (*Hous of Fame* 520-21)
>
> Thesiphone, thow help me for t'endite
> This woful vers, that wepen as I write.
>
> > (*Troilus* I. 6-7)

The last two examples illustrate a further point: Chaucer's "enditing" is not identified with, or confined to, verse composition.

> And they ben versified communely
> Of six feet, which men clepen *exametron*.
> In prose eek ben endited many oon.
>
> *(Monk's Tale* B² 1978-80)

> So yif me myght to ryme and ek endyte.
>
> *(Parlement of Foules* 119)

As the activity is distinguished from simple recording or communicating, the quality it confers is distinguished from the aural beauty of good versification, or the ornamentation of sense provided by figures of speech. While in practice "enditing" often seems to involve amplification, the drawing-out of a matter at length,

> What that she (Dido) wrot er that she dyde;
> And nere hyt to long to endyte,
> By God, I wolde hyt here write.
>
> *(Hous of Fame* 380-82)

> It nedeth nat al day thus for to endite.
>
> *(Legend of Good Women* G 310)

> What sholde I alday of his wo endyte?
>
> *(Knight's Tale* A 1380)

the verb itself does not denote any particular choice of rhetorical figure; it is the effort to achieve decorous rather than decorated composition. To choose ornaments for the occasion in a merely formulaic or automatic way is "scryvenyssh." Pandarus' counsel recalls that rules for epistolary decorum are provided in the handbooks of the *ars dictaminis*. "Enditing," in Chaucer's usage, however, is not to confer a particular style upon a matter, but to infuse it with style itself—an intentional design that conveys meaning. Its propriety emanates not from the social character of the participants in the rhetorical transaction, but from the ethical and emotional importance of the matter itself to the human community at large.

Though the term denotes composition in an appropriate style, Chaucer does not use it to refer to the stylistic propriety of low characters or light matters. When the verb takes an object specifying the topic of discourse, the narrative content "endited," the "matere" belongs to the narrative and tonal repertory of noble rather than churlish story: "batailles" (*Troilus* V. 1767; *Knight's Tale* A 2741), "wo" (*Knight's Tale* A 1380), "love" (*Hous of Fame* 634), "traitorie" (*Man of Law's Tale* B¹ 781); not that of "japes" or "harlotrie." The "matere" for "enditing" seems to be the rhetor's "sovereyn notabilitees" (*Nun's Priest's Tale* B² 4397), matter of awesome and universal human significance: a "case" (*Franklin's Tale* F 1550), a "storie" (*Anelida* 9; *Second Nun's Tale* G 80).

In the *Canterbury Tales* the verb is used only in or for the more consciously rhetorical performers—the Knight (A 1209, 1380, 1872, 2741), Squire (*General Prologue* 95), Man of Law (*General Prologue* 325, B¹ 781), Monk (B² 3170, 3858), Nun's Priest (B² 4397), Clerk (E 17, 41, 933, 1148), Franklin (F 1550), Second Nun (G 32, 80)—in short, all those figures whose performances include a great deal of preliminary and interspersed comment that refers attention to their manner of speech.

The reference of the term slightly overlaps that of *making* in Chaucer's usage (some instances are discussed in what follows), but there are important differences in connotation and context, and it is these, rather than mutually exclusive meanings, that are significant for the present purpose.

14. Chaucer uses the verb *to make* hundreds of times, and in dozens of instances to refer to verbal composition—of "vers," "bokes," "complaints," "minstralcies," "lays," "dytees," "songs," "balades," and the like—a list with a strong preponderance of performance rather than "textual" modes. See J.S.P. Tatlock and Arthur G. Kennedy, *A Concordance to the Complete Works of Chaucer* (Washington, D.C.: Carnegie Institution, 1927), s.v. *made, make, maker, making.* Even books, when conceived as "made," seem to be seen as at least potentially presentation pieces rather than texts for private study or contemplation. Chaucer uses the verb to refer to his own literary activity and that of his contemporaries; he rarely, however (with the important exceptions discussed herein), uses it absolutely, without specifying an object, to mean "to compose (pleasurable) verse"; a rare instance of this common French usage is *Complaint of Venus* 82.

He uses the noun *making* for literary composition generally. It does not denote any specific form or genre, but it more often refers to contemporary than ancient composition, and more often to literary activity with a recreative rather than instructive content or rhetorical aim.

He does not often use the noun *maker* to refer to any writer, however; nearly all of his uses of the word refer to God the Creator. One exception is *Boece* III. 6, 745-50, "makere of dytees that highten tragedies," glossing "tragedien" (L. *tragicus*); the other, discussed herein (*Troilus* V. 1787), refers to Chaucer himself.

For an excellent account of Chaucer's conception of "making," its differences from "poetry," and the relation of his use of the term to the vernacular poetics of his French contemporaries, see Glending Olson, "Deschamps' *Art de Dictier* and Chaucer's Literary Environment," *Speculum* 48 (1973): 714-23; and idem, "Making and Poetry in the Age of Chaucer," forthcoming in *Comparative Literature*; also Robert O. Payne, *The Key of Remembrance* (New Haven: Yale University Press, 1963), pp. 55-56.

In two instances Chaucer has paired "making" and "enditing": *General Prologue* 95 (Squire) and 325 (Man of Law); see note 22. They are not wholly distinct activities; "making" however, seems to connote pleasurable social composition for the court or any group considered as a coterie or cult; "enditing" suggests composition for an unspecified group or audience, emphasizing matter of more general worldly significance. On the multiple functions served by the late-medieval rhetor, which might include the creation of public displays as well as the household entertainments for the ruling house, see Gordon Kipling, *The Triumph of Honour* (Leiden: Brill, 1977). On "courtly makers" and the game of love, see John Stevens, *Music and Poetry in the Early Tudor Court* (Lincoln: University of Nebraska Press, 1961), esp. pp. 164, 206, 212.

15. Chaucer does not refer to any living writer, including himself, as a "poet." He applies the term to the ancients, such as "Virgile, Ovide, Omer, Lucan, and Stace" (*Troilus* V. 1792), Martianus Capella (*Merchant's Tale* E 1732), and to Orpheus (*Boece* III. m. 12, 1115-20), where it renders L *vates*. Among the "moderns" he uses it only

for Dante (*Monk's Tale* B² 2650; *Wife of Bath's Tale* D 1125), and Petrarch (*Clerk's Tale* E 31). *Poetry* is used for the work of these writers seen as a treasury of myths and fables, and for the cultural authority it wields. "Poetry" is a repository of "sentence," of morally substantial beauty; it is seen as a fund of classical moral and philosophical lore, as well as narrative matters, and may provide figures, fables, and wisdom to the "maker," whose activity is seen as that of giving it pleasing and available form. See Olson, "Making and Poetry"; on the different status of Boccaccio in this scheme from that Chaucer accords Dante and Petrarch, see Thomas J. Garbáty, "*Troilus* V. 1786-92 and V. 1807-27: An Example of Poetic Process," *Chaucer Review* 11 (1977): 299-305; and Donald McGrady, "Chaucer and the *Decameron* Reconsidered," *Chaucer Review* 12 (1977): 1-26.

16. The position of the reader I am describing here, as out of the world of common wisdom and mutual appearance while he is reading, corresponds to that by which Walter Benjamin characterizes the reader of a novel as distinguished from the hearer or teller of traditional stories. See "The Storyteller," in *Illuminations*, tr. Harry Zohn, ed. Hannah Arendt, esp. pp. 86-87; his remarks on the isolation of the novelist, who in his work "gives evidence of the profound perplexity of the living" but "is himself uncounseled, and cannot counsel others," seems an apt description of the Clerk's performance, as the following discussion will suggest.

17. See my article "The Idea of Public Poetry in the Reign of Richard II," *Speculum* 53 (1978): 94-114.

18. See Olson, "Deschamps' *Art de Dictier*," p. 717; Stevens, *Music and Poetry*, pp. 154-202.

19. See my essay "The *Physician's Tale* and Love's Martyrs: 'Ensamples Mo than Ten' as a Method in the *Canterbury Tales*," *Chaucer Review* 8 (1973): 9-32.

20. The Second Nun's prologue to her tale invokes the Virgin as, in effect, the Muse of this performance, to

> do me endite
> Thy maydens deeth, that wan thurgh her merite
> The eterneel lyf, and of the feend victorie.
>
> (G 32-34)

21. The possibility that the Man of Law's preface is either a satirical dig at "moral Gower," or part of a standing joke Chaucer shares with his fellow poet, does not preclude this reading, nor is it precluded by it. See Alfred David, "Man of Law"; John H. Fisher, *John Gower: Moral Philosopher and Friend of Chaucer* (New York: New York University Press, 1964), pp. 285-92. Whether aimed at Gower or not, the Man of Law's assessment of the moral value in this kind of poetry is a comic portrait of a believable contemporary sensibility, one opinionated member of a possible audience for both poets. Chaucer implies that any notion of moral art that cannot explain what is lacking in the Man of Law's view is not yet adequate.

22. In the General Prologue portrait of the Man of Law, Chaucer associates "making" and "enditing" as if they were similar skills: "Therto he koude endite and make a thyng" (325). While both terms may refer to literary composition, the context—a list of the Man of Law's skills as a lawyer—introduces at least some ambiguity, suggesting that both may refer to the writing of legal instruments or documents: the making of a charge or accusation (*OED* s.v. *indict*¹) or a proclamation (†*indict*²); and the writing of a legal

process, bringing a charge, pleading a cause, making a transaction (*OED* s.v. *thing* I.2, 3,4,5). The *OED* offers this line (s.v. *thing* II.13) as its first citation to illustrate the meaning: "an individual work of literature or art, a composition; a writing, piece of music, etc."; I am not convinced that this sense can be drawn unambiguously from the line. The ambiguity of reference to both legal and literary writing strikes me as both intentional and comic, supporting exactly what Chaucer does with the Man of Law as performer generally: namely, to suggest that the power of legal instruments to "indict" and of literary instruments to "endite" have very different practical force and use in the world, a difference the lawyer himself does not entirely grasp. He evidently sees literary "enditing" as advocating the conduct it refers to, and he is for this reason pompously pleased to find recorded in Chaucer's "sermons" no "unkynde abhominacions." The Man of Law's entire performance provides Chaucer with an occasion to consider in what senses fictions may be said to affirm anything, and the differernces between the literary and legal conceptions of truth and virtue.

23. Chaucer uses the verb in the *Legend* in the following places: G 69, 72, 73, 342, 364, 366, 437, 549, 573, 579, 618.

24. *Phaedrus* 275, tr. W. C. Helmbold and W. G. Rabinowitz (Indianapolis: Bobbs Merrill, 1956), pp. 68-70. See also Stanley Fish, *Self-Consuming Artifacts* (Berkeley and Los Angeles: University of California Press, 1972), pp. 15-20.

25. See Garbáty, "*Troilus* V: 1786-92 and V: 1807-27." There is disagreement as to what constitutes the "comedye." Garbáty views it as Troilus' ascent to the eighth sphere, from which cosmic perspective his sorrow is changed to laughter. Donald Howard, however, takes it to refer to the *Canterbury Tales*, which provide a tonal counterpart to *Troilus*; see *The Idea of the Canterbury Tales* (Berkeley and Los Angeles: University of California Press, 1976), pp. 30-45.

26. The injunction to avoid "envye" tends to support the identification of the poem's initial context and company with the court:

Envye—I preye to God yeve hire myschaunce!—
Is lavender in the grete court alway,
For she ne parteth, neyther nyght ne day,
Out of the hous of Cesar; thus seyth Dante.

(*LGW* G 333-36)

27. The accepted reading of the verb in 1788 is not "to compose in verse" but "to match" (see Garbáty, "*Troilus* V. 1786-92 and V. 1807-27"; and Richard C. Boys, "An Unusual Meaning of 'Make' in Chaucer," *MLN* 52 [1937]: 351-53; *MED* s.v. *make*). Yet "makere" in the preceding line—which is momentarily (and mistakenly) heard as in apposition to "God" ("God thi makere"), and thereby briefly (mis)understood as "creator"—and "makyng" in the following line, which can also be read as a near-synonym (as it is identical in etymological meaning) for "poesye" in the next line (that is, do not envy other poetry, but rather be reverently subject to it), both create the verbal equivalent of an optical illusion around "make," and cause one to hear the meaning "to compose," "to create," anyway. This ghost reading shadows the first, and shifts the speaker's wish to a more general sense: "send me the power to create again," rather than "send me the power to make the opposite kind of poem to this one."

The effect of the optical illusions does not stop here, however. The first momentary misreading leaves a residue that parallels the writer's "making" with the creative act of the Divine word; the third, by making the distinction between the pursuit of "makyng" and that of "poesye" finally consist in a different spirit (reverence rather than envy), tends to reduce the difference one heard at first between the objects or arts themselves. The stanza needs still closer analysis as a study of Chaucerian poetic process; these suggestions are confined to the present purpose.

28. This is essentially the view of Alfred David, *The Strumpet Muse* (Bloomington: Indiana University Press, 1976).

29. See Strohm, "Chaucer's Audience," pp. 30–31 on the taste of Richard II and the court generally for French love poetry; also Edith Richert, "King Richard II's Books," *The Library*, 4th ser., 13 (1933): 144–47.

30. See, for example, D. A. Pearsall, "The Squire as Story-Teller," *University of Toronto Quarterly* 34 (1964): 82–92; Robertson, "Chaucer's Franklin."

31. Dorothee Metlitzki, *The Matter of Araby in Medieval England* (New Haven: Yale University Press, 1977), pp. 137–60.

32. On the rhetorical uses of this characteristic Chaucerian device, and their significance for his theory of poetry, see Morton Bloomfield's remarks on the strategy of "answering a querulous objector," in "The Gloomy Chaucer," in *Veins of Humor*, ed. Harry Levin, *Harvard English Studies* 3 (Cambridge: Harvard University Press, 1972), pp. 64–66.

33. The literary role of "vavasours" in romances was to provide hospitality, to entertain knights-errant; see Pearcy, "Chaucer's Franklin and the Literary Vavasour."

34. The Monk's "enditing" of false Fortune, like that for which the Man of Law is praised in the General Prologue (325; see note 22), sustains the dual sense of the term—the legal sense "to charge, accuse" (> Modern English *indict*), and the rhetorical sense "to decry, complain" (> Modern English *indite*)—and reminds us of the forensic aspect of such a public ethical appeal, of the way the rhetoric of complaint implicitly invites and directs an audience's feelings as moral actors.

35. Cf. Petrarch, "Letter to Posterity" (*Seniles* XVIII.1) in *Selected Sonnets, Odes and Letters*, ed. and tr. Thomas G. Bergin (New York: Appleton Century Crofts, 1966), p. 3; also Ernest Hatch Wilkins, *Life of Petrarch* (Chicago: University of Chicago Press, 1961), pp. 246–48. A letter Petrarch wrote to accompany a copy of his Latin translation of the tale of Griselda (*Decameron* X.10), which he sent to Boccaccio in 1373 (*Seniles* XVII.2), describes the unique sweetness of the life in letters ("I am not fitted for other kinds of work"), and denies that he has sought fame or office: "(Only apparently) have I lived with princes; in reality, the princes lived with me. . . . I should never have submitted to any conditions which would, in any degree, have interfered with my liberty or my studies" (Bergin, pp. 12–17; see also Wilkins, pp. 236–39).

36. *The Decameron*, tr. G. H. McWilliam (Harmondsworth: Penguin, 1972), IX, Conclusion, p. 731.

 *Stephen J. Greenblatt*

Improvisation and Power

> What is a Wife & what is a Harlot?
> What is a Church? & What
> Is a Theatre? are they Two & not One?
> can they Exist Separate?
> Are not Religion & Politics the Same Thing?
> —Blake, *Jerusalem*

In his influential study of modernization in the Middle East, *The Passing of Traditional Society*, the sociologist Daniel Lerner defines the West as a "mobile society," a society characterized not only by certain enlightened and rational public practices but also by the inculcation in its people of a "*mobile sensibility* so adaptive to change that rearrangement of the self-system is its distinctive mode." While traditional society, Professor Lerner argues, functions on the basis of a "highly constrictive personality," one that resists change and is incapable of grasping the situation of another, the mobile personality of Western society "is distinguished by a high capacity for identification with new aspects of his environment," for he "comes equipped with the mechanisms needed to incorporate new demands upon himself that arise outside of his habitual experience." Those mechanisms Professor Lerner subsumes under the single term *empathy*, which he defines as "the capacity to see oneself in the other fellow's situation." In the West this capacity was fostered first by the physical mobility initiated by the Age of Exploration, then confirmed and broadened by the mass media. "These," he writes, "have peopled the daily world of their audience with sustained, even intimate, experience of the lives of others. 'Ma Perkins,' 'The Goldbergs,' 'I Love Lucy'—all these bring us friends we never met, but whose joys and sorrows we intensely 'share.'" And the international diffusion of the mass media means a concomitant diffusion of psychic mobility and hence of modernization: "In

57

our time, indeed, the spread of empathy around the world is accelerating."[1]

To test the rate of this acceleration, Professor Lerner devised a set of questions that he and his assistants put to a cross section of the inhabitants of the Middle East, to porters and cobblers, as well as grocers and physicians. The question began, "If you were made editor of a newspaper, what kind of a paper would you run?" and I confess myself in complete sympathy with that class of respondents who, like one shepherd interviewed in a village near Ankara, gasped "My God! How can you say such a thing? . . . A poor villager . . . master of the whole world."[2] Professor Lerner invariably interprets such answers as indicative of a constrictive personality incapable of empathy, but in fact the Turkish shepherd, with his Tamburlainian language, reintroduces the great missing term in the analysis of modernization, and that term is *power.* For my own part, I would like in this paper to delineate the Renaissance origins of the "mobile sensibility" and, having done so, to shift the ground from "I Love Lucy" to *Othello* in order to demonstrate that what Professor Lerner calls *empathy,* Shakespeare calls *Iago.*

To help us move from the contemporary Middle East to the early seventeenth century, let us dwell for a moment on Professor Lerner's own concept of Renaissance origins: "Take the factor of physical mobility," he writes, "which initiated Western take-off in an age when the earth was underpopulated in terms of the world man-land ratio. Land was to be had, more or less, for the finding. The great explorers took over vast real estate by planting a flag; these were slowly filled with new populations over generations."[3] It didn't exactly happen this way. Land does not become "real estate" quite so easily, and the underpopulation was not found but created by those great explorers. Demographers of Mesoamerica now estimate, for example, that the population of Hispaniola in 1492 was 7 or 8 million, perhaps as high as 11 million. Reduction to that attractive man-land ratio was startlingly sudden: by 1501, enslavement, disruption of agriculture, and, above all, European disease had reduced the population to some 700,000; by 1512, to 28,000.[4] The unimaginable massiveness of the death-rate did not, of course, go unnoticed; European observers took it as a sign of God's determination to cast down the idolators and open the New World to Christianity.

With the passage from the sociologist's bland world of ceremonial flag-planting in an empty landscape to violent displacement and insidious death, we have already moved toward Shakespeare's tragedy, and we move still closer if we glance at an incident recounted in 1525 by Peter Martyr in the Seventh Decade of *De Orbe Novo*. Faced with a serious labor shortage in the gold mines as a result of the decimation of the native population, the Spanish in Hispaniola began to raid neighboring islands. Two ships reached an outlying island in the Lucayas (now called the Bahamas) where they were received with awe and trust. The Spanish learned through their interpreters that the natives believed that after death their souls were first purged of their sins in icy northern mountains, then borne to a paradisal island in the south whose beneficent, lame prince offered them innumerable pleasures: "The soules inioy eternall delightes, among the dancings, and songes of young maidens, and among the embracements of their children, and whatsoeuer they loued heeretofore; they babble also there, that such as growe olde, waxe young againe, so that all are of like yeeres full of ioy and mirth." When the Spanish understood these imaginations, writes Martyr, they proceeded to persuade the natives "that they came from those places, wher they should see their parents, & children, & al their kindred, & friends that were dead: & should inioy al kind of delights, together with ye imbracements & fruition of beloued things." Thus deceived, the entire population of the island passed "singing and reioycing," Martyr says, onto the ships and were taken to the goldmines of Hispaniola. The Spanish, however, reaped less profit than they had anticipated; when they grasped what had happened to them, the Lucayans, like certain German Jewish communities during the Crusades, undertook mass suicide: "Becomming desperate, they either slewe themselues, or choosing to famish, gaue vppe their faint spirites, beeing perswaded by no reason, or violence, to take foode."[5]

Martyr, it appears, feels ambivalent about the story. He is certain that God disapproves of such treachery, since many of those who perpetrated the fraud subsequently died violent deaths; on the other hand, he opposes those who would free enslaved natives, since bitter experience has shown that even those Indians who have apparently been converted to Christianity will, given the slightest opportunity revert to "their auncient and natiue vices" and turn savagely against those who had instructed them "with fatherly charity."[6] For our purposes Martyr's ambivalence is less important than the power of his story to evoke a crucial Renaissance mode of behavior that links Lerner's "empathy" and Shakespeare's Iago: I shall call that mode *improvisation*, by which I mean the ability to both capitalize on the unforeseen and transform given materials into one's own scenario. The "spur of the moment" quality of improvisation is not as critical here as the opportunistic grasp of that which seems fixed and established. Indeed, as Castiglione and others in the Renaissance well understood, the impromptu character of an improvisation is itself often a calculated mask, the product of careful preparation.[7] What is essential is the Europeans' ability again and again to insinuate themselves into the preexisting political, religious, even psychic, structures of the natives and to turn those structures to their advantage. The process is as familiar to us by now as the most tawdry business fraud, so familiar that we assume a virtually universal diffusion of the necessary improvisational talent, but that assumption is almost certainly misleading. There are periods and cultures in which the ability to insert onself into the consciousness of another is of relatively slight importance, the object of limited concern; others in which it is a major preoccupation, the object of cultivation and fear. Professor Lerner is right to insist that this ability is a characteristically (though not exclusively) Western mode, present to varying degrees in the classical and medieval world and greatly strengthened from the Renaissance onward; he misleads only in insisting further that it is an act of imaginative generosity, a sympathetic appreciation of the situation of the other fellow. For when he speaks confidently of the "spread of empathy around the world," we must understand that he is speaking of the exercise of Western power, power that is creative as well as destructive, but that is scarcely ever wholly disinterested and benign.

To return to the Lucayan story, we may ask ourselves what conditions exist in Renaissance culture that make such an improvisation possible. It depends first upon the ability and willingness to play a role, to transform oneself, if only briefly and with mental reservations, into another. This necessitates the acceptance of disguise, the ability to effect a divorce, in Ascham's phrase, between the tongue and the heart. Such role playing in turn depends upon the transformation of another's reality into a manipulable fiction. The Spanish had to perceive the Indian's religious beliefs as illusions, "imaginations," as Martyr's English translator calls them. Lucayan society, Martyr observes, is based upon a principle of reverent obedience fostered by a set of religious fables that "are deliuered by worde of mouth and tradition from the Elders to the younger, for a most sacred and true hystorie, insomuch as he who but seemed to thinke otherwise, shoulde bee thrust out of the society of menne." The Lucayan king performs the supreme sacral functions and partakes fully in the veneration accorded to the idols, so that if he were to command one of his subjects to cast himself down from a precipice, the subject would immediately comply. The king uses this absolute power to ensure the just distribution, to families according to need, of the tribe's food, all of which is stored communally in royal granaries: "They had the golden age, mine and thine, the seedes of discord, were farre remoued from them." Martyr then perceives the social function of

Lucayan religious concepts, the native apparatus for their trans-
mission and reproduction, and the punitive apparatus for the
enforcement of belief. In short, he grasps Lucayan religion as an
ideology, and it is this perception that licenses the transformation
of "sacred and true hystorie" into "crafty & subtil imaginations"
that may be exploited.[8]

If improvisation is made possible by the subversive perception of
another's truth as an ideological construct, that construct must at
the same time be grasped in terms that bear a certain structural
resemblance to one's own set of beliefs. An ideology that is perceived as entirely alien would permit no point of histrionic entry:
it could be destroyed but not performed. Thus the Lucayan religion, in Martyr's account, is an anamorphic representation of
Catholicism: there are "Images" carried forth with solemn pomp
on "the holy day of adoration"; worshippers kneel reverently before these images, sing "hymns," and make offerings, "which at
night the nobles diuide among them, as our priests doe the cakes
or wafers which women offer";[9] there are "holy relics" about
which the chief priest, standing in his "pulpit," preaches; and as
we have seen, there is absolution for sin, purgatory, and eternal
delight in paradise. The European account of the native religion
must have borne some likeness to what the Lucayans actually believed; why else would they have danced, singing and rejoicing,
onto the Spanish ships? But it is equally important that the religion is conceived as analogous to Catholicism, close enough to
permit improvisation, yet sufficiently distanced to protect European beliefs from the violence of fictionalization. The Spanish
were not compelled to perceive their own religion as a manipulable human construct; on the contrary, the compulsion of their
own creed was presumably strengthened by their contemptuous
exploitation of an analogous symbolic structure.

This absence of reciprocity is an aspect of the total economy
of the mode of improvisation that I have sketched here. For
what we may see in the Lucayan story is an early manifestation

of an exercise of power that was subsequently to become vastly important and that remains a potent force in our lives: the ownership of another's labor conceived as involving no supposedly "natural" reciprocal obligation (as in feudalism), but rather functioning by concealing the very fact of ownership from the exploited who believe that they are acting freely and in their own interest. Of course, once the ships reached Hispaniola, this concealed ownership gave way to direct enslavement; the Spanish were not capable of continuing the improvisation into the mines. And it is this failure to sustain the illusion that led to the ultimate failure of the enterprise, for, of course, the Spanish did not want dead Indians but live mineworkers. It would take other, subtler minds, in the Renaissance and beyond, to perfect the means to sustain indefinitely an indirect enslavement.

I have called improvisation a central Renaissance mode of behavior, but the example on which I have focused is located on a geographical margin and might only seem to bear out Immanuel Wallerstein's theory that Western Europe in the sixteenth century increasingly established its ownership of the labor and resources of those located in areas defined as peripheral.[10] But I would argue that the phenomenon I have described is found in a wide variety of forms closer to home. It may be glimpsed, to suggest two significant instances, in the relationship of Tudor power to Catholic symbolism and the characteristic form of rhetorical education.

The Anglican Church and the monarch who was its Supreme Head did not, as radical Protestants demanded, eradicate Catholic ritual, but rather improvised within it in an attempt to assume its power. Thus, for example, in the Accession Day celebration of 1590, we are told that the Queen, sitting in the Tilt gallery,

> did suddenly hear a music so sweet and so secret, as every one thereat greatly marvelled. And hearkening to that excellent melody, the earth as it were opening, there appears a Pavilion, made of white Taffeta, being in proportion like unto the sacred Temple of the Virgins Vestal. This temple seemed to consist upon pillars of porphyry, arched like unto a

Church, within it were many lamps burning. Also, on the one side an
Altar covered with cloth of gold; and thereupon two wax candles burning
in rich candlesticks; upon the Altar also were laid certain Princely presents,
which after by three Virgins were presented unto her Majesty.[11]

This secular epiphany permits us to identify two of the characteristic operations of improvisation: displacement and absorption.
By *displacement* I mean the process whereby a prior symbolic
structure is compelled to coexist with other centers of attention
that do not necessarily conflict with the original structure but
are not swept up in its gravitational pull; indeed, as here, the
sacred may find itself serving as an adornment, a backdrop, an
occasion for a quite secular phenomenon. By *absorption* I mean
the process whereby a symbolic structure is taken into the ego so
completely that it ceases to exist as an external phenomenon; in
the Accession Day ceremony, instead of the secular prince humbl-
ing herself before the sacred, the sacred seems only to enhance
the ruler's identity, to express her power.[12]

Both displacement and absorption are possible here because the
religious symbolism was already charged with the celebration of
power. What we are witnessing is a shift in the institution that
controls and profits from the interpretation of such symbolism, a
shift mediated in this instance by the classical scholarship of
Renaissance humanism. The invocation of the Temple of the
Vestal Virgins is the sign of that transformation of belief into
ideology that we have already examined; the Roman mythology,
deftly keyed to England's Virgin Queen, helps to fictionalize
Catholic ritual sufficiently for it to be displaced and absorbed.

This enzymatic function of humanism leads directly to our
second instance of domestic improvisation, for the cornerstone
of the humanist project was a rhetorical education. In *The Tudor
Play of Mind*, Joel Altman has recently demonstrated the central
importance for English Renaissance culture of the *argumentum
in utramque partem*, the cultivation of the scholar's power to
speak equally persuasively for diametrically opposed positions.

The practice permeated intellectual life in the early sixteenth century and was, Altman convincingly argues, one of the formative
influences on the early drama.[13] It is in the spirit of such rhetorical mobility that Erasmus praises More, the greatest figure of
early Tudor humanism, for his ability "to play the man of all
hours with all men" and that Roper's *Life of Sir Thomas More*
informs its readers that as a boy in Cardinal Morton's household
More distinguished himself by his dazzling improvisations: "Though
he was young of years, yet would he at Christmas-tide suddenly
sometimes step in among the players, and never studying for the
matter, make a part of his own there presently among them,
which made the lookers-on more sport than all the players be-
side."[14]

The hagiographical bias of Roper's and most subsequent writing
on More has concealed the extent to which this improvisational
gift is closely allied to a control of power in the law courts and the
royal service: the mystification of manipulation as disinterested
empathy begins as early as the sixteenth century. As a corrective,
we need only read one of More's controversial works, such as
The Confutation of Tyndale's Answer, whose recurrent method is
through improvisation to transform the heretic's faith into a fiction, then absorb it into a new symbolic structure that will ridicule
or consume it. Thus Tyndale had written:

> Synne we thorow fragilyte neuer so ofte, yet as sone as we repent and
> come in to the ryght waye agayne, and vnto the testament whych god
> hath made in Crystes blood: our synnes vanysh awaye as smoke in the
> wynde, and as darkness at the commynge of lyght, or as thou cast a lytle
> blood or melke into the mayne see.

More responds by maliciously improvising on Tyndale's text:

> Neyther purgatory nede to be fered when we go hens, nor penauns nede
> to be done whyle we be here/but synne and be sory and syt and make
> mery, and then synne agayne and then repent a lytell and ronne to ye
> ale & wasshe away the synne, thynke ones on goddys promyse and then do

what we lyste. For hopynge sure in that, kyll we .x. men on a day we cast
but a lytell blood in to the mayne see.

Having thus made a part of his own, More continues by labeling
Tyndale's argument about penance as "but a pece of hys poetrye"
—an explicit instance of that fictionalization we have witnessed
elsewhere—and concludes,

Go me to Martyn Luther. . . . Whyle that frere lyeth with his nonne, &
woteth well he doth nought, and sayth styll he doth well: let Tyndale
tell me what repentynge is that. He repenteth euery mornynge, and to
bedde agayne euery nyghte/thynketh on goddys promyse fyrste, and
then go synne agayne vppon trust of goddys testament/and then he call-
eth it castynge of a lytell mylk in to the mayne see.[15]

Improvisation here obviously does not intend to deceive its
original object but to work upon a third party, the reader, who
might be wavering between the reformers and the Catholic Church.
If the heretic speaks of sin redeemed by God's testament as milk,
More returns that milk to sin, then surpasses the simple reversal
by transforming it to semen, while he turns the sea that imaged
for Tyndale the boundlessness of divine forgiveness into the sexual insatiability of Luther's nun.

These perversions of the reformer's text are greatly facilitated
by the fact that the text was already immersed in an intensely
charged set of metaphorical transformations—that is, More seizes
upon the brilliant instability of Tyndale's prose with its own
nervous passage from Christ's blood to sin conceived progres-
sively as smoke, darkness, blood, and finally milk. More's artful
improvisation makes it seem that murder and lust lay just beneath the surface of the original discourse, as a kind of dark sub-
text, and he is able to do so more plausibly because both violence
and sexual anxiety are in fact powerful underlying forces in
Tyndale's prose as they are in More's. That is, once again, there is
a haunting structural homology between the improvisor and his
other.

I hope that by now *Othello* seems virtually to force itself upon

us as the supreme symbolic expression of the cultural mode I
have been describing, for violence, sexual anxiety, and improvisation are the materials out of which the drama is constructed. To
be sure, there are many other explorations of these materials in
Shakespeare—one thinks of Richard III wooing Anne[16] or, in
comedy, of Rosalind playfully taking advantage of the disguise
that exile has forced upon her—but none so intense and radical.
In Iago's first soliloquy, Shakespeare goes out of his way to emphasize the improvised nature of the villain's plot:

> Cassio's a proper man, let me see now,
> To get this place, and to make up my will,
> A double knavery . . . how, how? . . . let me see,
> After some time, to abuse Othello's ear,
> That he is too familiar with his wife:
> He has a person and a smooth dispose,
> To be suspected, fram'd to make women false:
> The Moor a free and open nature too,
> That thinks men honest that but seems to be so:
> And will as tenderly be led by the nose . . .
> As asses are.
> I ha't, it is engender'd; Hell and night
> Must bring this monstrous birth to the world's light.
>
> (I, iii, 390–402)[17]

I will try shortly to cast some light on why Iago conceives of his
activity here as sexual; for the moment, we need only to observe
all of the marks of the impromptu and provisional, extending to
the ambiguity of the third-person pronoun: "to abuse Othello's
ear/That he is too familiar with his wife." This ambiguity is
felicitous; indeed, though scarcely visible at this point, it is the
dark essence of Iago's whole enterprise that is, as I shall argue, to
play upon Othello's buried perception of his own sexual relations
with Desdemona as adulterous.[18]

What I have called the marks of the impromptu extend to Iago's
other speeches and actions through the course of the whole play. In
act 2, he declares of his conspiracy, "'tis here, but yet confus'd;/

Knavery's plain face is never seen, till us'd," and this half-willed confusion continues through the agile, hectic maneuvers of the last act until the moment of exposure and silence. To all but Roderigo, of course, Iago presents himself as incapable of improvisation, except in the limited and seemingly benign form of banter and jig.[19] And even here he is careful, when Desdemona asks him to improvise her praise, to declare himself unfit for the task:

> I am about it, but indeed my invention
> Comes from my pate as birdlime does from frieze,
> It plucks out brain and all: but my Muse labours,
> And thus she is deliver'd.
>
> (II, i, 125–28)

Lurking in the homely denial of ability is the image of his invention as birdlime, and hence a covert celebration of his power to ensnare others. Like Jonson's Mosca, Iago is fully aware of himself as an improvisor and revels in his ability to manipulate his victims, to lead them by the nose like asses, to possess their labor without their ever being capable of grasping the relation in which they are enmeshed. Such is the relation Iago establishes with virtually every character in the play, from Othello and Desdemona to such lowly figures as Montano and Bianca. For the Spanish colonialists, improvisation could only bring the Lucayans into open enslavement; for Iago, it is the key to a mastery whose emblem is the "duteous and knee-crooking knave" who dotes "on his own obsequious bondage" (I, i, 45–46), a mastery invisible to the servant, a mastery, that is, whose character is essentially ideological. Iago's attitude toward Othello is nonetheless colonial: though he finds himself in a subordinate position, the ensign regards his black general as "an erring barbarian" whose "free and open nature" is a fertile field for exploitation. However galling it may be to him, Iago's subordination is a kind of protection, for it conceals his power and enables him to play upon the ambivalence of

Othello's relation to Christian society: the Moor is at once the institution and the alien, the conqueror and the infidel, the agent of "civility" and the Lucayan. Iago can conceal his malicious intentions toward "the thick-lips" behind the mask of dutiful service and hence prolong his improvisation as the Spaniards could not. To be sure, the play suggests, Iago too must ultimately destroy the beings he exploits and hence undermine the profitable economy of his own relations, but that destruction may be long deferred, deferred in fact for precisely the length of the play.[20]

If Iago then holds over others a possession that must constantly efface the signs of its own power, how can it be established, let alone maintained? We will find a clue, I think, in what we have been calling the *process of fictionalization* that transforms a fixed symbolic structure into a flexible construct ripe for improvisational entry. This process is at work in Shakespeare's play where we may more accurately identify it as *submission to narrative self-fashioning*. When in Cyprus Othello and Desdemona have been ecstatically reunited, Iago astonishes Roderigo by informing him that Desdemona is in love with Cassio. He has no evidence, of course—indeed we have earlier seen him "engender" the whole plot entirely out of his fantasy—but he proceeds to lay before his gull all of the circumstances that make this adultery plausible: "mark me, with what violence she first lov'd the Moor, but for bragging, and telling her fantastical lies; and will she love him still for prating?" (II, i, 221–23). Desdemona cannot long take pleasure in her outlandish match: "When the blood is made dull with the act of sport, there should be again to inflame it, and give satiety a fresh appetite, loveliness in favour, sympathy in years, manner and beauties" (II, i, 225–29). The elegant Cassio is the obvious choice: "Didst thou not see her paddle with the palm of his hand?" Iago asks. To Roderigo's objection that this was "but courtesy," Iago replies, "Lechery, by this hand: an index and prologue to the history of lust and foul thoughts" (II, i, 251–55). The metaphor makes explicit what Iago has been doing all along:

constructing a narrative into which he inscribes ("by this hand") those around him. He does not need a profound or even reasonably accurate understanding of his victims; he would rather deal in probable impossibilities than improbable possibilities. And it is eminently probable that a young, beautiful Venetian gentlewoman would tire of her old, outlandish husband and turn instead to the handsome, young lieutenant: it is, after all, one of the master plots of comedy.

What Iago as inventor of comic narrative needs is a sharp eye for the surfaces of social existence, a sense, as Bergson says, of the mechanical encrusted upon the living, a reductive grasp of human possibilities. These he has in extraordinarily full measure.[21] Above all, he is sensitive to habitual and self-limiting forms of discourse, to Cassio's reaction when he has had a drink or when someone mentions Bianca, to Othello's rhetorical extremism, to Desdemona's persistence and tone when she pleads for a friend; and, of course, he is demonically sensitive to the way individuals interpret discourse, to the signals they ignore and those to which they respond.

We should add that Iago includes himself in this ceaseless narrative invention; indeed, as we have seen from the start, a successful improvisational career depends upon role-playing that is in turn allied to the capacity, as Professor Lerner defines *empathy*, "to see onself in the other fellow's situation." This capacity requires above all a grasp that one is not forever fixed in a single, divinely sanctioned identity, an ability to imagine one's nonexistence so that one can exist for a moment in another and as another. In the opening scene Iago gives voice to this hypothetical self-cancellation in a line of eerie simplicity: "Were I the Moor, I would not be Iago" (I, i, 57).[22] What is disturbing in this comically banal expression—as, for that matter, in Professor Lerner's definition of empathy—is that the imagined self-loss conceals its opposite: a ruthless displacement and absorption of the other. *Empathy*, as its derivation from *einfühlung* suggests, may be a feeling of oneself into an object, but that object may have to be drained of its own substance before it will serve as an appropriate vessel. Certainly in *Othello*, where all relations are embedded in power and sexuality, there is no realm where the subject and object can merge in the unproblematic accord affirmed by the theorists of empathy.[23] As Iago himself proclaims, his momentary identification with the Moor is a strategic aspect of his malevolent hypocrisy:

> In following him, I follow but myself.
> Heaven is my judge, not I for love and duty,
> But seeming so, for my peculiar end.

> (I, i, 58–60)

Exactly what that "peculiar end" is remains opaque. Even the general term *self-interest* is suspect: Iago begins his speech in a declaration of self-interest—"I follow him to serve my turn upon him"—and ends in a declaration of self-division: "I am not what I am."[24] We tend, to be sure, to hear the latter as "I am not what I seem," hence as a simple confirmation of his public deception. But "I am not what I am" goes beyond social feigning: not only does Iago mask himself in society as the honest ancient, but in private he tries out a bewildering succession of brief narratives that critics have attempted, with notorious results, to translate into motives. These inner narratives—shared, that is, only with the audience—continually promise to disclose what lies behind the public deception, to illuminate what Iago calls "the native act and figure" of his heart, and continually fail to do so; or rather, they reveal that his heart is precisely a series of acts and figures, each referring to something else, something just out of our grasp. "I am not what I am" suggests that this elusiveness is permanent, that even self-interest, whose transcendental guarantee is the divine "I am what I am," is a mask.[25] Iago's constant recourse to narrative, then, is both the affirmation of absolute self-interest and the affirmation of absolute vacancy; the oscillation between the two

incompatible positions suggests in Iago the principle of narrativity
itself, cut off from original motive and final disclosure. The only
termination possible in his case is not revelation but silence.

The question remains: Why would anyone submit, even unconsciously, to Iago's narrative fashioning? Why would anyone submit to another's narrative at all? For an answer we may return to
our observation that there is a structural resemblance between
even a hostile improvisation and its object. In *Othello* the characters have always already experienced submission to narrativity.
This is clearest and most important in the case of Othello himself. When Brabantio brings before the Signiory the charge that
his daughter has been seduced by witchcraft, Othello promises
to deliver "a round unvarnish'd tale . . ./Of my whole course of
love" (I, iii, 90–91), and at the heart of this tale is the telling of
tales:

> Her father lov'd me, oft invited me,
> Still question'd me the story of my life,
> From year to year; the battles, sieges, fortunes,
> That I have pass'd:
> I ran it through, even from my boyish days,
> To the very moment that he bade me tell it.[26]

                                                    (I, iii, 128–33)

The telling of the story of one's life—the conception of one's
life as a story—is a response to public inquiry: to the demands of
the Senate, sitting in judgment or, at the least, to the presence of
an inquiring community. When, as recorded in the fourteenth-
century documents Le Roy Ladurie has brilliantly studied, the
peasants of the Languedoc village of Montaillou are examined by
the Inquisition, they respond with a narrative performance:
"About 14 years ago, in Lent, towards vespers, I took two sides
of salted pork to the house of Guillaume Benet of Montaillou, to
have them smoked. There I found Guillemette Benet warming
herself by the fire, together with another woman; I put the salted

meat in the kitchen and left."[27] And when the Carthaginian queen calls upon her guest to "tell us all things from the first beginning, Grecian guile, your people's trials, and then your journeyings," Aeneas responds, as he must, with a narrative of the destiny decreed by the gods.[28] So too Othello before the Senate or earlier in Brabantio's house responds to questioning with what he calls his "trauel's history" or, in the Folio reading, as if noting the genre, his "trauellours history." This history, it should be noted, is not only of events in distant lands and among strange peoples: "I ran it through," Othello declares, from childhood "To the very moment that he bade me tell it." We are on the brink of a Borges-like narrative that is forever constituting itself out of the materials of the present instant, a narrative in which the story-teller is constantly swallowed up by the story. That is, Othello is pressing up against the condition of all discursive representations of identity. He comes dangerously close to recognizing his status as a text, and it is precisely this recognition that the play as a whole will reveal to be insupportable. But, at this point, Othello is still convinced that the text is his own, and he imagines only that he is recounting a lover's performance.

In the forty-fifth sonnet of Sidney's *Astrophil and Stella*, Astrophil complains that while Stella is indifferent to the sufferings she has caused him, she weeps piteous tears at a fable of some unknown lovers. He concludes,

> Then thinke my deare, that you in me do reed
> Of Lovers ruine some sad Tragedie:
> I am not I, pitie the tale of me.

In *Othello* it is Iago who echoes that last line—"I am not what I am," the motto of the improvisor, the manipulator of signs that bear no resemblance to what they profess to signify—but it is Othello himself who is fully implicated in the situation of the Sidney sonnet: that one can win pity for oneself only by becoming a tale of oneself, and hence by ceasing to be oneself. Of course, Othello thinks that he has triumphed through his narrative self-fashioning:

> she thank'd me,
> And bade me, if I had a friend that lov'd her,
> I should but teach him how to tell my story,
> And that would woo her. Upon this hint I spake:
> She lov'd me for the dangers I had pass'd,
> And I lov'd her that she did pity them.

(I, iii, 163-68)

But Iago knows that an identity that has been fashioned as a story can be unfashioned, refashioned, inscribed anew in a different narrative: it is the fate of stories to be consumed or, as we say more politely, interpreted. And even Othello, in his moment of triumph, has a dim intimation of this fate: half a dozen lines after he has recalled "the Cannibals, that each other eat," he remarks complacently, but with an unmistakable undertone of anxiety, that Desdemona would come "and with a greedy ear/Devour up my discourse" (I, iii, 149-50).

Paradoxically, in this image of rapacious appetite Othello is recording Desdemona's *submission* to his story, what she calls the consecration of her soul and fortunes "to his honours, and his valiant parts" (I, iii, 253). What he has both experienced and narrated she can only embrace as narration:

> My story being done,
> She gave me for my pains a world of sighs;
> She swore i'faith 'was strange, 'twas passing strange;
> 'Twas pitiful, 'twas wondrous pitiful;
> She wish'd she had not heard it, yet she wish'd
> That heaven had made her such a man.[29]

(I, iii, 158-63)

It is, of course, characteristic of early modern culture that male submission to narrative is conceived as active, entailing the fashioning of one's own story (albeit within the prevailing conventions), and female submission as passive, entailing the entrance into marriage in which, as Tyndale writes, the "weak vessel" is put "under the obedience of her husband, to rule her lusts and wanton appetites." Sara, Tyndale explains, "before she was married, was Abraham's sister, and equal with him; but, as soon as she was married, was in subjection, and became without comparison inferior; for so is the nature of wedlock, by the ordinance of God."[30] As least for the world of Renaissance patriarchs, this account is fanciful in its glimpse of an original equality; most women must have entered marriage, like Desdemona, directly from paternal domination. "I do perceive here a divided duty," she tells her father before the Venetian Senate; "you are lord of all my duty,"

> but here's my husband:
> And so much duty as my mother show'd
> To you, preferring you before her father,
> So much I challenge, that I may profess,
> Due to the Moor my lord.[31]

(I, iii, 184–89)

She does not question the woman's obligation to obey, invoking instead only the traditional right to transfer her duty. Yet though Desdemona proclaims throughout the play her submission to her husband—"Commend me to my kind lord," she gasps in her dying words—that submission does not accord wholly with the male dream of female passivity. She was, Brabantio tells us,

> A maiden never bold of spirit,
> So still and quiet, that her motion
> Blush'd at her self,

(I, iii, 94–96)

yet even this self-abnegation in its very extremity unsettles what we may assume was her father's social expectation: "So opposite to marriage that she shunned / The wealthy curled darlings of our nation" (I, ii, 67–68). And, of course, her marriage choice is, for Brabantio, an act of astonishing disobedience, explicable only as the somnambulistic behavior of one bewitched or drugged. He views her elopement not as a transfer of obedience but as theft or treason or a reckless escape from what he calls his "guardage." Both he and Iago remind Othello that her marriage suggests not submission but deception:

> She did deceive her father, marrying you;
> And when she seem'd to shake and fear your looks,
> She lov'd them most.[32]

(III, iii, 210–11)

As the sly reference to Othello's "looks" suggests, the scandal of Desdemona's marriage consists not only in her failure to receive her father's prior consent, but in her husband's blackness. That blackness—the sign of all that the society finds frightening and dangerous—is the indelible witness to Othello's permanent status as an outsider, no matter how highly the state may value his services or how sincerely he has embraced its values.[33] The safe passage of the female from father to husband is irreparably disrupted, marked as an escape: "O heaven," Brabantio cries, "how got she out?" (I, i, 169).

Desdemona's relation to her lord Othello should, of course, lay to rest any doubts about her proper submission, but it is not only Brabantio's opposition and Othello's blackness that raise such doubts, even in the midst of her intensest declarations of love. There is rather a quality in that love itself that unsettles the orthodox schema of hierarchical obedience and makes Othello perceive her submission to his discourse as a devouring of it. We may perceive this quality most clearly in the exquisite moment of the lovers' ecstatic reunion on Cyprus:

> *Oth.* It gives me wonder great as my content
> To see you here before me: O my soul's joy,
> If after every tempest come such calmness,
> May the winds blow, till they have waken'd death,
> And let the labouring bark climb hills of seas,
> Olympus-high, and duck again as low

As hell's from heaven. If it were now to die,
'Twere now to be most happy, for I fear
My soul hath her content so absolute,
That not another comfort, like to this
Succeeds in unknown fate.
Des.   The heavens forbid
But that our loves and comforts should increase,
Even as our days do grow.
Oth.   Amen to that, sweet powers!
I cannot speak enough of this content,
It stops me here, it is too much of joy.

(II, i, 183–97)

Christian orthodoxy in both Catholic and Protestant Europe could envision a fervent mutual love between husband and wife, the love expressed most profoundly by St. Paul in words that are cited and commented upon in virtually every discussion of marriage:

> So men are bound to love their own wives as their own bodies. He that loveth his own wife, loveth himself. For never did any man hate his own flesh, but nourisheth and cherisheth it, even as the Lord doth the congregation: for we are members of his body, of his flesh and of his bones. For this cause shall a man leave father and mother, and shall be joined unto his wife, and they two shall be one flesh. This mystery is great, but I speak of Christ and of the congregation.[34]

Building upon this passage and upon its source in Genesis, sixteenth-century commentators could write that marriage is a "high, holy, and blessed order of life, ordained not of man, but of God, yea and that not in this sinful world, but in paradise that most joyful garden of pleasure."[35] But like the Pauline text itself, all such discussions of married love begin and end by affirming the larger order of authority and submission within which marriage takes its rightful place. The family, as William Gouge puts it, "is a little Church, and a little Commonwealth . . . whereby trial may be made of such as are fit for any place of authority, or of subjection in Church or Commonwealth."[36]

In Othello's passionate greeting, the proper sentiments of a Christian husband sit alongside something else: a violent oscillation between heaven and hell, a momentary possession of the soul's absolute content, an archaic sense of monumental scale, a dark fear—equally archaic, perhaps—of "unknown fate." Nothing *conflicts* openly with Christian orthodoxy, but the erotic intensity that informs almost every word is experienced in tension with it. This tension is less a manifestation of some atavistic "blackness" specific to Othello than a manifestation of the colonial power of Christian doctrine over sexuality, a power visible at this point precisely in its inherent limitation.[37] That is, we glimpse in this brief moment of erotic intensity the *boundary* of the orthodox, the strain of its control, the potential disruption of its hegemony by passion. This scene, let us stress, does not depict rebellion or even complaint—Desdemona invokes "the heavens" and Othello answers, "Amen to that, sweet powers!" Yet the plural here eludes, if only slightly, a serene affirmation of orthodoxy: the powers in their heavens do not refer unmistakably to the Christian God, but rather are the nameless transcendent forces that protect and enhance erotic love. To perceive the difference, we might recall that if Augustine argues, against the gnostics, that God had intended Adam and Eve to procreate in Paradise, he insists at the same time that our first parents would have experienced sexual intercourse without the excitement of the flesh. How then could Adam have had an erection? Just as there are persons, Augustine explains, "who can move their ears, either one at a time, or both together" and others who have "such command of their bowels, that they can break wind continuously at pleasure, so as to produce the effect of singing," so before the Fall Adam would have had fully rational, willed control of the organ of generation and thus would have needed no erotic arousal.[38] "Without the seductive stimulus of passion, with calmness of mind and with no corrupting of the integrity of the body, the husband would lie upon the bosom of his wife," and in this calm union, the semen could reach the womb "with the integrity of the female genital organ being preserved, just as now, with that same integrity being safe, the menstrual flow of blood can be emitted from the womb of a virgin."[39] Augustine grants that even Adam and Eve, who alone could have done so, failed to experience this "passionless generation," since they were expelled from Paradise before they had a chance to try it, but the ideal of edenic placidity remains as a reproach to all fallen sexuality, a condemnation of its inherent degradation and violence.[40]

The rich and disturbing pathos of the lovers' passionate reunion in *Othello* derives then not only from our awareness that Othello's premonition is tragically accurate—this is the summit of his joy—but from a rent, a moving ambivalence, in his experience of the ecstatic moment itself. The "calmness" of which he speaks may express gratified desire, but, as the repeated invocation of death suggests, it may equally express the longing for a final *release* from desire, from the dangerous violence, the sense of extremes, the laborious climbing and falling out of control that are experienced in the tempest. To be sure, Othello *welcomes* this tempest, with its charge of erotic feeling, but he does so for the sake of the ultimate consummation that the experience can call into being: "If after every tempest comes such calmness. . . ." That which men most fear to look upon in the storm—death—is for Othello that which makes the storm endurable. If the death he invokes may figure not the release from desire but its fulfillment—for *death* is a common Renaissance term for orgasm—this fulfillment is characteristically poised between an anxious sense of self-dissolution and a craving for decisive closure. If Othello's words suggest an embrace of sexuality, they suggest simultaneously that for him sexuality is a menacing voyage to reach a longed-for haven; it is one of the dangers to be passed. Othello embraces the erotic as a supreme form of romantic narrative, a tale of risk and violence issuing forth at last in a happy and final tranquility.

Desdemona's response is in an entirely different key:

> The heavens forbid
> But that our loves and comforts should increase,
> Even as our days do grow.

This is spoken to allay Othello's fear, but may it not instead augment it? For if Othello characteristically responds to his experience by shaping it as a story, Desdemona's reply denies the possibility of such narrative control and offers instead a vision of unabating increase. Othello says "Amen" to this vision, but it arouses in him a feeling at once of overflowing and inadequacy: "I cannot speak enough of this content,/It stops me here, it is too much of joy." Desdemona has once again devoured up his discourse, and she has done so precisely in bringing him comfort and content.[41] Rather than simply confirming male authority, her submission eroticizes everything to which it responds, from the "disastrous chances" and "moving accidents" Othello relates, to his simplest demands,[42] to his very mistreatment of her:

> my love doth so approve him,
> That even his stubbornness, his checks and frowns,—
> Prithee unpin me,—have grace and favour in them.[43]

(IV, iii, 19-21)

The other women in the play, Bianca and Emilia, both have moments of disobedience to the men who possess and abuse them —in the case of Emilia, it is a heroic disobedience for which she pays with her life.[44] Desdemona performs no such acts of defiance, but her erotic submission, conjoined with Iago's murderous cunning, far more effectively, if unintentionally, subverts her husband's carefully fashioned identity.

We will examine more fully the tragic process of this subversion, but it is important to grasp first that Othello's loss of himself—a loss depicted discursively in his incoherent ravings—arises not only from the fatal conjunction of Desdemona's love and Iago's hate, but also from the nature of that identity, from what we have called his submission to narrative self-fashioning. We may invoke

in this connection Lacan's observation that the source of the subject's frustration in psychoanalysis is ultimately neither the silence
nor the reply of the analyst:

> Is it not rather a matter of frustration inherent in the very discourse of the
> subject? Does the subject not become engaged in an ever-growing dispos-
> session of that being of his, concerning which—by dint of sincere portraits
> which leave its idea no less incoherent, of rectifications which do not suc-
> ceed in freeing its essence, of stays and defenses which do not prevent his
> statue from tottering, of narcissistic embraces which become like a puff of
> air in animating it—he ends up by recognizing that this being has never
> been anything more than his construct in the Imaginary and that this
> construct disappoints all of his certitudes? For in this labor which he
> undertakes to reconstruct this construct *for another*, he finds again the
> fundamental alienation which made him construct it *like another one*, and
> which has always destined it to be stripped from him *by another*.[45]

Shakespeare's military hero, it may be objected, is far removed
from this introspective project, yet I think it is no accident that
every phrase of Lacan's critique of psychoanalysis seems a brilliant
reading of *Othello*, for I would propose that there is a deep resemblance between the reconstruction of the self in analysis—at least
as Lacan conceives it—and Othello's self-fashioning. The resemblance is grounded in the dependence of even the innermost self
upon a language that is always given from without and upon
representation before an audience. I do not know if such are the
conditions of human identity, but they are unmistakably the conditions of theatrical identity, where existence is conferred upon a
character by the playwright's language and the actor's performance. And in *Othello* these governing circumstances of the
medium itself are reproduced and intensified in the hero's situation: his identity depends upon a constant performance, as we
have seen, of his "story," a loss of his own origins, an embrace and
perpetual reiteration of the norms of another culture. It is this
dependence that gives Othello, the black mercenary, a relation to
Christian values that is the existential equivalent of a religious

vocation; he cannot allow himself the moderately flexible adherence that most ordinary men have toward their own formal beliefs. Christianity is the alienating yet constitutive force in Othello's identity, and if we seek a discursive mode that will link Lacan's analysis and Shakespeare's play, we will find it in *confession*.

Othello himself invokes before the Venetian Senate the absolute integrity of confession, conceived, it appears, not as the formal auricular rite of penitence but as a generalized self-scrutiny in God's presence:

> as faithful as to heaven
> I do confess the vices of my blood,
> So justly to your grave ears I'll present
> How I did thrive in this fair lady's love,
> And she in mine.[46]

(I, iii, 123-26)

The buried identification here between the vices of the blood and mutual thriving in love is fully exhumed by the close of the play, when confession has become a virtually obsessional theme.[47] Theological and juridical confession are fused in Othello's mind when, determined first to exact a deathbed confession, he comes to take Desdemona's life:

> If you bethink yourself of any crime,
> Unreconcil'd as yet to heaven and grace,
> Solicit for it straight. . . .
> Therefore confess thee freely of thy sin,
> For to deny each article with oath
> Cannot remove, nor choke the strong conceit,
> That I do groan withal: thou art to die.

(V, ii, 26-28, 54-57)

The sin that Othello wishes Desdemona to confess is adultery, and her refusal to do so frustrates the achievement of what in theology was called "a good, complete confession."[48] He feels the outrage of the thwarted system that needs to imagine itself merciful, sacramental, when it disciplines:

> thou dost stone thy heart,
> And makest me call what I intend to do
> A murder, which I thought a sacrifice.

(V, ii, 64–66)

We are at last in a position to locate the precise nature of the symbolic structure into which Iago inserts himself in his brilliant improvisation: this structure is the centuries-old Christian doctrine of sexuality, policed socially and psychically, since the Fourth Lateran Council of 1215, by confession. To Iago, the Renaissance skeptic, this system has a somewhat archaic ring, as if it were an earlier stage of development that his own modern sensibility had cast off.[49] If Othello seems in Iago's presence at once an old man and a child, it is because the West has characteristically confounded cultural and chronological primitivism, so that the "extravagant and wheeling stranger," the "barbarian," must at the same time be perceived as both aged and childish. Like the Lucayan religion to the conquistadors, the orthodox doctrine that governs Othello's sexual attitudes—his simultaneous idealization and mistrust of women—seems to Iago sufficiently close to be recognizable, sufficiently distant to be manipulable. We watch him manipulate it directly at the beginning of act 4 when he leads Othello through a brutally comic parody of the late medieval confessional manuals with their casuistical attempts to define the precise moment at which venial temptation passes over into mortal sin:

> *Iago* To kiss in private?
> *Oth.*   An unauthoriz'd kiss.
> *Iago* Or to be naked with her friend abed,
>   An hour, or more, not meaning any harm?
> *Oth.* Naked abed, Iago, and not mean harm?
>   It is hypocrisy against the devil:
>   They that mean virtuously, and yet do so,
>   The devil their virtue tempts, and they tempt heaven.
> *Iago* So they do nothing, 'tis a venial slip.

(IV, i, 2–9)

Iago in effect assumes an extreme version of the laxist position in such manuals in order to impel Othello toward the rigorist version that viewed adultery as one of the most horrible of mortal sins, more detestable, in the words of the *Eruditorium penitentiale*, "than homicide or plunder," and hence formerly deemed punishable, as several authorities remind us, by death.[50] Indeed in the mid-sixteenth century, Tyndale's erstwhile collaborator, George Joy, called for a return to the Old Testament penalty for adulterers. "God's law," he writes, "is to punish adultery with death for the tranquility and commonwealth of His church." This is not an excessive or vindictive course; on the contrary, "to take away and to cut off putrified and corrupt members from the whole body, lest they poison and destroy the body, is the law of love."[51] When Christian magistrates leave adultery unpunished, they invite more betrayals and risk the ruin of the realm, for, as Protestants in particular repeatedly observe, the family is an essential component of an interlocking social and theological network. Hence adultery is a sin with the gravest of repercussions; in the words of the great Cambridge divine, William Perkins, it

> destroyeth the Seminary of the Church, which is *a godly seed* in the family, and it breaketh the covenant between the parties and God; it robs another of the precious ornament of chastity, which is a gift of the Holy Ghost; it dishonors their bodies and maketh them temples of the devil; and the Adulterer maketh his family a Stews.[52]

It is in the bitter spirit of these convictions that Othello enacts the grotesque comedy of treating his wife as a strumpet and the tragedy of executing her in the name of justice, lest she betray more men.

But we still must ask how Iago manages to persuade Othello that Desdemona has committed adultery, for all of the cheap tricks Iago plays seem somehow inadequate to produce the unshakable conviction of his wife's defilement that seizes Othello's soul and drives him mad. After all, as Iago taunts Othello, he cannot achieve the point of vantage of God whom the Venetian women let "see the pranks/They dare not show their husbands" (III, iii, 206–7):

> Would you, the supervisor, grossly gape on,
> Behold her topp'd?

(III, iii, 401–2)

How then, without "ocular proof" and in the face of both love and common sense, is Othello so thoroughly persuaded? To answer this, we must recall the syntactic ambiguity we noted earlier—"to abuse Othello's ear,/That he is too familiar with his wife"—and turn to a still darker aspect of orthodox Christian doctrine, an aspect even more centrally inscribed in the confessional system. *Omnis amator feruentior est adulter* goes the Stoic epigram, and St. Jerome does not hesitate to draw the inevitable inference: "An adulterer is he who is too ardent a lover of his wife."[53] Jerome quotes Seneca: "All love of another's wife is shameful; so too, too much love of your own. A wise man ought to love his wife with judgment, not affection. Let him control his impulses and not be borne headlong into copulation. Nothing is fouler than to love a wife like an adulteress. . . . Let them show themselves to their wives not as lovers, but as husbands."[54] The words echo through more than a thousand years of Christian writing on marriage, and, in the decisive form given them by Augustine and his commentators, remain essentially unchallenged by the leading Reformers of the sixteenth and early seventeenth century. The "man who shows no modesty or comeliness in conjugal intercourse," writes Calvin, "is committing adultery with his wife," and the *King's Book*, attributed to Henry VIII, informs its readers that in lawful matrimony a man may break the Seventh Commandment "and live unchaste with his own wife, if he do unmeasurably and inordinately serve his or her fleshly appetite or lust."[55]

In the Augustinian conception, as elaborated by Raymond of Peñaforte, William of Rennes, and others, there are four motives for conjugal intercourse: to conceive offspring; to render the marital debt to one's partner so that he or she might avoid incontinence; to avoid fornication oneself; and to satisfy desire. The first two motives are without sin and excuse intercourse; the third is a venial sin; the fourth—to satisfy desire—is mortal. Among the many causes that underlie this institutional hostility to desire is the tenacious existence, in various forms, of the belief that pleasure constitutes a legitimate release from dogma and constraint. Thus when asked by the Inquisition about her happy past liaison with the heretical priest of Montaillou, the young Grazide Lizier replies with naive frankness, "In those days it pleased me, and it pleased the priest, that he should know me carnally, and be known by me; and so I did not think I was sinning, and neither did he." "With Pierre Clergue," she explains "I liked it. And so it could not displease God. It was not a sin." For the peasant girl, apparently, pleasure was the guarantee of innocence: "But now, with him, it does not please me any more. And so now, if he knew me carnally, I should think it a sin."[56] A comparable attitude, derived not from peasant culture but from the troubadours, evidently lies behind the more sophisticated courtship of Romeo: "Thus from my lips, by thine my sin is purged."[57]

It should not surprise us that churchmen, Catholic and Protestant alike, would seek to crush such dangerous notions, nor that they would extend their surveillance and discipline to married couples and warn that pleasure in the marriage bed is at least a potential violation of the Seventh Commandment. "Nothing is more vile," says Raymond's influential *summa*, "than to love your wife in adulterous fashion."[58] The conjugal act may be without sin, writes the rigorist Nicolaus of Ausimo, but only if "in the performance of this act there is no enjoyment of pleasure."[59] Few *summas* take so extreme a position, but virtually all are in agreement that the active pursuit of pleasure in sexuality is damnable, for as Jacobus Ungarelli writes in the sixteenth century, those who undertake intercourse for pleasure "exclude God from their minds,

act as brute beasts, lack reason, and if they begin a marriage for
this reason, are given over to the power of the devil."[60]

Confessors then must determine if the married penitent has a
legitimate excuse for intercourse and if the act has been performed
with due regard for "matrimonial chastity." And, as Ambrose
observed, even the most plausible excuse is shameful in the old:
"Youths generally assert the desire of having children and think to
excuse the heat of their age by the desire for generation. How
much more shameful for the old to do what is shameful for the
young to confess."[61] Othello himself seems eager to ward off this
shame; he denies before the Senate that he seeks

> To please the palate of my appetite,
> Nor to comply with heat, the young affects
> In me defunct. . . .[62]

(I, iii, 262-64)

But Desdemona makes no such disclaimer; indeed her declaration
of passion is frankly, though by no means exclusively, sexual:

> That I did love the Moor, to live with him,
> My downright violence, and scorn of fortunes,
> May trumpet to the world: my heart's subdued
> Even to the utmost pleasure of my lord.[63]

(I, iii, 247-51)

This moment of erotic intensity, this frank acceptance of pleasure
and submission to her spouse's pleasure, is, I would argue, as much
as Iago's slander the cause of Desdemona's death, for it awakens
the deep current of sexual anxiety in Othello, anxiety that with
Iago's help expresses itself in quite orthodox fashion as the perception of adultery.[64] Othello unleashes upon Cassio—"Michael Cassio,
/That came a-wooing with you" (III, iii, 71)—the fear of pollution,
defilement, and brutish violence that is bound up with his own
experience of sexual pleasure, while he must destroy Desdemona
both for her excessive experience of pleasure and for awakening
such sensations in himself.

Such is the achievement of Iago's improvisation on the orthodox sexual doctrine in which Othello believes; true to that doctrine, pleasure itself becomes for Othello pollution, a defilement of his property in Desdemona and in himself.[65] It is at the level of this dark, sexual revulsion that Iago has access to Othello, access assured, as we should expect, by the fact that beneath his cynical modernity and professed self-love Iago reproduces in himself the same psychic structure. He is as intensely preoccupied with adultery, while his anxiety about his own sexuality may be gauged from the fact that he conceives his very invention, as the images of engendering suggest, as a kind of demonic semen that will bring forth monsters.[66] Indeed Iago's discourse—his assaults on women, on the irrationality of eros, on the brutishness of the sexual act—reiterates virtually to the letter the orthodox terms of Ungarelli's attack on those who seek pleasure in intercourse.

The improvisational process we have been discussing depends for its success upon the concealment of its symbolic center, but as the end approaches, this center becomes increasingly visible. When, approaching the marriage bed on which Desdemona has spread the wedding sheets, Othello rages, "Thy bed, lust stain'd, shall with lust's blood be spotted" (V, i, 36), he comes close to revealing his tormenting identification of marital sexuality—limited perhaps to the night he took Desdemona's virginity—and adultery.[67] The orthodox element of this identification is directly observed—"this sorrow's heavenly,/It strikes when it does love" (V, ii, 21-22)—and on her marriage bed/deathbed, Desdemona seems at last to pluck out the heart of the mystery:

> *Oth.* Think on thy sins.
> *Des.* They are loves I bear to you.
> *Oth.* And for that thou diest.
> *Des.* That death's unnatural, that kills for loving.

> (V, ii, 39-42)

The play reveals at this point not the unfathomable darkness of human motives but their terrible transparency, and the horror of the revelation is its utter inability to deflect violence. Othello's identity is entirely caught up in the narrative structure that drives him to turn Desdemona into a being incapable of pleasure, a piece of "monumental alabaster," so that he will at last be able to love her without the taint of adultery: "Be thus, when thou art dead, and I will kill thee,/And love thee after" (V, ii, 18–19). It is as if Othello had found in a necrophilic fantasy the secret solution to the intolerable demands of the rigorist sexual ethic, and the revelation that Cassio has not slept with Desdemona leads only to a doubling of this solution, for the adulterous sexual pleasure that Othello had projected upon his lieutenant now rebounds upon himself.[68] Even with the exposure of Iago's treachery, then, there is for Othello no escape—rather a still deeper submission to narrative, a reaffirmation of the self as story, but now split suicidally between the defender of the faith and the circumcised enemy who must be destroyed. Lodovico's bizarrely punning response to Othello's final speech—"O bloody period!"—insists precisely upon the fact that it was a speech, that this life fashioned as a text is ended as a text.

Finally, we may ask, is there any escape from narrativity for Shakespeare? Montaigne, who shares many of Shakespeare's most radical perceptions, invents in effect a brilliant mode of *nonnarrative* self-fashioning: "I cannot keep my subject still. It goes along befuddled and staggering, with a natural drunkenness. I take it in this condition, just as it is at the moment I give my attention to it."[69] Shakespeare by contrast remains throughout his career the supreme purveyor of "empathy," the fashioner of narrative selves, the master improvisor. Where Montaigne withdrew to his study, Shakespeare became the presiding genius of a popular, urban art form with the capacity to foster psychic mobility in the service of Elizabethan power; he became the principal maker of what we may see as the prototype of the mass media Professor Lerner so admires.

To an envious contemporary like Robert Greene, Shakespeare

seems a kind of green-room Iago, appropriating for himself the labors of others, and at the least we must grant that it would have seemed fatal to be imitated by him. He possessed a limitless talent for entering into the consciousness of another, perceiving its deepest structures as a manipulable fiction, reinscribing it into his own narrative form.[70] If in the late plays he experiments with controlled disruptions of narrative, moments of eddying and ecstasy, these invariably give way to reaffirmations of self-fashioning through story.

Shakespeare approaches his culture not, like Marlowe, as rebel and blasphemer, but rather as dutiful servant, content to improvise a part of his own within its orthodoxy. And if after centuries that improvisation has been revealed to us as embodying an almost boundless challenge to the culture's every tenet, a devastation of every source, the author of *Othello* would have understood that such a revelation scarcely matters. After all, the heart of a successful improvisation lies in concealment, not exposure; and besides, as we have seen, even a hostile improvisation reproduces the relations of power that it hopes to displace and absorb. If there are intimations in Shakespeare of a release from the complex narrative orders in which everyone is inscribed, these intimations do not arise from bristling resistence or strident denunciation—the mood of a Jaques or Timon. They arise paradoxically from a peculiarly intense *submission* whose downright violence undermines everything it was meant to shore up, the submission depicted not in Othello or Iago but in Desdemona. As both the play and its culture suggest, the arousal of intense, purposeless pleasure is only superficially a confirmation of existing values, established selves.[71] In Shakespeare's narrative art, liberation from the massive power structures that determine social and psychic reality is glimpsed in an *excessive* aesthetic delight, an erotic embrace of those very structures—the embrace of a Desdemona whose love is more deeply unsettling than even an Iago's empathy.

NOTES

1. Daniel Lerner, *The Passing of Traditional Society: Modernizing the Middle East* rev. ed. (New York: Free Press, 1964), pp. 49-53.

2. Ibid., p. 24.

3. Ibid., p. 65.

4. The figures are from Sherburne Cook and Woodrow W. Borah, *Essays in Population History: Mexico and the Caribbean* (Berkeley and Los Angeles: University of California Press, 1971), pp. 376-411.

5. Peter Martyr (Pietro Martire d'Anghiera), *De Orbe Novo*. I have used the translation of M. Lok in *A Selection of Curious, Rare, and Early Voyages and Histories of Interesting Discoveries* (London: R. H. Evans, 1812), pp. 623, 625. The Seventh Decade was finished in the middle of 1525. On Peter Martyr, see Henry R. Wagner, "Peter Martyr and His Works," *Proceedings of the American Antiquarian Society* 56 (1946): pp. 238-88. There is a rather pallid modern translation of *De Orbe Novo* by Francis A. MacNutt (New York: Putnam's, 1912).

6. Martyr, *De Orbe Novo*, p. 627.

7. It is the essence of *sprezzatura* to create the impression of a spontaneous improvisation by means of careful rehearsals. Similarly, the early English drama often strove for this effect; see, for example, Henry Medwall's *Fulgens and Lucres* (1497), where the seemingly incidental conversation of "A" and "B" is fully scripted.

8. Martyr, *De Orbe Novo*, pp. 623, 618, 625.

9. Ibid., p. 622.

10. Immanuel Wallerstein, *The Modern World-System: Capitalist Agriculture and the Origins of the European World-Economy in the Sixteenth Century* (New York: Academic Press, 1974).

11. Roy Strong, *The Cult of Elizabeth: Elizabethan Portraiture and Pageantry* (London: Thames and Hudson, 1977), p. 153.

12. As an example of the operation of displacement in the visual arts, one may consider Breughel's *Christ Bearing the Cross*, where the mourning figures from Van der Weyden's great *Descent from the Cross* are pushed out to the margin of the canvas and the swirling, festive crowd all but obscures Christ. Similarly, for absorption we may invoke Durer's self-portrait of 1500 where the rigidly frontalized, verticalized, hieratic figure has taken into itself the Christ Pantocrator.

13. Joel B. Altman, *The Tudor Play of Mind: Rhetorical Inquiry and the Development of Elizabethan Drama* (Berkeley and Los Angeles: University of California Press, 1978). See also Jackson I. Cope, *The Theater and the Dream: From Metaphor to Form in Renaissance Drama* (Baltimore: The Johns Hopkins University Press, 1973), esp. ch. 4-6. Cope argues brilliantly for the central importance of improvisation in the drama of the Renaissance, but for him improvisation is in the service finally of "a real coherence," of "the eternal order" of the myths of renewal (p. 210). One passes, by means of an apparent randomness, a chaotic flux, to a buried but all-powerful form. Improvisation is the mask of providence, and Cope concludes his study with a discussion of *The Tempest* as a "mythic play" of natural resurrection and Christian doctrine. I would argue that the final effect of improvisation in Shakespeare is the reverse: we always begin with a notion of the inescapability of form, a sense that there are no suprises, that narrative

triumphs over the apparent disruptions, that even the disruptions serve narrative by confirming the presence of the artist as a version of the presence of God. And through improvisation we pass, only partially and tentatively, to a sense that in the very acts of
homage to the great formal structures, there open up small but constant glimpses of the
limitations of those structures, of their insecurities, of the possibility of their collapse.

14. Erasmus, *Praise of Folly*, trans. Hoyt Hopewell Hudson (New York: Modern
Library, 1941), p. 2. See also Erasmus's observation on More in a letter to Ulrich von
Hutten: "He is not offended even by professed clowns, as he adapts himself with marvelous dexterity to the tastes of all; while with ladies generally and even with his wife,
his conversation is made up of humour and playfulness" (*Epistles*, trans. F. M. Nichols,
3 vols. [New York: Russell & Russell, 1962], 3:392). William Roper, *The Life of Sir
Thomas More*, ed. Richard S. Sylvester and Davis P. Harding (New Haven: Yale University Press, 1962), p. 198. See my "More, Role-Playing, and *Utopia*," *Yale Review* 67
(1978):517-36.

15. Thomas More, *The Confutation of Tyndale's Answer*, ed. Louis A. Schuster,
Richard C. Marius, James P. Lusardi, and Richard J. Schoeck, in *The Complete Works of
St. Thomas More* (New Haven: Yale University Press, 1973), 8:90-92. My attention
was drawn to this passage by Professor Louis L. Martz who discussed it in a lecture at
the Folger conference "Thomas More: The Man and His Age." On More's "art of improvisation" see Martz, "The Tower Works," in *St. Thomas More: Action and Contemplation*, ed. Richard S. Sylvester (New Haven: Yale University Press, 1972), pp. 63-65.

16. Richard III virtually declares himself an improvisor: "I clothe my naked villainy /
With odd old ends stol'n forth of holy writ" (I, iii, 335-36). He gives a fine demonstration of his agility when he turns Margaret's curse back on herself. Behind this trick perhaps is the fact that there were in the popular culture of the Renaissance formulaic
curses and satirical jigs into which any names could be fitted; see Charles Read Basker-
vill, *The Elizabethan Jig and Related Song Drama* (Chicago: University of Chicago Press,
1929), pp. 66-67.

17. All citations of *Othello* are to the Arden edition, ed. M. R. Ridley (Cambridge:
Harvard University Press, 1958). Iago's description of Cassio, "a finder out of occasions"
(II, i, 240-41), is a far more apt description of himself as improvisor.

18. This perception on Othello's part is the subject of a powerful unpublished essay,
"On the Language of Sexual Pathology in *Othello*," by Professor Edward Snow of
George Mason University.

19. Iago's performance here, which Desdemona unnervingly characterizes as "lame and
impotent," is one of the ways in which he is linked to the playwright or at least to the
Vice-like "presenter" of a play; see Bernard Spivack, *Shakespeare and the Allegory of
Evil: The History of a Metaphor in Relation to His Major Villains* (New York: Columbia
University Press, 1958).

20. One might argue that Shakespeare, like Marx, sees the exploiter as doomed by the
fact that he must reduce his victim to nothingness, but where Marx derives a revolutionary optimism from this process, Shakespeare derives the tragic mood of the play's end.

21. "The wine she drinks is made of grapes," Iago says in response to Roderigo's
idealization of Desdemona, and, so reduced, she can be assimilated to Iago's grasp of the
usual run of humanity. Similarly, in a spirit of ironic connoisseurship, he observes
Cassio's courtly gestures, "If such tricks as these strip you out of your lieutenantry, it
had been better you had not kiss'd your three fingers so oft, which now again you are
most apt to play the sir in: good, well kiss'd, an excellent courtesy" (II, 9, 171-75). He

is watching a comedy of manners. For Iago as a "portrait of the artist," see Stanley Edgar Hyman, *Iago: Some Approaches to the Illusion of His Motivation* (New York: Atheneum, 1970), pp. 61–100.

22. The simplicity is far more apparent than real. When Iago says, "Were I the Moor, I would not be Iago," is the *I* in both halves of the line the same? Does it designate a hard, impacted self-interest prior to social identity, or are there two distinct, even opposing selves? Were I the Moor, I would not be Iago, because the "I" always loves itself and the creature I know as Iago hates the Moor he serves or, alternatively, because as the Moor I would be other than I am now, free of the tormenting appetite and revulsion that characterize the servant's relation to his master and that constitute my identity as Iago. I would be radically the same/I would be radically different. The rapacious ego underlies all institutional structure/the rapacious ego is constituted by institutional structures. The vertigo intensifies if we add the sly preceding line: "It is as sure as you are Roderigo, /Were I the Moor, I would not be Iago." One imagines that Roderigo would unconsciousnessly touch himself at this point to make sure that he *is* Roderigo.

Iago is a master of the vertiginous confounding of self and other, being and seeming:

> Men should be what they seem,
> Or those that be not, would they might seem none.

> (III, iii, 130–31)

> He's that he is; I may not breathe my censure,
> What he might be, if, as he might, he is not,
> I would to Heaven he were!

> (IV, i, 267–69)

23. See, for example, Theodor Lipps:

> The specific characteristic of esthetic pleasure has now been defined. It consists in this: that it is the enjoyment of an object, which however, so far as it is the object of *enjoyment*, is not an object, but myself. Or, it is the enjoyment of the ego, which however, so far as it is esthetically enjoyed, is not myself but objective.
>
> Now, all this is included in the concept empathy. It constitutes the very meaning of this concept. Empathy is the fact here established, that the object is myself and by the very same token this self of mine is the object. Empathy is the fact that the antithesis between myself and the object disappears, or rather does not yet exist. ("Empathy, Inner Imitation, and Sense-Feelings," in *A Modern Book of Esthetics*, ed. Melvin Rader [New York: Holt, Rinehart and Winston, 1960], p. 376.)

To establish this "fact," Lipps must posit a wholly esthetic dimension and what he calls an "ideal," as opposed to a "practical," self. For Shakespeare there is no realm of the purely esthetic, no space defined by the intersection of negative capability and the willing suspension of disbelief, and no separation of an "ideal" from a "practical" self.

24. To complicate matters further, both declarations occur in a cunning performance for his dupe Roderigo; that is, Iago is saying what he presumes Roderigo wants to believe.

25. Thus Iago invokes heaven as the judge of his self-interested hypocrisy, for *self* and *interest* as stable entities both rely ultimately upon an absolute Being.

26. Elsewhere, too, Othello speaks as if aware of himself as a character: "Were it my cue to fight," he tells the incensed Brabantio and his own followers, "I should have known it,/Without a prompter" (I, ii, 83–84). His acceptance of the commission to

to fight the Turks is likewise couched in an inflated diction that suggests he is responding to a cue:

> The tyrant custom, most grave senators,
> Hath made the flinty and steel couch of war
> My thrice-driven bed of down: I do agnize
> A natural and prompt alacrity
> I find in hardness, and would undertake
> This present wars against the Ottomites.

(I, iii, 229-34)

27. Emmanuel Le Roy Ladurie, *Montaillou: The Promised Land of Error*, trans. Barbara Bray (New York: Braziller, 1978), pp. 8-9. In a review-essay, Natalie Zemon Davis calls attention to the narrative structure of the testimony, a structure she attributes not to the pressure of the Inquisition but to the form of village culture: "Some of these details were probably remembered over the decades—good memories are part of oral culture—but most form a reconstructed past: from a general memory of an event, a narrative is created that tells with verisimilitude how the event could have unfolded. The past is a story" ("Les Conteurs de Montaillou," *Annales: Economies, Sociétés, Civilisations* 34 [1979]:70).

On narrativity as a mode, see Louis Marin, *Utopiques: Jeux d'Espaces* (Paris: Minuit, 1973); Svetlana Alpers, "Describe or Narrate? A Problem in Realistic Representation," *New Literary History* 7 (1976-77):15-41; Leo Bersani, "The Other Freud," *Humanities in Society* 1 (1978):35-49.

On self-fashioning, see my "Marlowe and Renaissance Self-Fashioning," in *Two Renaissance Mythmakers: Christopher Marlowe and Ben Jonson*, ed. Alvin B. Kernan, Selected Papers from the English Institute, 1975-76, new series, no. 1 (Baltimore: The Johns Hopkins University Press, 1977), pp. 41-69.

28. *The Aeneid of Virgil*, trans. Allen Mandelbaum (New York: Bantam Books, 1972), I:1049-51.

29. I reluctantly accept the Quarto's *sighs* for the Folio's *kisses*; the latter need not, as editors sometimes claim, suggest an improbable immodesty but rather may express Othello's perception of Desdemona's nature, hence what her love has given him. Moreover, the frank eroticism of *kisses* is in keeping with Desdemona's own speeches; it is Othello who emphasizes a pity that she voices nowhere in the play itself. On the other hand, *sighs* admits a simpler reading and by no means excludes the erotic.

There is another interpretive problem in this speech that should be noted: the last two lines are usually taken as a continuation of Desdemona's actual response, as recalled by Othello. But they may equally be his interpretation of her feelings, in which case they may say far more about Othello than about Desdemona. A competent actor could suggest either possibility. There is a further ambiguity in the *her* of "made her such a man"; I hear *her* as accusative, but the dative cannot be ruled out.

30. William Tyndale, *The Obedience of a Christian Man* (1527-1528), in *Doctrinal Treatises and Introductions to Different Portions of the Holy Scriptures*, ed. Henry Walter (Cambridge: Parker Society, 1848), p. 171.

31. Both the Folio and the Second Quarto read "You are the Lord of duty," but the paradox of an absolute duty that must nevertheless be divided is suggestive.

32. Iago is improvising on two earlier remarks of Brabantio:

> and she, in spite of nature,
> Of years, of country, credit, everything,
> To fall in love with what she fear'd to look on?

(I, iii, 96-98)

> Look to her, Moor, have a quick eye to see:
> She has deceiv'd her father, may do thee.

(I, iii, 292-93)

In a society troubled by clandestine marriage, the circumstances of Desdemona's union already brand her as faithless, even at the moment Othello stakes his life upon her faith, while, quite apart from these circumstances, it could seem that for the male psyche depicted in the play the very act of leaving her father borders obscurely on sexual betrayal.

33. See George K. Hunter, "Othello and Colour Prejudice," *Proceedings of the British Academy, 1967* 53 (1968):139-63.

A measure of the complex significance of Othello's blackness may be taken from a glance at the competing interpretive possibilities of Desdemona's "I saw Othello's visage in his mind" (I, iii, 252):

"Do not be surprised that I have married an older black man who looks to you grotesque and terrifying. I have married not a face, a complexion, but a mind: a resolute, Christián mind."

"I saw Othello's valuation of himself, his internal image, the picture he has in his mind of his own face. I saw how much he had at stake in his narrative sense of himself, how much his whole existence depended upon this sense, and I was deeply drawn to this 'visage.'"

"I saw Othello's visage—his blackness, his otherness—in his mind as well as his complexion: there is a unity in his being. I am subdued to precisely this quality in him."

34. Ephesians 5:28-32, as quoted in the marriage liturgy (*The Book of Common Prayer, 1559*, ed. John Booty [Charlottesville: University Press of Virginia, 1976], p. 297). The passage is cited by Arthur Kirsch, "The Polarization of Erotic Love in 'Othello'," *Modern Language Review* 73 (1978):721; though it differs in its emphases and method, Kirsch's essay draws conclusions that closely parallel several of my own.

35. Thomas Becon, cited in William and Malleville Haller, "The Puritan Art of Love," *Huntington Library Quarterly* 5 (1941-42):244-45.

36. William Gouge, cited in Haller, "Puritan Art of Love," p. 246.

37. From its inception, Christianity competed fiercely with other sexual conceptions and practices. For a detailed and moving study of one episode in this struggle, see Le Roy Ladurie's *Montaillou*, Michel Foucault has attempted the beginnings of a modern history of the subject in *La volonté de savoir* (Paris: Gallimard, 1976).

38. St. Augustine, *The City of God*, trans. Marcus Dods (New York: Modern Library, 1950), bk. 14, chap. 24, p. 473.

39. Ibid., chap. 26, p. 475.

40. Cf. Lucretius: "Lovers' passion is storm-tossed, even in the moment of fruition, by waves of delusion and incertitude. . . . They clasp the object of their longing so tightly that the embrace is painful. They kiss so fiercely that teeth are driven into lips. All this

because their pleasure is not pure, but they are goaded by an underlying impulse to hurt the thing, whatever it may be, that gives rise to these budding shoots of madness" (*The Nature of the Universe*, trans. Ronald Latham [Baltimore: Penguin, 1951], pp. 163–64).

41. Richard Onorato has called my attention to the way Iago, who is watching this scene, subsequently used the word *content*. "Nothing can, nor shall content my soul," he tells himself, "Till I am even with him, wife, for wife" (II, i, 293–94). Later, when under his influence Othello has bade "farewell content" (III, iii, 354), Iago proffers the consoling words, "Pray be content" (III, iii, 457).

42. When Othello asks Desdemona to leave him a little to himself, she replies, "Shall I deny you? no, farewell, my lord" (III, iii, 87).

43. "Prithee unpin me" requires that the actress, as she speaks these words, call attention to Desdemona's erotic submission to Othello's violence.

44. As Gabrielle Jackson pointed out to me, Emilia feels that she must explain her refusal to observe her husband's commands to be silent and go home:

> Good gentlemen, let me have leave to speak,
> 'Tis proper I obey him but not now:
> Perchance, Iago, I will ne'er go home.

> (V, ii, 196–98)

The moment is felt as a liberating gesture and redeems her earlier, compliant theft of the handkerchief, but it is both too late and fatal. The play does not hold out the wife's disobedience as a way of averting tragedy.

45. Jacques Lacan, *The Language of the Self: The Function of Language in Psychoanalysis*, trans. Anthony Wilden (Baltimore: The Johns Hopkins University Press, 1968), p. 11.

46. In effect, Othello invokes larger and larger spheres of self-fashioning: Othello to Desdemona, Othello to Desdemona and Brabantio, Othello to the Senate; Othello to heaven.

47. The word *confession* and its variants (*confess'd, confessions*) is repeated eighteen times in the course of the play, more often than in any other play in the canon.

48. See Thomas N. Tentler, *Sin and Confession on the Eve of the Reformation* (Princeton, N.J.: Princeton University Press, 1977). Tentler's fine book has largely superseded Henry Charles Lea, *A History of Auricular Confession and Indulgences in the Latin Church*, 3 vols. (Philadelphia: Lea Brothers, 1896), still useful, however, for its massive detail. There are powerful speculations upon the importance of this material in Michel Foucault, *La volonté de savoir*.

49. This is a frequent response in the literature of colonialism; we may encounter it in Spenser's *View of the Present State of Ireland* where he sees the Irish as living in certain respects as the English did before the civilizing influence of the Norman Conquest. The terms *chronological* and *cultural primitivism* are from Arthur O. Lovejoy and George Boas, *Primitivism and Related Ideas in Antiquity* (Baltimore: The Johns Hopkins University Press, 1935).

50. Tentler, *Sin and Confession*, p. 229. The *Eruditorium penitentiale* points out that in cases of necessity it is possible to kill or steal justifiably, "but no one may fornicate knowingly without committing a mortal sin." Tentler observes, "This kind of thinking is an exaggeration even of medieval puritanism. Yet it is also true that the climate of religious opinion allowed and perhaps even encouraged such exaggerations" (p. 229). Cf. Francis Dillingham: "Julius Caesar made a law that if the husband or the wife found

either in adultery, it should be lawful for the husband to kill the wife or the wife the husband. Death then by the light of nature is fit punishment for adulterers and adulteresses" (*Christian Oeconomy or Houshold Government* [London: John Tapp, 1609], p. 13).

51. George Joy, *A Contrarye (to a certayne manis) Consultacion: That Adulterers ought to be punyshed wyth death* (London, 1559), pp. G4^V, A4^V.

52. William Perkins, *A Godly and Learned Exposition of Christ's Sermon on the Mount* (Cambridge: Thomas Brooke and Cantrell Legge, 1608), p. 111. For similar material, see Robert V. Schnucker, "La position puritaine a l'égard de l'adultère," *Annales: Economies, Sociétés, Civilisations* 27 (1972): 1379-88.

53. Quoted, with a mass of supporting material, in John T. Noonan, Jr., *Contraception: A History of Its Treatment by the Catholic Theologians and Canonists* (Cambridge: Harvard University Press, 1966), p. 80. The Stoic marital doctrine, Noonan observes, "joined the Stoic distrust of pleasure and the Stoic insistence on purpose" (p. 47); early Christians embraced the doctrine and hardened its formulation in combatting the gnostic sects.

54. Noonan, *Contraception*, p. 47.

55. John Calvin, *Institutes of the Christian Religion*, bk. 2, chap. 8, section 44, quoted in Lawrence Stone, *The Family, Sex, and Marriage in England, 1500-1800* (New York: Harper and Row, 1977), p. 499; *The King's Book, or A Necessary Doctrine and Erudition for Any Christian Man* (1543), ed. T. A. Lacey (London: Society for Promoting Christian Knowledge, 1932), pp. 111-12. See likewise John Rogers, *The Glasse of Godly Loue* (1569), ed. Frederick J. Furnivall, New Shakespeare Society, ser. 6, no. 2 (London: N. Trubner, 1876), p. 185: "Also there ought to be a temperance between man and wife, for God hath ordained marriage for a remedy or medicine, to assuage the heat of the burning flesh, and for procreation, and not beastly for to fulfill the whole lusts of the devilish mind and wicked flesh." In the seventeenth century William Perkins informs his readers about the "holy manner" in marital intercourse involves moderation, "for even in wedlock, excess in lusts is no better than plain adultery before God" (*Christian Oeconomie*, trans. Thomas Pickering [London: Felix Kyngston, 1609], p. 113).

56. Le Roy Ladurie, *Montaillou*, pp. 151, 157. In fact the priest, who was, in Le Roy Ladurie's words, "an energetic lover and incorrigible Don Juan" (p. 154), held a somewhat different position. "One woman's just like another," he told Grazide's mother, "The sin is the same, whether she is married or not. Which is as much as to say that there is no sin about it at all" (p. 157). Le Roy Ladurie interprets his views on love as follows: "Starting from the Cathar proposition that 'any sexual act, even between married persons, is wrong,' he applied it to suit himself. Because everything was forbidden, one act was no worse than another" (pp. 158-59).

57. I, v, 107. Le Roy Ladurie quotes from the *Brévaire d'amour*: "A lady who sleeps with a true lover is purified of all sins . . . the joy of love makes the act innocent, for it proceeds from a pure heart" (*Montaillou*, p. 159).

58. Tentler, *Sin and Confession*, p. 174.

59. Tentler, *Sin and Confession*, p. 181: hoc est in executione ipsius actus nulla voluptatis delectatione teneatur.

60. Tentler, *Sin and Confession*, p. 183. For a humanist version of these notions, see the following aphorism from Juan Luis Vives's *Introductio ad Sapientiam*:

> The pleasure of the body is, like the body itself, vile and brutal.
> Sensual delectation bores the soul and benumbs the intellect.

Sensual delectation is like robbery, it vilifies our soul. This is the reason why even the most corrupted man seeks secrecy and abhors witnesses.

Sensual pleasure is fleeting and momentaneous, totally beyond any control and always mixed with frustration.

Nothing debilitates more the vigor of our intellect than sexual pleasure. (Carlos G. Norena, *Juan Luis Vives* [The Hague: Martinus Nijhoff, 1970], p. 211)

For an attenuated modern version, see the first televised speech delivered from the Sistine Chapel on 27 August 1978 by Pope John Paul I; the Pope prayed that families "may be defended from the destructive attitude of sheer pleasure-seeking, which snuffs out life." (*San Francisco Chronicle*, 28 August 1978, p. 1).

61. Noonan, *Contraception*, p. 79.

62. A major textual crux, and I have taken the liberty, for the sake of clarity and brevity, to depart from Ridley's reading, which is as follows:

the young affects
In my defunct, and proper satisfaction,
But to be free and bounteous of her mind.

As Ridley says, "after all the discussion, Othello's meaning is moderately clear. He is too mature to be subjugated by physical desire"; but he goes on to read *proper* as "justifiable," where I would read it as "my own." Ridley's *moderately* should be emphasized.

63. Yet another crux: the Quarto reads "very quality" instead of "utmost pleasure." I find the latter more powerful and persuasive, particularly in the context of Desdemona's further mention (line 255) of "The rites for which I love him."

64. Desdemona is, in effect, a kind of mirror reversal of Cordelia: where the latter is doomed in the first act of the play by her refusal to declare her love, the former is doomed precisely for such a declaration.

Professor Spivack, along with most critics of the play, sees Iago as the enemy of the religious bond in marriage (*Shakespeare and the Allegory of Evil*, pp. 49-50); I would argue that it is precisely the nature of this bond, as defined by rigorists, that torments Othello.

65. On *property*, see Kenneth Burke:

Iago may be considered 'consubstantial' with Othello in that he represents the principles of jealousy implicit in Othello's delight in Desdemona as a private spiritual possession. Iago, to arouse Othello, must talk a language that Othello knows as well as he, a language implicit in the nature of Othello's love as the idealization of his private property in Desdemona. This language is the dialectical opposite of Othello's; but it so thoroughly shares a common ground with Othello's language that its insinuations are never for one moment irrelevant to Othello's thinking. Iago must be cautious in leading Othello to believe them as *true*: but Othello never for a moment doubts them as *values*. (*A Grammar of Motives* [Berkeley and Los Angeles: University of California Press, 1969], p. 414)

As so often happens, I discovered that Burke's brilliant sketch had anticipated the shape of much of my argument. Burke has an essay on the ritual structure of the play in *Hudson Review* 4 (1951): 165-203.

66. I have read two powerful unpublished essays that analyze the male sexual anxieties in the play at a level prior to or beneath the social and doctrinal one discussed here:

Edward Snow, "On the Language of Sexual Pathology in *Othello*" and C. L. Barber, "'I'll pour this pestilence into his ear': *Othello* as a Development from *Hamlet*."

67. In act 4, Othello had first thought of poisoning Desdemona and then was persuaded by Iago to "strangle her in her bed, even the bed she hath contaminated" (IV, i, 203–4). The blood he fantasizes about later may be simply an expression of violence (as he had earlier declared, "I will chop her into messes" [IV, i, 196]), but it is tempting to see it as a projection of the blood that marked her loss of virginity and hence, in his disturbed formulation, as "lust's blood." I have seen, via the academic samizdat, an unpublished essay by Stanley Cavell that sensitively explores the anxiety over virginity, staining, and impotence in the play.

68. Like Oedipus, Othello cannot escape the fact that it is he who has committed the crime and must be punished.

We should, in fairness, call attention to the fact that Othello in the end views his wife as "chaste," but the language in which he does so reinforces the orthodox condemnation of pleasure: "cold, cold, my girl, / Even like thy chastity" (V, ii, 276–77). Indeed, the identification of the coldness of death with marital chastity seems to me a *confirmation* of the necrophilic fantasy.

69. "Of Repentance," in *The Complete Essays of Montaigne*, trans. Donald M. Frame (Stanford: Stanford University Press, 1958), pp. 610–11. It is hardly irrelevant for our purposes that Montaigne describes this method in an essay in which he rejects the confessional system.

70. On Shakespeare's talent for entering into the consciousness of others and giving supreme expression to incompatible perspectives, see Norman Rabkin's concept of *complementarity*: *Shakespeare and the Common Understanding* (New York: Free Press, 1967).

In *The Anxiety of Influence* (New York: Oxford University Press, 1973), Harold Bloom remarks, "Shakespeare is the largest instance in the language of a phenomenon that stands outside the concern of this book: the absolute absorption of the precursor" (p. 11).

71. On pleasure and the threat to established order, see Georges Bataille, *Death and Sensuality: A Study of Eroticism and the Taboo* (New York: Walker, 1962), and Mikhail Bakhtin, *Rabelais and His World*, trans. Hélène Iswolsky (Cambridge: M.I.T. Press, 1968).

I have also been influenced here by Michel Foucault, *Discipline and Punish: The Birth of the Prison*, trans. Alan Sheridan (New York: Pantheon, 1971), and by Leo Bersani, "The Subject of Power," *Diacritics* 7 (1977): 2–21.

 *René Girard*

"To Entrap the Wisest":
A Reading of *The Merchant of Venice*

The criticism of *The Merchant of Venice* has been dominated by two images of Shylock that appear irreconcilable. It is
my contention that both images belong to the play and that far
from rendering it unintelligible their conjunction is essential to
an understanding of Shakespeare's dramatic practice.

The first image is that of the Jewish moneylender in the late-
medieval and modern book of anti-Semitism. The mere evocation
of that Jewish stereotype suggests a powerful system of binary
oppositions that does not have to be fully developed to pervade
the entire play. First comes the opposition between Jewish greed
and Christian generosity, between revenge and compassion, between the crankiness of old age and the charm of youth, between
the dark and the luminous, the beautiful and the ugly, the gentle
and the harsh, the musical and the unmusical, and so on.

There is a second image that comes only after the stereotype has
been firmly implanted in our minds; at first it does not make as
strong an impression as the first, but it gathers strength later on
because the language and behavior of the Christian characters repeatedly confirm the rather brief but essential utterances of Shylock himself on which it primarily rests.

The symmetry between the explicit venality of Shylock and the
implicit venality of the other Venetians cannot fail to be intended
by the playwright. It is true that Bassanio's courtship of Portia is
presented primarily as a financial operation. In his plea for Antonio's financial support, Bassanio mentions first the wealth of the
young heiress, then her beauty, then finally her spiritual qualities.
Those critics who idealize the Venetians write as if the many textual clues that contradict their view were not planted by the
author himself, as if their presence in the play were a purely

fortuitous matter, like the arrival of a bill in the morning mail when one really expects a love letter. On every possible occasion Shakespeare pursued the parallel between the amorous venture of Bassanio and the typical Venetian business of Antonio, his commerce on the high seas. Observe, for instance, the manner in which Gratiano, who is just back from Belmont and still flushed with the success of this expedition, addresses Salerio:

> Your hand, Salerio. What's the news from Venice?
> How doth that royal merchant, good Antonio?
> I know he will be glad of our success.
> We are the Jasons, we have won the fleece.
> *Sal.* I would you have won the fleece that he hath lost.
>
> (III, ii, 241–46)*

The truth is that Bassanio and friends have done exactly that. Even if Antonio's losses turned out to be real, Portia's conquest would more than make up financially for Antonio's ships.

Regarding this symmetry between Shylock and the Venetians, many good points have been made. I will mention only one, for the sole reason that I have not found it in the critical literature on the play. If I am not original, please accept my apologies.

Act 3, scene 2, Bassanio wants to reward his lieutenant for his services, and he tells Gratiano and Nerissa that they will be married simultaneously with Portia and himself, in a double wedding ceremony—at Portia's expense we may assume. "Our feast," he says, "shall be much honored in your marriage." Upon which the elated Gratiano says to his fiancée: "We'll play with them the first boy for a thousand ducats" (III, ii, 214–17).

These young people have ample reason to be joyous, now that their future is made secure by Bassanio's clever stroke with the caskets, and this bet sounds harmless enough, but Shakespeare is not addicted to pointless social chitchat and must have a purpose. Gratiano's baby will be two thousand ducats cheaper than An-

*All citations of *The Merchant of Venice* are to the edition published by J. M. Dent in London in 1894.

tonio's pound of flesh. Human flesh and money in Venice are constantly exchanged for one another. People are turned into objects of financial speculation. Mankind has become a commodity, an exchange value like any other. I cannot believe that Shakespeare did not perceive the analogy between Gratiano's wager and Shylock's pound of flesh.

Shylock's pound of flesh is symbolical of Venetian behavior. The Venetians appear different from Shylock, up to a point. Financial considerations have become so natural to them and they are so embedded into their psyches that they have become not quite but almost invisible; they can never be identified as a distinct aspect of behavior. Antonio's loan to Bassanio, for instance, is treated as an act of love and not as a business transaction.

Shylock hates Antonio for lending money without interest. In his eyes, the merchant spoils the financial business. We can read this as the resentment of vile greed for noble generosity within the context of the first image, but we may prefer another reading that contributes to the second image. The generosity of Antonio may well be a corruption more extreme than the caricatural greed of Shylock. As a rule, when Shylock lends money, he expects more money in return, and nothing else. Capital should produce capital. Shylock does not confuse his financial operations with Christian charity. This is why, unlike the Venetians, he can look like the embodiment of greed.

Venice is a world in which appearances and reality do not match. Of all the pretenders to Portia's hand, Bassanio alone makes the right choice between the three caskets because he alone is a Venetian and knows how deceptive a splendid exterior can be. Unlike his foreign competitors who obviously come from countries where things still are more or less what they seem to be, less advanced countries we might say, he instinctively feels that the priceless treasure he seeks must hide behind the most unlikely appearance.

The symbolic significance of choosing lead rather than the gold and silver selected by the two foreigners faithfully duplicates the whole relationship between the true Venetians and the foreign Shylock. When the two alien pretenders reach avidly for the two precious metals, just like Shylock, they look like personifications of greed; in reality they are rather naive, whereas Bassanio is anything but naive. It is characteristic of the Venetians that they look like the very picture of disinterestedness at the precise moment when their sly calculations cause the pot of gold to fall into their lap.

The generosity of the Venetians is not feigned. Real generosity makes the beneficiary more dependent on his generous friend than a regular loan. In Venice a new form of vassality prevails, grounded no longer in strict territorial borders but in vague financial terms. The lack of precise accounting makes personal indebtedness infinite. This is an art Shylock has not mastered since his own daughter feels perfectly free to rob and abandon him without the slightest remorse. The elegance of the décor and the harmony of the music must not lead us to think that everything is right with the Venetian world. It is impossible, however, to say exactly what is wrong. Antonio is sad but he cannot say why, and this unexplained sadness seems to characterize the whole Venetian business aristocracy as much as Antonio himself.

Even in Shylock's life, however, money and matters of human sentiment finally become confused. But there is something comical in this confusion because, even as they become one, money and sentiment retain a measure of separateness, they remain distinguishable from each other and we hear such things as "My daughter! Oh, my ducats! Oh, my daughter!/Fled with a Christian! Oh, my Christian ducats!" (II, viii, 15–16) and other such ridiculous utterances you would never catch in a Venetian mouth.

There is still another occasion upon which Shylock, goaded by his Venetian enemies, confuses financial matters with other passions, and it is the affair of his loan to Antonio. In the interest of his revenge, Shylock demands no interest for his money, no positive guarantees in case of default, nothing but his infamous pound of flesh. Behind the mythical weirdness of the request, we have one spectacular instance of that complete interpenetration between the financial and the human that is characteristic less of Shylock than of the other Venetians. Thus Shylock appears most scandalous to the Venetians and to the spectators when he stops resembling himself to resemble the Venetians even more. The spirit of revenge drives him to imitate the Venetians more perfectly than before, and, in his effort to teach Antonio a lesson, Shylock becomes his grotesque double.

Antonio and Shylock are described as rivals of long standing. Of such people we often say that they have their differences, but this expression would be misleading. Tragic—and comic—conflict amounts to a dissolving of differences that is paradoxical because it proceeds from the opposite intention. All the people involved in the process seek to emphasize and maximize their differences. In Venice, we found, greed and generosity, pride and humility, compassion and ferocity, money and human flesh, tend to become one and the same. This undifferentiation makes it impossible to define anything with precision, to ascribe one particular cause to one particular event. Yet on all sides it is the same obsession with displaying and sharpening a difference that is less and less real. Here is Shylock, for instance, in act 2, scene 5: "Well thou shalt see, thy eyes shall be thy judges,/The difference between Old Shylock and Bassanio" (II, v, 1–2). The Christians too are eager to demonstrate that they are different from the Jews. During the trial scene, it is the turn of the duke, who says to Shylock: "Thou shalt see the difference of our spirits" (IV, i, 368). Even the words are the same. Everywhere the same senseless obsession with differences becomes exacerbated as it keeps defeating itself.

The paradox is not limited to *The Merchant of Venice*. Everywhere in Shakespeare it is an essential component of the tragic and comic relationship. In *The Comedy of Errors*, the endless efforts of the twins to clear up the confusion created by that identity between them which they cannot recognize keeps generating more confusion. The theme of the identical twins, significantly, is borrowed from Plautus, and it is more than an allegory of the process I am talking about; it is its mythical transposition. We have an allusion to this process of undifferentiation, I believe, in a well-known line of *The Merchant*. When Portia enters the court she asks, "Which is the merchant and which is the Jew?" (IV, i, 174). Even if she has never met either Antonio or Shylock, we have a right to be surprised Portia cannot identify the Jewish money-lender at first sight, in view of the enormous difference, visible to all, that is supposed to distinguish him from the gracious Venetians. The line would be more striking, of course, if it came after rather than before the following one: "Antonio and old Shylock both stand forth" (IV, i, 175). If Portia were still unable to distinguish Shylock from Antonio once the two men have come forward together, the scene would explicitly contradict the primary image of Shylock, the stereotype of the Jewish money-lender. This contradiction would stretch the limits of dramatic credibility beyond the breaking point, and Shakespeare refrained from it, but he went as far as he could, I believe, here and elsewhere, to question the reality of a difference he himself, of course, had first introduced into his play. Even the structure of the line, with its two symmetrical questions, suggests the prevalence of symmetry between the two men. The repetition of the interrogative *which* occurs elsewhere in Shakespeare to suggest the perplexity of observers confronted with items that should be different enough to be clearly differentiated but no longer are. In *A Midsummer Night's Dream*, for instance, the undifferentiation of nature, the confusion of the year's four seasons, precedes and announces the undifferentiation of the four lovers, and the monstrous undifferentiation of Bottom, at the height of the midsummer madness:

> The spring, the summer,
> The childing autumn, angry winter change

Their wonted liveries, and the mazed world
By their increase, now knows not which is which.

(II, i, 111–14)

This analysis must lead to Shylock's famous tirade on reciprocity and revenge; we now have the context in which the meaning and purpose of the passage become unmistakable:

. . . if you tickle us,
Do we not laugh? if you poison us, do we not
Die? and if you wrong us, shall we not revenge?
If we are like you in the rest, we will resemble
You in that. If a Jew wrong a Christian, what
Is his humility? Revenge. If a Christian wrong
A Jew, what should his sufferance be by Christian
Example? Why, revenge. The villainy
You teach me, I will execute; and it shall go
Hard but I will better the instruction.

(III, i, 67–76)

The text insists above all on Shylock's personal commitment to revenge. It does not support the type of "rehabilitation" naively demanded by certain revisionists. But it unequivocally defines the symmetry and the reciprocity that govern the relations between the Christians and Shylock. It says the same thing as the line: "Which is the merchant and which is the Jew?" It is as essential, therefore, as it is striking, and it fully deserves to be singled out.

With his caricatural demand for a pound of flesh, Shylock does, indeed, "better the instruction." What we have just said in the language of psychology can be translated into religious terms. Between Shylock's behavior and his words, the relationship is never ambiguous. His interpretation of the law may be narrow and negative but we can count on him for acting according to it and for speaking according to his actions. In the passage on revenge, he alone speaks a truth that the Christians hypocritically deny. The truth of the play is revenge and retribution. The Christians manage to hide that truth even from themselves. They do not live by the law of charity, but this law is enough of a presence in their language to drive the law of revenge underground, to make this revenge almost invisible. As a result, this revenge becomes more subtle, skillful, and feline than the revenge of Shylock. The Christians will easily destroy Shylock but they will go on living in a world that is sad without knowing why, a world in which even the difference between revenge and charity has been abolished.

Ultimately we do not have to choose between a favorable and an unfavorable image of Shylock. The old critics have concentrated on Shylock as a separate entity, an individual substance that would be merely juxtaposed to other individual substances and remain unaffected by them. The ironic depth in *The Merchant of Venice* results from a tension not between two static images of Shylock, but between those textual features that strengthen and those features that undermine the popular idea of an insurmountable difference between Christian and Jew.

It is not excessive to say that characterization itself, as a real dramatic problem or as a fallacy, is at stake in the play. On the one hand Shylock is portrayed as a highly differentiated villain. On the other hand he tells us himself that there are no villains and no heroes; all men are the same, especially when they are taking revenge on each other. Whatever differences may have existed between them prior to the cycle of revenge are dissolved in the reciprocity of reprisals and retaliation. Where does Shakespeare stand on this issue? Massive evidence from the other plays as well as from *The Merchant* cannot leave the question in doubt. The main object of satire is not Shylock the Jew. But Shylock is rehabilitated only to the extent that the Christians are even worse than he is and that the "honesty" of his vices makes him almost a refreshing figure compared to the sanctimonious ferocity of the other Venetians.

The trial scene clearly reveals how implacable and skillful the Christians can be when they take their revenge. In this most curious performance, Antonio begins as the defendant and Shylock as the plaintiff. At the end of one single meeting the roles are reversed and Shylock is a convicted criminal. The man has done no actual harm to anyone. Without his money, the two marriages, the two happy events in the play, could not have come to pass. As his triumphant enemies return to Belmont loaded with a financial and human booty that includes Shylock's own daughter, they still manage to feel compassionate and gentle by contrast with their wretched opponent.

When we sense the injustice of Shylock's fate, we usually say: Shylock is a scapegoat. This expression, however, is ambiguous. When I say that a character in a play is a scapegoat, my statement can mean two different things. It can mean that this character is unjustly condemned from the perspective of the writer. The conviction of the crowd is presented as irrational by the writer himself. In this first case, we say that in that play there is a theme or motif of the scapegoat.

There is a second meaning to the idea that a character is a scapegoat. It can mean that, from the perspective of the writer, this character is justly condemned, but in the eyes of the critic who makes the statement, the condemnation is unjust. The crowd that condemns the victim is presented as rational by the writer, who really belongs to that crowd; only in the eyes of the critic are the crowd and the writer irrational and unjust.

The scapegoat, this time, is not a theme or motif at all; it is not made explicit by the writer, but if the critic is right in his allegations, there must be a scapegoat effect at the origin of the play, a collective effect probably, in which the writer participates. The critic may think, for instance, that a writer who creates a character like Shylock, patterned after the stereotype of the Jewish moneylender, must do so because he personally shares in the anti-Semitism of the society in which this stereotype is present.

When we say that Shylock is a scapegoat, our statement remains vague and critically useless unless we specify if we mean the scapegoat as theme or the scapegoat as structure, the scapegoat as an object of indignation and satire or the scapegoat as a passively accepted delusion.

Before we can resolve the critical impasse to which I referred at the beginning of my presentation we must reformulate it in the terms of this still unperceived alternative between the scapegoat as structure and the scapegoat as theme. Everyone agrees that Shylock is a scapegoat, but is he the scapegoat of his society only or of Shakespeare's as well?

What the critical revisionists maintain is that the scapegoating of Shylock is not a structuring force but a satirical theme. What the traditionalists maintain is that scapegoating, in *The Merchant of Venice*, is a structuring force rather than a theme. Whether we like it or not, they say, the play shares in the cultural anti-Semitism of the society. We should not allow our literary piety to blind us to the fact.

My own idea is that the scapegoat is both structure and theme in *The Merchant of Venice*, and that the play, in this essential respect at least, is anything any reader wants it to be, not because Shakespeare is as confused as we are when we use the word *scapegoat* without specifying, but for the opposite reason: he is so aware and so conscious of the various demands placed upon him by the cultural diversity of his audience; he is so knowledgeable in regard to the paradoxes of mimetic reactions and group behavior that he can stage a scapegoating of Shylock entirely convincing to those who want to be convinced and simultaneously undermine that process with ironic touches that will reach only those who can be reached. Thus he was able to satisfy the most vulgar as well as the most refined audiences. To those who do not want to challenge the anti-Semitic myth, or Shakespeare's own espousal of that myth, *The Merchant of Venice* will always sound like a confirmation of that myth. To those who do challenge these same beliefs, Shakespeare's own challenge will become perceptible. The play is not unlike a perpetually revolving object that, through some mysterious means, would always present itself to each viewer under aspects best suited to his own perspective.

Why are we reluctant to consider this possibility? Both intellectually and ethically, we assume that scapegoating cannot be and should not be a theme of satire and a structuring force at the same time. Either the author participates in the collective victimage and he cannot see it as unjust or he can see it as unjust and he should not connive in it, even ironically. Most works of art do fall squarely on one side or the other of that particular fence. Rewritten by Arthur Miller, Jean-Paul Sartre or Bertolt Brecht, *The Merchant* would be different indeed. But so would a *Merchant of Venice* that would merely reflect the anti-Semitism of its society, as a comparison with Marlowe's *Jew of Malta* immediately reveals.

If we look carefully at the trial scene, no doubt can remain that Shakespeare undermines the scapegoat effects just as skillfully as he produces them. There is something frightening in this efficiency. This art demands a manipulation and therefore an intelligence of mimetic phenomena that transcends not only the ignorant immorality of those who submit passively to victimage mechanisms but also the moralism that rebels against them but does not perceive the irony generated by the dual role of the author. Shakespeare himself must first generate at the grossly theatrical level the effects that he later undermines at the level of allusions.

Let us see how Shakespeare can move in both directions at the same time. Why is it difficult not to experience a feeling of relief and even jubilation at the discomfiture of Shylock? The main reason, of course, is that Antonio's life is supposed to be under an immediate threat. That threat stems from Shylock's stubborn insistence that he is entitled to his pound of flesh.

Now the pound of flesh is a mythical motif. We found earlier that it is a highly significant allegory of a world where human beings and money are constantly exchanged for one another, but it is nothing more. We can imagine a purely mythical context in which Shylock could really carve up his pound of flesh and

Antonio would walk away, humiliated and diminished but alive. In *The Merchant of Venice*, the mythical context is replaced by a realistic one. We are told that Antonio could not undergo this surgical operation without losing his life. It is certainly true in a realistic context, but it is also true, in that same context, that, especially in the presence of the whole Venetian establishment, old Shylock would be unable to perform this same operation. The myth is only partly demythologized, and Shylock is supposed to be capable of carving up Antonio's body in cold blood because, as a Jew and a moneylender, he passes for a man of unusual ferocity. This presumed ferocity justifies our own religious prejudice.

Shakespeare knows that victimage must be unanimous to be effective, and no voice is effectively raised in favor of Shylock. The presence of the silent Magnificoes, the élite of the community, turns the trial into a rite of social unanimity. The only characters not physically present are Shylock's daughter and his servant, and they are of one mind with the actual scapegoaters since they were the first to abandon Shylock after taking his money. Like a genuine Biblical victim, Shylock is betrayed "even by those of his own household."

As scapegoating affects more and more people and tends toward unanimity, the contagion becomes overwhelming. In spite of its judicial and logical nonsense, the trial scene is enormously performative and dramatic. The spectators and readers of the play cannot fail to be affected and cannot refrain from experiencing Shylock's defeat as if it were their own victory. The crowd in the theater becomes one with the crowd on the stage. The contagious effect of scapegoating extends to the audience. In *The Merchant of Venice*, at least, and perhaps in many other plays, the Aristotelian catharsis is a scapegoat effect.

As an embodiment of Venetian justice, the duke should be impartial, but at the very outset of the proceedings he commiserates with the defendant and launches into a diatribe against Shylock:

I am sorry for thee. Thou art come to answer
A stony adversary, an inhuman wretch,
Uncapable of pity, void and empty
From any dram of mercy.

(IV, i, 3-6)

These words set the tone for the entire scene. The Christian virtue par excellence, mercy is the weapon with which Shylock is clubbed over the head. The Christians use the word *mercy* with such perversity that they can justify their own revenge with it, give full license to their greed and still come out with a clear conscience. They feel they have discharged their obligation to be merciful by their constant repetition of the word itself. The quality of their mercy is not strained, to say the least. It is remarkably casual and easy. When the duke severely asks: "How shalt thou hope for mercy, rendering none?" (IV, i, 88), Shylock responds with impeccable logic: "What judgment shall I dread, doing no wrong?" (IV, i, 89).

Shylock trusts in the law too much. How could the law of Venice be based on mercy, how could it be equated with the golden rule, since it gives the Venetians the right to own slaves and it does not give slaves the right to own Venetians? How can we be certain that Shakespeare, who engineered that scapegoat effect so skillfully, is not fooled by it even for one second? Our certainty is perfect and it may well be much more than "subjective," as some critics would say. It may well be perfectly "objective" in the sense that it correctly recaptures the author's intention and yet it remains a closed book to a certain type of reader. If irony were demonstrable it would cease to be irony. Irony must not be explicit enough to destroy the efficiency of the scapegoat machine in the minds of those fools for whom that machine was set up in the first place. Irony cannot fail to be less tangible than the object on which it bears.

Some will object that my reading is "paradoxical." It may well be, but why should it be a priori excluded that Shakespeare can write a paradoxical play? Especially if the paradox on which the play is built is formulated most explicitly at the center of that very play. Shakespeare is writing, not without a purpose, I suppose, that appearances, especially the appearances of beautiful language, are "The seeming truth which cunning times put on / To entrap the wisest" (III, ii, 100-101). Shakespeare is writing, not without a purpose, that the worst sophistry, when distilled by a charming voice, can decide the outcome of a trial, or that the most unreligious behavior can sound religious if the right words are mentioned. Let us listen to the reasons given by Bassanio for trusting in lead rather than in silver or gold and we will see that they apply word for word to the play itself:

> The world is still deceived with ornament.
> In law, what plea so tainted and corrupt
> But being seasoned with a gracious voice,
> Obscures the show of evil? In religion,
> What damned error but some sober brow
> Will bless it, and approve it with a text,
> Hiding the grossness with fair ornament?
> There is no vice so simple but assumes
> Some mark of virtue on his outward parts.

(III, ii, 74-82)

This is so appropriate to the entire play that it is difficult to believe it a coincidence.

I see Bassanio's brief intervention during the trial scene as another sign of Shakespeare's ironic distance. As soon as Shylock begins to relent, under the pressure of Portia's skill, Bassanio declares his willingness to pay back the money Shylock is now willing to accept. In his eagerness to be finished with the whole unpleasant business, Bassanio shows a degree of mercy, but Portia remains adamant. Feeling her claws in Shylock's flesh, she drives them deeper and deeper in order to exact her own pound of flesh. Bassanio's suggestion bears no fruit but its formulation at this crucial moment cannot be pointless. It is the only reasonable solution to the whole affair but dramatically it cannot prevail because it is undramatic. Shakespeare is too good a playwright not to understand that the only good solution, from a theatrical standpoint, is the scapegoating of Shylock. On the other hand he wants to point out the unjust nature of the "cathartic" resolution that is forced upon him by the necessity of his art. He wants the reasonable solution to be spelled out somewhere inside the play.

Is it not excessive to say that scapegoating is a recognizable motif in *The Merchant of Venice*? There is one explicit allusion to the scapegoat in the play. It occurs at the beginning of Shylock's trial.

> I am a tainted wether of the flock,
> Meetest for death. The weakest kind of fruit
> Drops earliest to the ground, and so let me.
> You cannot better be employed, Bassanio,
> Than to live still and write mine epitaph.

(IV, i, 114–18)

Is there a difficulty for my thesis in the fact that Antonio rather than Shylock utters these lines? Not at all, since their mutual hatred has turned Antonio and Shylock into the doubles of each other. This mutual hatred makes all reconciliation impossible— nothing concrete separates the antagonists, no genuinely tangible issue that could be arbitrated and settled—but the undifferentiation generated by this hatred paves the way for the only type of resolution that can conclude this absolute conflict, the scapegoat resolution.

Antonio speaks these lines in reply to Bassanio, who has just asserted he would never let his friend and benefactor die in his place. He would rather die himself. Neither one will die, of course, or even suffer in the slightest. In the city of Venice, no Antonio or Bassanio will ever suffer as long as there is a Shylock to do the suffering for them.

There is no serious danger that Antonio will die, but he can really see himself, at this point, as a scapegoat in the making. Thus

Shakespeare can have an explicit reference to scapegoating without pointing directly to Shylock. There is a great irony, of course, not only in the fact that the metaphor is displaced, the scapegoat being the essence of metaphoric displacement, but also in the almost romantic complacency of Antonio, in his intimation of masochistic satisfaction. The quintessential Venetian, Antonio, the man who is sad without a cause, may be viewed as a figure of the modern subjectivity characterized by a strong propensity toward self-victimization or, more concretely, by a greater and greater interiorization of a scapegoat process that is too well understood to be reenacted as a real event in the real world. Mimetic entanglements cannot be projected with complete success onto all the Shylocks of this world, and the scapegoat process tends to turn back upon itself and become reflective. What we have, as a result, is a masochistic and theatrical self-pity that announces the romantic subjectivity. This is the reason why Antonio is eager to be "sacrificed" in the actual presence of Bassanio.

Irony is not demonstrable, I repeat, and it should not be, otherwise it would disturb the catharsis of those who enjoy the play at the cathartic level only. Irony is anticathartic. Irony is experienced in a flash of complicity with the writer at his most subtle, against the larger and coarser part of the audience that remains blind to these subtleties. Irony is the writer's vicarious revenge against the revenge that he must vicariously perform. If irony were too obvious, if it were intelligible to all, it would defeat its own purpose because there would be no more object for irony to undermine.

The reading I propose can be strengthened, I believe, through a comparison with other plays, notably *Richard III*. When Shakespeare wrote this play, his king's identity as a villain was well established. The dramatist goes along with the popular view, especially at the beginning. In the first scene, Richard presents himself as a monstrous villain. His deformed body is a mirror for the self-confessed ugliness of his soul. Here too we are dealing with a stereotype, the stereotype of the bad king that can be said to be generated or revived by the unanimous rejection of the scapegoat king, the very process that is reenacted in the last act after gathering momentum throughout the play.

If we forget for a while the introduction and the conclusion to focus on the drama itself, a different image of Richard emerges. We are in a world of bloody political struggles. All adult characters in the play have committed at least one political murder or benefited from one. As critics like Murray Krieger and Ian Kott have pointed out, the War of the Roses functions as a system of political rivalry and revenge in which every participant is a tyrant and a victim in turn, always behaving and speaking not according to permanent character differences but to the position he occupies at any moment within the total dynamic system. Being the last coil in that infernal spiral, Richard may kill more people more cynically than his predecessors, but he is not essentially different. In order to make the past history of reciprocal violence dramatically present, Shakespeare resorts to the technique of the curse. Everyone keeps cursing everyone else so vehemently and massively that the total effect is tragic or almost comic according to the mood of the spectator; all these curses mutually cancel each other until the end, when they all converge against Richard and bring about his final undoing, which is also the restoration of peace.

Two images of the same character tend to alternate, one highly differentiated and one undifferentiated. In the case of *The Merchant of Venice* and *Richard III* some fairly obvious reasons can be invoked; in both plays, the theme was a sensitive one, dominated by social and political imperatives regarding which Shakespeare felt skeptical, obviously, but that he could not attack openly. The method he devised permitted an indirect satire, highly effective with the knowledgeable few and completely invisible to the ignorant multitude, avid only of the gross *catharsis* Shakespeare never failed to provide.

Some kind of social and political interpretation is unavoidable, I believe, but it is not incompatible, far from it, with a more radical approach.

Great theater is necessarily a play of differentiation and undifferentiation. The characters will not hold the interest of the audience unless the audience can sympathize with them or deny them its sympathy. They must be highly differentiated, in other words, but any scheme of differentiation is synchronic and static. In order to be good, a play must be dynamic rather than static. The dynamics of the theater are the dynamics of human conflict, the reciprocity of retribution and revenge; the more intense the process, the more symmetry you tend to have, the more everything tends to become the same on both sides of the antagonism.

In order to be good a play must be as reciprocal and undifferentiated as possible but it must be highly differentiated, too, otherwise the spectators will not be interested in the outcome of the conflict. These two requirements are incompatible, but a playwright who cannot satisfy both simultaneously is obviously not a great playwright; he will produce either plays too differentiated, which will be labeled *pièces à thèse* because they will be experienced as insufficiently dynamic, or plays too undifferentiated, in order to have a lot of action, or suspense, as we say, but this suspense will appear pointless and will be blamed for a lack of intellectual and ethical content.

The successful playwright can fulfill the two contradictory requirements simultaneously, even though they are contradictory. How does he do it? In many instances he does not seem fully aware of what he is doing; he must do it in the same instinctive manner as the spectators who passionately identify with one antagonist. Even though the assumed difference between the two always translates itself into reciprocal and undifferentiated behavior, our view of the conflict tends to be static and differentiated.

We can be certain, I believe, that such is not the case with Shakespeare. Shakespeare is fully conscious of the gap between the difference of the static structure and the nondifference of

tragic action. He fills his plays with ironic allusions to the gap between the two and he does not hesitate to widen that gap still
further, as if he knew that he could do this with impunity and that
in all probability he would be rewarded for doing it; far from
destroying his credibility as a creator of "characters" he would
increase the overall dramatic impact of his theater and turn his
plays into those dynamic and inexhaustible objects upon which
critics can comment endlessly without ever putting their finger on
the real source of their ambiguity.

In *Richard III* we have examples of this practice no less striking
than in *The Merchant of Venice*. Anne and Elizabeth, the two
women who have most suffered at the hands of Richard, cannot
resist the temptation of power, even at the cost of an alliance with
him, when Richard himself diabolically dangles this toy in front of
them. After cursing Richard abundantly and discharging in this
manner all her moral obligations, Anne literally walks over the
dead body of her father to join hands with Richard. A little later
Elizabeth walks over the dead bodies of two of her children,
symbolically at least, in order to deliver a third one into the
bloody hands of the murderer.

These two scenes are structurally close, and they generate a
crescendo of abomination that cannot be without a purpose.
These two women are even more vile than Richard, and the only
character who is able to point out this vileness, thus becoming in a
sense the only ethical voice in the whole play, is Richard himself,
whose role, *mutatis mutandis*, is comparable to that of Shylock in
The Merchant of Venice.

It is Shakespeare's genius that he can do such things. And he
does them, not to generate irony only, but for the sake of dramatic efficiency. He knows that by doing them, he creates uneasiness
among the spectators, he places upon them a moral burden with
which they cannot deal in terms of the scapegoat values presented
at the outset. The demand for the expulsion of the scapegoat is

paradoxically reinforced by the very factors that make this expulsion arbitrary.

I fully agree that, in the case of plays like *Richard III* or *The Merchant of Venice*, an infinite number of readings is possible, and this infinity is determined by "the play of the signifier." I do not agree that this play is gratuitous, and that it is in the nature of all signifiers as signifiers to produce such infinite play. The literary signifier always becomes a victim. It is a victim of the signified, at least metaphorically, in the sense that its play, its *différence*, or what you will, is almost inevitably sacrificed to the one-sidedness of a single-minded differentiated structure à la Lévi-Strauss. The sacrificed signifier disappears behind the signified. Is this victimage of the signifier nothing but a metaphor, or is it mysteriously connected to the scapegoat as such in the sense that it is rooted in that ritual space where the major signifier is also a victim, not merely in the semiotic sense, this time, but in the sense of Shylock or of Richard III? The play of the signifier, with its arbitrary interruption for the sake of a differentiated structure, operates exactly like the theatrical and ritual process, with its conflictual undifferentiation suddenly resolved and returned to static differentiation through the elimination of a victim. Everything I have said suggests that to Shakespeare, at least, all these things are one and the same. The process of signification is one with the scapegoat resolution of the crisis in which all significations are dissolved, then reborn—the crisis that is described at length in *Troilus and Cressida* and designated as the "crisis of Degree." The evidence from ritual as well as from mythology suggests that Shakespeare may well be right. Long before *deciders* acquired its more abstract significance—to decide—it meant to cut with a knife, to immolate a sacrificial victim.

Those who think that the problem of textuality can be disposed of with no regard for the victims to which literary texts allude should have a close look at *The Merchant of Venice*.

 *Lennard J. Davis*

A Social History of Fact and Fiction: Authorial Disavowal in the Early English Novel

Authors of English novels of the seventeenth and early eighteenth centuries almost always begin their works with a preface asserting that they are presenting not a fiction but a factual account of some real series of events. Linked to this assertion is the companion one that the author, rather than being the creator of the work, is in fact only the literary editor of someone else's papers, journals, or oral hstory. Aphra Behn, for example, in the beginning of her novel *Oroonoko*, writes, "I do not pretend, in giving you the history of this Royal Slave, to entertain my Reader with Adventures of a feign'd hero. . . ." She continues with the corollary: "What I could not be witness of, I received from the mouth of the chief actor of this history."[1] The pattern here is a familiar one—affirmation of veracity and denial of authorship—and is a predictable feature of early novels. The question I should like to pose is why such an odd tack should have become so universally adopted by writers of early English novels? Why should most of these seventeenth- and early eighteenth-century novelists have chosen deliberately to claim that instead of writing fictions, they were only recording facts?

This problem can be explained away by saying that authorial disavowal was merely a convention established to steer around the puritan sanction against nondidactic, imaginative tales and stories. In this sense, the author was protected against the charge of writing fictions—which most puritans regarded as nothing more than lies or falsehoods. Alternatively, authorial disavowal can be dismissed as conventional humility; the eighteenth-century novelist was being circumspect in the same way an Elizabethan gentleman poet might have been in finding it distasteful to openly solicit a printer for his works. In both these explanations, authors are seen as knowingly setting up minor deceptions to defend themselves in advance against moral condemnation. The use of authorial disavowal, then, is seen as a technique for covering one's ground morally much in the same manner as embarrassed government officials do legally when they ritualistically repeat such phrases as "to the best of my ability" or "as far as I can remember" during Senate hearings.

As is perhaps obvious, such attempts to account for authorial disavowal seem insufficient or incomplete. If authors were trying to avoid the puritan sanction against writing fictions, it is difficult to see what the benefit of lying about the truthfulness of a work would have been. Essentially religious men, like Defoe and Richardson, would by lying only compound their sins—hardly fooling anyone, least of all God. Defoe specifically condemns lying of all sorts in *Serious Reflections . . . of Robinson Crusoe* and pointedly chastises authors who make up stories but "vouch their story with more assurance than others, and vouch also that they knew the persons who were concerned in it."[2] If, on the other hand, authors were being conventionally humble, it is hard to believe that so many authors could have been so humble. Defoe, for example, not known for his humility in other respects, seems unlikely to have gone in for this kind of self-effacement. Or Richardson, so full of pride and pomposity, cannot be imagined to have shielded himself under the aegis of editorship merely to prevent the applause that he seemed to have courted so strenuously anyway.

Another way of accounting for authorial disavowal has been to see the device as a means of making novels appear more realistic. According to this view, writers more or less deliberately increase the "distance," to use Wayne Booth's term,[3] between themselves and their novels by implying that the narrative has a legitimate autonomy of its own, the author being merely the editor of a manuscript *trouvé*. This technique is then seen as simply another device in the early novelist's repertoire to achieve what Ian Watt has called "formal realism."[4] So writers who want to achieve this formal realism need only maintain that their work is true, talk in great detail about the variety of objects that are part of daily life, and introduce low-life characters into their work. Although this attempt to explain authorial disavowal is perhaps the most persuasive by virtue of its justification on the grounds of formal realism, it is also an explanation that is incomplete insofar as it attempts to explain only the stylistic effect of disavowal—not the origin, significance, or even necessity of such a device. The more pressing concern is why a writer should have cared to make his narrative more realistic in the first place. Even the use of the words *realistic* or *realism* begs the question by implying that there was available to particular writers during the seventeenth century the concept of realism that they might freely choose to adopt. In fact, according to the *Oxford English Dictionary*, the word *realism* itself was not used in English until the mid-nineteenth century, and there was no parallel word to describe the concept of realism before that time. Fielding's use of the term "comic epic-poem in prose" hardly seems a handy substitute.[5] It is possible that a concept of factual verisimilitudinous narrative existed without the specific nomenclature. However, as I hope to demonstrate, during the seventeenth and eighteenth centuries there seems to have been much confusion about the nature of that narrative discourse that we have come to call "realistic." The important issue for English culture at that time seems to have been not simply how to be more realistic, or even how to achieve formal realism, but whether it was possible to write fictions at all without maintaining that they were factual.

One further point about the notion that authorial disavowal merely serves to heighten realism can be made: since the use of this technique was so widespread in the beginning of the eighteenth century, it should be clear that its effect on the reading public surely would have become lessened by overuse. The wonder is that

Samuel Richardson, in his original preface to *Pamela* in the mid-eighteenth century, should have used, once again, the device that had been used by Aphra Behn some seventy years before. If the aim of distancing an author from his work is to create heightened realism, the technique could only have worked if most readers had a dulled if not retarded sense of observation after seeing the same device for so many years. More likely, it seems that readers would have attained a kind of perceptual fatigue over some three generations and could no longer be expected to believe that narratives beginning with authorial disavowal were automatically more realistic. Indeed, as Harry Levin has noted, "Fiction approximates truth, not by concealing art but by exposing artifice."[6] That is, realism is based not on the extended and continued use of a particular convention, as in the case of authorial disavowal, but in the continual rejection of earlier accepted conventions. Indeed, by the year 1727, Mary Davys noted in her book *The Accomplished Rake or Modern Fine Gentleman* that "probably feigned stories," that is, novels that "pretend to write true histories" but that "give themselves the utmost liberty of feigning," have been "for some time . . . out of use and fashion."[7] Davys's opinion, while somewhat premature in its announcement of the retirement of the novel, still indicates that at least some readers during the first quarter of the eighteenth century found the technique of authorial disavowal rather a bit tired and played out. If this was the case, then the plea of formal realism cannot be made for the novelists' habit of claiming that their works were not fictions.

I would suggest here that to understand the phenomenon of authorial disavowal we need to go beyond the idea that its use is only conventional. If authorial disavowal is a convention, we need to ask further what the significance of that convention is. What myths does it uphold? And what myths are upheld by it? In this sense, we need to treat literary conventions with the care that Roland Barthes has studied popular conventions with in *Mythologies* or the way Michel Foucault has explored the manner in which political domination manifests itself in even the minor conventions and rituals of institutional life and thought. In effect, we need to look at authorial disavowal as something more than a neutral habit or personal tic of novelists, and to consider this phenomenon as a significant and historically particular sign of a transformation in the discourse of narrative.

In doing this, the first fact that must strike us as crucial is that early novelists, by denying the fictitious quality of their work, are openly claiming to be part of one *discourse* (to use Foucault's term)—that of history or journalism—rather than that of another—fiction. The fact is that novelists of the seventeenth and eighteenth centuries were, for the most part, more closely related in their work to the journalistic discourse than to any other. Eliza Haywood was a journalist; Defoe and Fielding both wrote for and edited various newspapers; Richardson printed newspapers; Aphra Behn was, too, a writer of political as well as literary pieces, and Bunyan was a pamphleteer; Swift was deeply involved with political writing and journalism. What is striking is that all these authors moved between fact and fiction with a freedom not afforded to most novelists of the twentieth century. We may expect our novelists to write occasional pieces for the *New York Times Sunday Magazine*, or, as in the case of Norman Mailer, to write journalism of a sort, but these novelists serve the function of in-house literary backbenchers and seldom if ever report or investigate news. We do not expect to see the byline of a novelist as a newswriter in every issue of a newspaper the way a reader of the eighteenth century might well have expected to read Defoe in every issue of the *Review* or Mrs. Haywood in the *Female Spectator*. These writers of the eighteenth century seem to have been journalists first and novelists second, as was Defoe, who did not embark on his first novel until he was in his sixties.

This connection between fiction and journalism has, it turns out, a considerable prehistory. Even the fact that novelists frequently claimed their works were true can be seen as a partial carry-over from journalism. News ballads and early newsbooks of the sixteenth and seventeenth centuries could almost always be expected to contain somewhere the assertion that the event they related was true and not a fiction. One commonly read headlines such as: "True and dreadful new tidings of blood and brimstone which God hath caused to rain from Heaven" or "The True Description of a Monsterous Child Born in The Ile of Wight."[8] Frequently, too, news would be registered with the Stationers Company as having been sworn to be true by a justice.[9] This overniceness as to the truthfulness of news seems to have been a defense against the commonly accepted notion during the sixteenth and seventeenth centuries that much news was simply fabricated. Journalists were often depicted as "lying stationers" profiting unwholesomely from news by publishing "whisperings, mutterings, and bare suppositions."[10] News, until well into the seventeenth century, always carried with it the signification that it was all lies for the consumption of the lower classes. Hence, newspapers frequently bore such defensive subtitles as the one attached to *Mercurius Civicus*, which proclaimed itself "*London's Intelligencer or Truth impartially related from thence to the whole Kingdom to prevent misinformation.*"[11] This routine assertion that newspapers were not writing lies but were presenting the truth seems to have continued on into the early novel.

If both the novelist and the journalist (who, as we have seen, were frequently the same) were impelled to insist on the factuality of their writings during the seventeenth century, it is possible to point to a certain ontological insecurity in the categories of fact and fiction in English narrative of this period. The case here is unusual precisely because one is confronted not simply with a journalist or a biographer asserting that the facts of his or her story are true. Rather, what seems unusual is that the insistence on veracity in these cases is made during a time when there was no standard veracious discourse in the realm of narrative. That is to say, no narrative form had become the locus of what we might call today nonfiction. Certainly the study of law and theology had a claim to the virtue of factuality, but these discourses were not strictly part of the narrative tradition. The Bible was clearly a true narrative for the readers of the time, but the Bible is certainly in a case by itself. History, too, during the sixteenth and seventeenth centuries was in a rather nonobjective mode. For instance, Sir Walter Raleigh allowed that historians might invent historical events as long as no contradictory records were available.[12] Sir Philip Sidney's dictum in *An Apology for Poetry* (1595) that poetry was truer than history should also be understood in this context.

The word *novel* itself seems to contain this sense of ontological uncertainty. In the late sixteenth and early seventeenth century, *novel*, according to the *Oxford English Dictionary*, could apply to either a fictional tale, like those found in the *Decameron* or *Cents Nouvelles Nouvelles*, or a journalistic report in the form of a printed ballad or flying sheet. The word *novel* seems to have been used interchangeably with the word *news*—and both were applied freely to writings that were about true or fictional events, quotidian or supernatural occurrences, and incidents that may have been recent or several decades old. For this semantic parity to have existed, the concept of news must have carried no special signification of factuality, as the word *novel* must have carried no signification of being fictional. Titles like *A Sack Full of News* (1557), *News from Antwerp* (1580), and *News From Hell* (1606) all reveal differing degrees of factuality in their range from jest-book to news ballad to religious-satirical commentary. Even the news reports themselves were hardly to be considered factual, as we have seen. These tales of criminals, the supernatural, domestic disputes, and freaks of nature were in fact quite like the material that appeared in imaginative novels of the time such as Thomas Deloney's *Thomas of Reading* (1598) or Robert Greene's *A Notable Discovery of Cozenage* (1591).

If a novel, then, at the end of the sixteenth century carried no special sense of being a fictional work, clearly by the mid-eighteenth century the meaning of the word had changed. It now could be counted on to signify a longish piece of narrative fiction —distinguished from romance for the most part—but strongly implying imaginative and not factual narrative. William Congreve in the preface to *Incognita* (1692) was able to give his well-known definition of the novel as a story of a familiar nature filled with "accidents and odd events, such which not being so distant from our belief."[13] Congreve's definition is not essentially different from Clara Reeve's some ninety years later, in which she defines novels as "familiar relations of such things as pass everyday before our eyes . . . we are affected by the joys or distresses, of the person in the story, as if they were our own."[14] The congruence of Congreve's and Reeve's definitions of the novel should indicate what seems fairly obvious to us: the establishment of the novel as a distinct form—now unrelated to news or journalism—had been accomplished in the eighteenth century.

What we have seen is that the novel, at least in semantic terms, seems to have moved from a parity with journalism to a separate identity as fictional work. During the sixteenth and seventeenth centuries novels and news reports were not seen as clearly fictional or as clearly factual; in other words, narrative during this time seems to have been categorized in ways that did not depend on the distinction between fact and fiction. This undifferentiated, general category of narrative can be referred to as the *news/novels* discourse for the sake of convenience.

Confirmation of this hypothesis of the undifferentiated category of news/novels can be found in the laws and statutes that were used to regulate what could be printed. Here, one finds too the absence of any category of uniquely fictional narrative until well into the eighteenth century. For example, the Licensing Act of 1662, which would last in one form or another until 1695, contains an unconscious definition of the news/novels discourse. The act assigned the licensing of all historical works and political writings to the secretary of state, all legal works to the lord chancellor and the judges, all work on religion, philosophy, and physics to the Archbishop of Canterbury and the Bishop of London.[15] Aside from the interesting way that discourses are apportioned and assigned to various sectors of the state, the striking fact for us is that there is no mention in the act of fiction, tales, or imaginative stories. This absence may have been due to mere oversight, or to the fact that such works were outside the jurisdiction of the law. However, since various kinds of tales and ballads had been specifically mentioned in earlier laws,[16] one must assume that perhaps the general category of "historical and political works" could have included fiction, tales, and novels as well as news and histories. That is, the general category could have been the news/novels discourse about which we have been speaking.

This hypothetical news/novels discourse seems to receive further confirmation in the Licensing Act of 1663, legislated one year after the previous licensing act, which grouped various kinds of printed matter into what one must infer was the unconscious—and in that sense more or less obvious—categories present in the mind of a seventeenth-century reader. The resulting taxonomy of discourses, according to the language of the act, identifies specifically one distinct category that encompasses "all narratives, advertisements, intelligencers, diurnals and other books of public intelligence."[17] What is significant here is that in listing all possible kinds of printed matter, the writers of the act saw fit to lump together all narrative—whether factual or fictional—into one discrete grouping. What is perhaps more interesting is that the act equates this undifferentiated mass of narratives with "intelligencers, diurnals and other books of public intelligence"—that is, with newspapers and newsbooks. In this act, narrative was seen as a kind of subdivision or element of a larger journalistic discourse that was popular and constitutively social.

Among many, two points are important here. First, these publications mentioned by the act as being part of the news/novels discourse share the common denominator of writing about and being interested in events that happened in the recent past. This interest distinguishes these narratives from history and romance, for example, which tend to treat mainly the distant past. In this sense, we are dealing with the "new" and the "novel." The second common denominator among these narratives of recentness is the fact that all were published in serial form. The serial format of both newspapers and novelistic narratives is significant because serialization was a kind of signifier of the news/novels discourse. Fictional works were frequently difficult to tell from factual ones not only on the basis of content, but on the basis of their printed form as well. Rogue's tales, like *The English Rogue* (1665–1671) by Richard Head and Francis Kirkman, were printed over a period of years. *Poor Robin's Memoirs* (1677) was published virtually weekly in single half-sheets as if it were a kind of newspaper, as was *The English Guzman or Captain Hilton's Memoirs* (1683). Such serialized criminal tales might end up each week with the last-line salutation of "I bid you farewell till next week," or "Enough for a Penny till next."[18] These tag lines are evidence that the notion of the continuing story is shared by both serialized newspapers and serialized novels.

The quality of serial publication and the quality of recentness are not accidentally shared by these narratives; they are crucially interrelated and interdependent—and both are deeply implicated in the development of the journalistic discourse. The serial format of news, the fact that since 1621 newspapers were published at regular intervals, revealed what was one of the latent benefits of the typographical technology—the capacity for printed works to comment on, record, and disseminate a continuous account and record of public events on a regular basis and with only the delayed immediacy of—at most—the passage of a week. In this sense, journalism's contribution to the world of narrative discourse was the establishment of a mode of presenting the past, more specifically the recent past, without the powerful retrospective implications of a treatise on history. Journalism's invention was the use of a kind of mediated or median past tense, roughly the equivalent of the past imperfect, which signaled to the reader that what was being treated was neither the remote past (which was reserved for historical narratives or romances) nor the present (which would be confined to monologue, lyric, or drama). This median past tense was clearly dependent on both serial publication and a middle-class interest in the new, the novel. The fact that newspapers could write about events as recent as those of last week gave to print the capacity to approach the recapture of recent time past. Serial publication permitted a regularly published, continuous, and co-terminous transcription of reality. These developments in narrative, I would argue, were major ones to seventeenth-century culture, permitting, among other things, language to become the transcriber of recentness and immediacy. If, as Northrop Frye says, romance was the aristocracy's re-creation of an idealized and distant past,[19] then this new journalistic narrative seems to be linked to the middle-class's desire for a more recent and less idealized moment. Journalism seems to have given to society, and particularly to the middle and lower classes, a way of describing reality that coincided temporarily with that reality, that kept running alongside of that reality, without necessarily holding up a mirror to it.

Before continuing, I wish to make clear that in saying that the news/novels discourse was structurally indifferent to fact or fiction as a definer of genre, I do not mean to imply that people during the seventeenth century were incapable of knowing the difference between fact and fiction. I have no doubt that they could tell, in their daily life, the real from the imaginary. What I am saying is that in the limited sphere or discourse of printed prose narrative, the factuality or fictionality of a work was not crucial to defining the genre of that work before approximately the second quarter of the eighteenth century. I should also point out that nowhere am I maintaining that there is an absolute distinction between fact and fiction to which we can now comfortably point and say, "There it is." Rather, as Northrop Frye has written, it would seem that "everything in words is plasmatic, and truth and falsehood represent the direction or tendencies in which verbal structures go, or are thought to go."[20] The ground rules for my argument require the reader to kick the stone along with Dr. Johnson and concede that there are at least consentual attitudes toward what is true and false, and that, at least in the cataloguing of books in the twentieth century, it is important to establish whether a work is fictional or factual, although there will always be works that defy this categorization.[21]

So, the news/novels discourse, while structurally indifferent to fact and fiction during the seventeenth century, could be described as being defined by its interest in recentness and immediacy, its transcription of reality, and its link with information dissemination—which is the aspect of this discourse that marks it as distinctly social and popular.

Then at what point did distinguishing between factual and fictional narratives become significant to the English culture and why? Of course we cannot point to a single moment, an obvious kink in the historical continuum, but what seems clear is that the period from 1700 to 1750 was a crucial one in the separation of factual narratives from fictional ones. This separation was not entirely unmotivated or accidental; and it is not as if the attempt to distinguish the factual from the fictional had never been made before the eighteenth century. In fact, since the beginning of the news/novels discourse, which one might date as starting with the early news ballads of the 1530s, the government had begun to perceive the dangers inherent in a printed information network that it could not control. The monarchy and then the Parliament tried to distinguish between factual (hence potentially libelous) narratives and fictional ones. From the reign of Henry VIII to that of Queen Anne the government repeatedly tried to control dissent expressed through the printed word. But the state's attempts to control factual narratives were ineffective until the eighteenth century because the lawmakers defined news not in terms of its content but in terms of its mode of publication. The problem for the state during the sixteenth and seventeenth centuries was how to go about restricting journalism when no distinct category of news existed apart from the more general category of prose narrative. In effect, the government could not define legally—hence regulate—what constituted fact. Frequently one finds publications defined in legal statutes on the basis of their format alone. Thus, for example, a monopoly was granted to Thomas Symcock by James I for ballads, briefs, and other "things printed on one side of the paper."[22] This apparently arbitrary category of one-sided printed matter seems to define a segment of print that includes the literary, political, journalistic—whether these include the factual or the fictional. The laws fail, to my knowledge, to mention the banning of news per se.

Even the Stamp Act of 1712, specifically designed to decimate opposition newspapers, does not ban *news* but the *format* of pamphlets, papers, and newspapers. The Stamp Act specified that publications of half-sheet size be printed on paper that had a half-penny stamp affixed to it, and those of a whole-sheet size be taxed with a one-penny stamp.[23] There was no mention of the taxing of news, although it must have been evident to all[24] that only newspapers and pamphlets were published in this format and were therefore to be crushed. Obviously the problem for the government was that printers could fairly easily circumvent these legal restrictions by changing the design and format of their publications, which is exactly what they did to avoid the Stamp Act's effect. The act stated that papers of less than one sheet had to pay a tax on "every printed copy," while editions longer than one sheet had to pay the tax "in one printed copy," and printers interpreted this accidental distinction to produce the fanciful—but legal—reading that newspapers of a single sheet paid *per copy*, but longer publications paid only *per edition*. So printers simply expanded their traditionally single-sheet publications to one and a half sheets and thereby had to pay only three shillings for each edition.

It was not until the revision of the Stamp Act in 1724[25] that an English law specifically defined what constituted news by taxing all journals, mercuries, and newspapers of any format—particularly distinguishing between pamphlets and newspapers. This action struck a decisive wedge between news (which was taxable now) and fiction (which was not), and one can actually see in the newspapers printed after 1724 that news items were segregated onto one specially stamped page, while other items were moved over to what became the nontaxable literary pages.[26] The legislative action of 1724 is by no means the single act that separated fact from fiction, but it is a kind of symbolic watershed. After this action, government regulations and judicial rulings began to recognize the distinct category of news. But the next quarter of a century was still a time of much confusion concerning the precise definition of news and consequently of novels.[27] The extent to which fact and fiction were independnt and interdependent was still a pressing concern.

The full history of government regulation of the press, and particularly the use of seditious libel laws to suppress opposition writing, is too lengthy to go into here.[28] But what this rather selective history of journalism reveals is that eighteenth-century attitudes toward fact and fiction were by no means simple. If novelists, who were really journalists, claimed to be writing factual accounts, which were really fictional, then perhaps it is possible to say that the eighteenth century might have held notions of fact and fiction that were considerably different from those of our own. The case for such a possibility becomes stronger when we consider that for a news story to appear in print during the eighteenth century, it frequently had to be cast in the form of fiction or allegory to avoid violating the harassing seditious libel laws; Dr. Johnson did this when he wrote accounts of the English parliamentary sessions for the *Gentleman's Magazine* in an allegorized and anagramized version that chronicled the debates of the "Senate of Liliput."[29]

The rather paradoxical situation arising as a result of this state of affairs was that works of fiction were appearing in print claiming to be true—while news items were appearing in print claiming to be fictional. This unusual situation leads one to suspect that during this time some major cultural realignment was occurring in which fact and fiction figured prominently.

The novels themselves acted as focuses for these questions. The problem of authorial disavowal, with which I began this paper, can now be placed in the context of this general cultural transformation of narrative. When, for example, Defoe writes in the Preface to *Robinson Crusoe*, "The Editor believes the thing to be a just history of fact; neither is there any appearance of fiction in it,"[30] we can see his denial of fictionality as more than mere convention. As Defoe moves through his other novels, he reveals an ambivalence, a shifting, a slippage in his use of authorial disavowal, and consequently a change in his attitude toward fact and fiction. In *The Farther Adventures of Robinson Crusoe* Defoe no longer avers that his work is strictly factual but allows that parts of his novel are, as he says, "Invention or Parable."[31] In the preface to his next book, *Colonel Jack*, Defoe muddies the waters further by saying, "Nor is it of any concern to the reader whether it [the book] be an exact historical relation of real facts, or whether the hero of it intended to present us, at least in part with a moral romance."[32] Here Defoe retains the guise of editor, but allows that the work itself might be fiction or moral romance, and that if the work is indeed fiction, then the fault lies with the author of the work—Colonel Jack himself. Defoe is playing a shrewd game here, refusing to pledge himself either to fact or fiction, news or novels. In *Moll Flanders*, Defoe—still as editor—allows that the work may be fictionalized but again places the blame on Moll herself for being unreliable, and advises the reader to "take it as he pleases."[33] In *Roxana*, the reader is told not that the work is true, but only that the story's "foundation is laid in truth of fact."[34] This last tactic allows Defoe to write fiction without writing lies.

In the progression of dodges, feints, and bluffs here, Defoe himself seems to be trying to work out some way of writing fiction that is not fiction. Defoe is not merely using a convention, he is trying to wrestle with and define a new conception of narrative that increasingly requires works to be either true or false. Defoe's solution is to tread a middle ground by claiming that his work is simultaneously true in one sense and not true in another. The interesting thing is that, despite obvious differences in levels of credence and sophistication, so many readers in the eighteenth century could tolerate such a provisional and qualified notion of what constituted a factual narrative. This willingness to let fact and fiction remain, at least to this extent, undifferentiated is a sign of the cultural confusion on this issue.

Defoe, of course, seems more or less obviously related to the development of journalism, and his works of pseudobiography are perhaps too openly newslike to confirm the general statements I have been making about the novel arising from a previous journalistic discourse. So I would like to consider at this juncture Samuel Richardson, whose work is generally seen as distinct from journalism and more closely related to spiritual autobiography and romance. I want to suggest here that Richardson's work was also intimately linked to the news/novels discourse and that much of his writing, too, emerged from the rupture between factual and fictional narratives.

Richardson begins the original version of *Pamela* with what must now be a familiar statement that the work he is presenting is factual and that he is merely the editor. However, Richardson wrote privately to a friend that he wanted his books "to be thought genuine; only so far kept up, I mean, as that they should not prefatically be owned not to be genuine."[35] The wording of this letter is somewhat paradoxical in saying that Richardson wanted the novel to be *thought* genuine but not to be *considered* genuine.

That is, he wanted the novel to be seen as partially or provisionally true only to the extent that it could not be charged with being outrightly false. Richardson's intent, along with that of Defoe, seems to have been to place his novel in a unique category of provisionally true narrative. As Richardson's now-famous letter to Stinstra suggests, the foundation for *Pamela* appears to have been "true" in some very limited sense of the word; Richardson claimed to have overheard in a tavern the story of a poor girl made rich and noble through marriage. But if the foundation for the story is true, in what sense can one say that the story is true?

An attack on Richardson by an anonymous author of a pamphlet entitled *Pamela Censured* reveals much about the extent to which the debate over fact and fiction was ongoing, detailed, and serious. The attack begins by saying that although Richardson offers us letters as "originals" and says that these constitute a "narrative which has its foundation in Truth," in reality anyone can reduce Richardson's formulation to its "modestest construction" in common sense and say that "Pamela is a Romance form'd in Manner of a literary correspondence founded on a tale which the Author had heard, and modell'd into its present shape. . . . And however true the foundation may have been, yet a few Removes and Transitions make it deviate into a downright Falsehood."[36] What the critic of *Pamela* is engaged in here is no less than a thoroughgoing analysis of the types, degrees, and categories of veracity that are embodied in the work. He considers that *Pamela* is founded on a tale, modeled into a shape, and thereby removed from the truth. Still, the critic refuses to say outrightly that *Pamela* is a fiction entirely. His analysis seems to reflect an awareness that narratives can be both truth and false in the special senses of those words, but his attitude also reflects a profound ambivalence.

The readers of *Pamela* and *Robinson Crusoe* must have been in a state of considerable ambivalence as to whether or not the works they were reading were true. Many did consider *Pamela* to be a true story, and one went so far as to write to the putative editor demanding, "Let us have Pamela as Pamela wrote it."[37] Even the French translator of *Pamela* considered the story "a true one" and that Richardson, as editor, "often sacrificed the story to moral instruction."[38] There were, on the other hand, those who refused to believe that Richardson was only editor; the author of *Pamela Censured* called Richardson a "half-editor, half-author."[39] But significantly even this attack allowed Richardson the title of "half-editor," as if it were too much a violation of the news/novels discourse to say that a work of such popularity could be entirely fictional. So, for an eighteenth-century reader of Defoe or Richardson, it would be literally impossible to know with any certainty whether books like *Pamela* were true or not. And as I have argued elsewhere at greater length[40] this ambivalence and uncertainty was itself one of the hallmarks of reader response to early English novels—certainly to those works before *Tom Jones*— a work that openly admits its fictionality.

The state of ambivalence I am discussing was no doubt furthered by the incidents that followed the publication of *Pamela* in 1740. In the following year there appeared a *Memoire of the Life of Lady H., The Celebrated Pamela.* This book averred that Lady Hesilrige, who did actually marry into the aristocracy, was the real Pamela, and other such publications as this no doubt caused many readers to wonder about the truth of Richardson's work. In early 1741 things grew murkier yet, when two booksellers, Chandler and Kelly, published a work called *Pamela's Conduct in High Life*, a sequel to Richardson's first two volumes. Richardson responded to this literary ambush by advertising that Chandler and Kelly were writing "without any other knowledge of the story than what they are able to collect from the two volumes already printed. [And that Richardson was] continuing the work himself, from materials that, perhaps, but for such a notorious invasion of his plan, he should not have published."[41] Although Richardson

calls himself an "author" here for the first time, he still per-
petuates the necessary state of ambivalence by implying that he
was editing "materials"—presumably some actual record or further letters—to which his rivals do not have access. However,
Chandler and Kelly claimed in an advertisement in the *London
Evening Post* that their book was published directly from Pamela's
"original papers" and was "regularly digested by a gentleman more
conversant in high life than the vain author of *Pamela*."[42]

Richardson had argued himself into a corner, and his dilemma
illustrates some of the tangible disadvantages of authorial disavowal. By denying that his work was fictional, Richardson had
to maintain that *Pamela* was based on actual records and documents. But, by taking this tack, he had no way of preventing other
authors from claiming to possess those very records and writing
from them. His problems were compounded by the fact that
Richardson was not really conversant with upper-class life and
therefore could not even have claimed to be the best or most
suitable editor of Pamela's letters. In this sense, Chandler and
Kelly could openly boast that their usurpation of Richardson's
book was not theft but an actual improvement. Clearly, during
this time when the Copyright Law of 1709 was still easily cir-
cumvented, authorial disavowal became distinctly unsuited for
maintaining fiscal control over one's writings. To claim that a
novel was purely fictional would be an advantage to writers like
Richardson since they could then maintain that the uniqueness
and originality of a novel came from its connection to a particular
author's imagination and not from its source in actual records.

However, for Richardson, it was morally and artistically important to maintain that his works were in some sense genuine.
His objection to novels in general were that they paid so little
attention to fact, to the real. To him, the Behns, the Manleys, the
Haywoods, are equated with a "set of wretches."[43] It was the un-
truthful aspect of continental romances that disgusted Richardson when he wrote, "I hate so much the French marvelous and all

unnatural machinery."[44] *Tom Jones*, too, was "a rambling collection of waking dreams in which probability was not observed,"[45] and *Shamela* received vituperation—predictably—as a misrepresentation of facts. Richardson's concern here is with establishing in narrative what he considered an innovative attention to factuality. Richardson wrote that narratives must be "very circumstantial" so as best to "maintain an air of probability" and "represent real life."[46]

Richardson claimed that he was founding a "new species of writing,"[47] and I think that Richardson meant this induced mutation in narrative to be different precisely because it had a new relationship to the problems of fact and fiction. What then was Richardson's innovation? Clearly not his epistolary style itself since, as Katherine Hornbeak has shown,[48] this form of writing was quite popular before Richardson. Richardson's innovation was what he called "spontaneous writing," that is, "letters [written] by parties themselves at the very time in which the events happened."[49] What was significant and unique in this innovation was the attempt to recapture recent time past and forcibly decrease the interval between event and transcription that would in some sense decrease the cognitive space between language and reality as well. The method of spontaneous writing permits Richardson to fashion language and narrative so as to cleave closer to the real in terms of both time and space—time in the sense that when Pamela writes, she writes close to the moment of doing; and space in the sense that the reader is presented with the letters themselves. Lovelace, perhaps more than any other character, comes closest to this ideal since he writes not only spontaneously but in shorthand, as well, so that he can attempt to asymtotically approach the immediacy of the originating moment. Because Richardson assembles these units of immediacy in a series of letters rather than a retrospective narrative, he is better able to give a continuous and coterminous account of reality by virtue of the serial format that letters afford.

By now it should be clear that the way I have been talking about spontaneous writing is the same way I have been talking about the innovations of journalism. In his own way, Richardson seems to have borrowed the concept of the mediated or median past tense that journalism had introduced. In both Richardson's novels and journalistic narratives, seriality, recentness, immediacy, and even dissemination of information are paramount. Just as journalism had permitted language to become in some sense an embodiment of and a memorial to those public events it recorded, so too spontaneous writing allowed Pamela, for example, to leave behind the only valid record of the events that transpired between herself and Lord B.

While I am not saying that Pamela is a journalist—even though she does keep a journal—it is significant that she is in some sense much sought after precisely because she does regularly and obsessively transcribe reality, although this is clearly not her only charm. Lord B. becomes, quite early on, the regular and even obsessive reader of her letters. He frequently expresses his readerly devotion with expressions like, "I long to see the particulars of your plot. . . and [am] desirous of reading all you write."[50] He also respects her attention to factuality in her narratives, reflected in her "great regard to truth,"[51] and even says that she writes "a very moving tale."[52] Moreover, Lady Davers, who has heard about Pamela's journalizing, wants to read her writings—precisely because she looks to Pamela's work as the only authentic record of what actually happened: "I understand child, says she, that you keep a journal of all matters that pass . . . I should delight to read all of his [Lord B.'s] stratagems, attempts, contrivances, menaces, and offers to you."[53] So, Lady Davers becomes part of Pamela's reading public, joining Lord B, and of course Pamela's parents, who value their daughter for her writing, too, which they read as if these communications were actually the monthly parts of a serialized novel. To Goodman Andrews and his wife, Pamela's accounts of her travails were "the delight of our spare hours," and like many novel readers they could not wait to finish the story and "so turned to the end; where we find . . . her virtue within view of its reward."[54]

So effective, in fact, is Richardson's attempt to have language cleave to reality that frequently Pamela is all but subsumed or replaced by her language. Thus Pamela's complex taming of Lord B. and his would-be seduction of her are worked out initially through his penetrating her epistolary integument by reading her private correspondence. He is "overcome" by her "charming manner of writing."[55] The scene in which Lord B. attempts to rape Pamela is virtually paralleled by his attempt to forcibly undress her to secure the letters that are hidden under her petticoats. Lord B. warns: "Now . . . it is my opinion that they are about you, and I never undressed a girl in my life; but I will now begin to strip my pretty Pamela; and I hope I shall not go far before I find them."[56] As he stoops to see if they are "about your knees with your garters,"[57] Pamela yields up her secret manuscript in despair. The metonymy in this scene of private letters in proximity to private parts is not to be overlooked, and the attempted forcible removal of Pamela's deepest secrets from under her petticoats sets up an equation between Pamela's physical and spiritual being and her own written account of that being, which for the moment is as important as her maidenhead for Lord B. to possess. In this symbolic sense, Pamela-the-heroine becomes replaced by Pamela-the-linguistic-simulacrum. This state of affairs is emphasized throughout the work by the particularly textual nature of Pamela's being. To the reader, her existence is manifestly constituted through the omnipresent machinery of spontaneous writing—letters, journals, texts —which stand perpetually between the reader and the writing heroine and have the effect of rendering Pamela's incarnation profoundly typographical—certainly more typographical than any written narrative before the work of Richardson. Even Mrs. Jewkes bears witness against Pamela's constant textualization of experience when she says to Pamela in understandable despair that certain matters "would better bear *talking* of, than *writing* about."[58]

Clarissa, too, shares this quality of typographical existence. She literally becomes the sum and total of her written account, which she actively pushed into publication. Clarissa's last act, the writing of her will, which was "published in compliance with the lady's order on her deathbed,"[59] as the original subtitle to the novel stated, is suggestive of the final replacement of herself by her language and her will incarnate in language. Clarissa says that she is "solicitous to have all those letters and materials preserved which will set my whole story on a true light." She continues, "The warning that may be given from those papers to all such young creatures as may have known or heard of me, may be of more efficacy to the end wished for, as I humbly presume to think, than my appearance could have been in a court of justice."[60] Clarissa's existence is more efficacious, as she says, in language than in personal appearance. It is Clarissa's written, printed story that is paramount, and the story itself replaces Clarissa and her temporal existence. As she writes of herself, "One day, sir, you will perhaps know all my story."[61] Even Anna Howe, seeing Clarissa's final remains, responds not as if she were viewing a corpse, but as if she had seen the concluding punctuation mark of a discourse, when she says, "And this all . . . of my Clarissa's story."[62] Clarissa's conscious attempt to put her writing in the hands of the public, to replace herself by her language, goes Pamela one better in the attempt to journalize experience.

What I have been suggesting is that the innovativeness of spontaneous writing lies in its ability to decrease the cognitive space between thought, reality, and language. In so doing, language itself comes to the forefront and takes the place, as it were, of the events or people that it describes. In journalism, the printed account becomes through the passage of time the archival record; in *Pamela* the character is memorialized and preserved in time by virtue of her own written account. I think that this new capacity of language can be called a major shift in culture; it is a transformation that has been described in detail elsewhere. Michel Foucault in *The Order of Things*[63] details precisely this changeover in linguistic capacity. Foucault notes that language, at least formal narrative language, in the middle ages served mainly as a mark or sign for another level of meaning that had to be reached through some hermeneutical or allegorical process. However, Foucault notes, by the time of the classical period (by which he means the late seventeenth and early eighteenth centuries) this interpretative demand of language has been dropped and replaced by verisimilitude or what Foucault refers to as a "discursivity of representation." Language is no longer a sign for some other level of meaning and reality, language becomes itself capable of verisimilitude, the representing of meaning and reality. So Foucault might not find it odd that in Richardson's novel the heroine is not so much Pamela as Pamela's language. There is no demand for interpretation in the novel—only a meticulous care for the material aspect of language—the fetishization of style and penmanship, the concern with the minutiae of sending and receiving, intercepting, forging, and the logophilia that demands every event be obsessively incarnated into the word.

In suggesting this "text-ualization" of experience, I am not saying that eighteenth-century novelists were actually twentieth-century French critics in powdered wigs and waistcoats. And I certainly do not mean to reduce all experience to language and so aestheticize all literary phenomena into an infinite regression of signifiers and signifieds. My belief is that far from having such an effect, the primacy or centrality of language as representation in these eighteenth-century novels shows us how fictional narrative is actually part of powerful discourse associated with journalism. This discourse did, it is true, transcribe reality into language—but it did so with the aim of increasing the numbers of those privy to information, of creating political ideologies, and of embodying social consciousness in the printed word. The nexus between news and novels is a powerful one because it allows us to see that fictional narratives, by participating in a journalistic discourse, are also part of an information-disseminating system that is by definition social. Raymond Williams has aptly referred to literature as social language and social practice[64]—and I think by showing that novels were part of the journalistic discourse, we can add dimensions to the concept of "social language."

If we can consider eighteenth-century novelists as actually being part of a public and popular news/novel discourse, then I think it is possible to understand the problem of authorial disavowal with which I began. Further, if even a writer like Richardson, who has been seen traditionally as a novelist in "recoil" from his environment seeking in his writing "the emotional satisfaction which ordinary life denied,"[65] can be seen as actually part of a social language and practice, then the usual notion of the novel as being an escape from experience can be challenged. Authors who denied their authorship and insisted that their works were true were, I would argue, attempting to make a statement about the real difficulties of finding their place in the midst of a discourse that was in the active process of rupture. As the news/novels discourse grew into the specialized subdiscourses of journalism and fiction, novelists still saw themselves as part of a news-synthesizing and disseminating system, but the works they were writing, while embodying the qualities of recentness, immediacy, memorialization, preservation, transcription, and dissemination, no longer could be seen as *news*. Richardson spoke about his role as novelist as if he were actually a journalist or editorial writer when he wrote, "And it is a glorious privilege, that a middling man enjoys who has preserved his independency, and can occasionally (though not stoically) tell the world what he thinks of that world."[66] Richardson here places novels clearly at the side of newspapers, saying in effect that novelists, instead of writing news of public events of a nation, were writing news of the ideology as it were of that nation. If novelists refused to concede that they were writing fictions, perhaps it was because fiction was too limiting a concept for them; they were in their own sense of themselves still writing news—only, in this case, news stripped of its reference to immediate public events.

Dickens may have thought that novels would mainly concern themselves with the romantic side of familiar things, but for the eighteenth-century novelists the factual side of public things was not entirely outside their realm of interest. With the advent of the category of the purely fictional and its antithetical category of the purely factual—a division our modern world acknowledges and relies upon—has also come a weakening and an isolation to the novelistic discourse. Fiction is now perceived for the most part as a separate and specialized discourse that has been canonized and valorized as aesthetic, and therefore removed from the world of public events. Even those contemporary novelists who oppose this limitation are working against a general and widely accepted view of fiction. Novels still report on the ideologies of our cultural moment, but they are treated as being part of a discourse that is no longer immanent, no longer energized as is news by its continual impingement on the world of things. Perhaps the most telling detail, finally, about the rupture between fact and fiction is presented to us each week in our own homes with Sunday breakfast. As we cleave the *New York Times* into its component parts, some of us reach for the news sections and others for the literary supplement. The word *supplement* evokes the contemporary role of novels, and is all the more ironic when we consider that before 1725 the literary and the journalistic elements of newspapers were virtually indistinguishable, serialized novels resting cheek by jowl with fabricated news stories, invented biographies, and the details of continental wars. The price we have paid for pure fiction is that now novels are regarded as supplementary, and authors who openly profess to be writing fictions are treated as people who are in a major sense not telling the truth.

NOTES

1. Aphra Behn, *Oroonoko* (New York: Norton, 1973), p. 1.

2. Daniel Defoe, *Serious Reflections . . . of Robinson Crusoe*, ed. G. H. Maynadier (New York: Crowell, 1903), p. 106.

3. Wayne Booth, *The Rhetoric of Fiction* (Chicago: University of Chicago Press, 1966), pp. 155-59.

4. Ian Watt, *The Rise of the Novel* (Berkeley and Los Angeles: University of California Press, 1964), pp. 31-34.

5. Henry Fielding, *Joseph Andrews and Shamela*, ed. Martin Battestin (Boston: Houghton Mifflin, 1961), p. 7.

6. Harry Levin, *The Gates of Horn* (New York: Oxford University Press, 1963), p. 51.

7. W. H. McBurney, ed., *Four Before Richardson: Selected English Novels, 1720-1727* (Lincoln: University of Nebraska Press, 1963), p. 235.

8. Edward Arber, *A Transcript of the Registers of the Company of Stationers of London, 1554-1640*, 5 vols. (London, 1875), III:91; Mathais A. Shaaber, *Some Forerunners of the Newspaper in England, 1476-1622* (Philadelphia: University of Pennsylvania Press, 1929), p. 145n.

9. See for example Arber, *Transcript*, II:663. Also, note Autolycus' speech in *The Winter's Tale* (IV, iv, 254-79).

10. John Fletcher, *The Fair Maid of the Inn* (London: John Tonson, 1711), p. 35; Richard Braithwait, *Whimzies, or a New Cast of Characters* (London: Felix Kingston, 1631), p. 20.

11. *Mercurius Civicus* (11-18 January 1643).

12. Sir Walter Raleigh, *The History of the World*, 5 vols. (London, 1687), II:xxiii, quoted in William K. Nelson, *Fact or Fiction: The Dilemma of the Renaissance Storyteller* (Cambridge: Harvard University Press, 1973), p. 43.

13. William Congreve, *Incognita; or Love and Duty Reconcil'd. A Novel*, ed. H.F.B. Brett-Smith (Oxford: Blackwell, 1922), pp. 5-6.

14. Clara Reeve, *The Progress of Romance*, 2 vols. (London: Colchester, 1785), I:iii.

15. 14 Charles II, c. 33.

16. Arber, *Transcript*, II:41, IV:529-36.

17. H. R. Fox Bourne, *English Newspapers: Chapters in the History of Journalism* (New York: Russell and Russell, 1966), p. 33.

18. *Poor Robin's Memoires with His Life and Adventures* 1 (10 December 1677):1-2.

19. Northrop Frye, *Anatomy of Criticism* (New York: Atheneum, 1970), pp. 303-10.

20. Northrop Frye, *The Secular Scripture* (Cambridge: Harvard University Press, 1976), p. 17.

21. Stanley Fish in his essay "How to Do Things With Austin and Searle: Speech Act Theory and Literary Criticism" (*MLN* 91 [1976]) would have it that the opposition between factual and fictional discourses is largely a matter of the arbitrary since all discourses refer to some pretended or assumed conventional system. Thus facts are only facts within a system that renders them factual. I would not deny this assumption but would only insist that the terms of the system itself seem to have changed during the period I am discussing. It is precisely in this way that narrative—having been seen earlier as incapable of sustaining facts—in the eighteenth century is arbitrarily (but not without

certain historical motivations) allowed to be the repository of factual discourse.

22. Arber, *Transcript*, V:lvii.

23. 10 Anne. c. 19.

24. See Swift's letters to Stella on the subject in Jonathan Swift, *Journal to Stella*, 2 vols., ed. Harold Williams (Oxford: Clarendon Press, 1948), II:553.

25. 11 George I. c. 8.

26. R. M. Wiles, *Serial Publication in England Before 1700* (Cambridge: At the University Press, 1937), pp. 36–37.

27. See for example *London Magazine* (May 1733) for a discussion on the question of what constitutes news.

28. See Joseph Frank, *The Beginnings of the English Newspaper, 1620-1660* (Cambridge: Harvard University Press, 1961); and Frederick Seaton Siebert, *Freedom of the Press in England, 1476-1776: The Rise and Decline of Government Control* (Urbana: University of Illinois Press, 1952).

29. See for example *Gentlemen's Magazine* 14 (March 1744):119-20 for an entry in which Walpole (anagramized as Walelop) condemns newspapers.

30. Daniel Defoe, *The Life and Surprizing Adventures of Robinson Crusoe* (Stratford-upon-Avon: Shakespeare Head, 1928), p. ix.

31. Ibid., p. x.

32. Daniel Defoe, *Colonel Jack* (Stratford-upon-Avon: Shakespeare Head, 1928), p. viii.

33. Daniel Defoe, *Moll Flanders* (Stratford-upon-Avon: Shakespeare Head, 1928), p. viii.

34. Daniel Defoe, *The Fortunate Mistress or . . . Roxana* (Stratford-upon-Avon: Shakespeare Head, 1928), p. ix.

35. Samuel Richardson, *Selected Letters*, ed. John Carroll (Oxford: Clarendon Press, 1964), p. 85.

36. *Pamela Censured* (Los Angeles: William Andrew Clark Memorial Library, 1976), p. 7.

37. Samuel Richardson, *Introduction to Pamela*, ed. Sheridan W. Baker, Jr. (Los Angeles: William Andrew Clark Memorial Library, 1954), p. xiii.

38. Richardson, *Selected Letters*, p. 223.

39. *Pamela Censured*, p. ix.

40. See Lennard J. Davis, *Factual Fictions: Studies in the Origins of the English Novel* (forthcoming).

41. *Daily Advertiser* (11 May 1741); *London Evening Post* (14-16 May 1741) in Alan Dugald McKillop, *Samuel Richardson: Printer and Novelist* (Hamden, Conn.: Shoe String Press, 1960), p. 54.

42. *London Evening Post* (6-9 June, 1741).

43. Richardson, *Selected Letters*, p. 173n.

44. Ibid., p. 53.

45. Ibid., p. 127.

46. Samuel Richardson, *Clarissa: Preface, Hints of Prefaces and Postscript* (Los Angeles: William Andrew Clark Memorial Library, 1964), p. 368.

47. Richardson, *Selected Letters*, p. 41.

48. Katherine Gee Hornbeak, *The Complete Letter Writer in England, 1568-1800* (Northampton, Mass.: Smith College Studies in Modern Languages, 1934).

49. Richardson, *Clarissa: Preface, Hints of Prefaces*, p. 366.

50. Samuel Richardson, *Pamela* (New York: Norton, 1958), p. 242.

51. Ibid., p. 243.

52. Ibid., p. 251.

53. Ibid., p. 482.

54. Ibid., p. 166.

55. Ibid., p. 83.

56. Ibid., p. 245.

57. Ibid.

58. Ibid., p. 144.

59. Samuel Richardson, *Clarissa*, ed. John Burrell (New York: Random House, 1950), p. x.

60. Samuel Richardson, *Clarissa*, ed. George Sherburn (Boston: Houghton Mifflin, 1962), p. 438.

61. Richardson, *Clarissa*, ed. Burrell, p. 661.

62. Ibid., p. 732.

63. Michel Foucault, *The Order of Things* (New York: Pantheon, 1970), pp. 3–120.

64. Raymond Williams, *Marxism and Literature* (Oxford: Oxford University Press, 1977), pp. 151–64.

65. Watt, *Rise of the Novel*, pp. 186, 191.

66. McKillop, *Samuel Richardson,* p. 15.

 *Terry Eagleton*

Text, Ideology, Realism

It would be possible to argue that the aim of "deconstructionist" criticism is to confront *ideology* with *textuality*. If ideology lays claim to an oppressive plentitude of meaning, then textuality is at hand to reveal its hidden places of "castration"; if ideology assumes a secure hierarchy of meanings, organized around some privileged set of transcendental signifiers that close it upon itself, then textuality will show how one signifier merely displaces, redoubles, and stands in for another in a potentially infinite chain that can be arrested only by violence. Textuality exposes those fissures, slippages, and self-mutilations that are as inevitable to ideological discourse as to any other, but that such discourse must at all costs repress; turning the frayed edge of ideology to the light, textuality plucks away at the points where it may be unraveled, skeptically refusing its apparent buoyancy in the name of a cunning of script that will embrace no meaning as self-sufficient.

All this we have learned from the work of Jacques Derrida and his growing progeny. And the radical challenge of such work, its power to illuminate and provoke, is surely not in doubt. Yet there are problems with such speculation, not least for a critic whose commitment to materialism extends beyond semantic boundaries into a theory of history itself. It is notable, to begin with, that such deconstructionism, for all its undoubted sophistication, is in danger of radically simplifying the whole problem of ideology itself. Ideology, in this parlance, is essentially synonymous with "metaphysics," which may in turn be defined as "logocentricity" or the "philosophy of presence." The ideological, in brief, is a matter of plenitude, deceptive transparency, discursive closure; and certainly, for Derrida himself, it can be found to share these constituents in common all the way from Plato to

Lévi-Strauss. Yet one flinches a little before such a sweeping
assertion, not least on the part of a critic notable for his myo-
pically tenacious attention to the margins and crevices of particular texts. What "deep structure" or transhistorical continuity—
concepts this very discourse has taught us to suspect—might be
at stake here? It may well be the case that the valorization of
speech over script, with all that it has been shown to imply, marks
the Western philosophical tradition throughout; but it is less clear
how helpful such an assertion is going to be when we are confronted with specific Western ideological formations. That they
will tend to laud speech and denigrate script we can, since Derrida,
confidently expect; but it is far from plain how much productive
insight we can derive from *that*. For even if there is indeed a fila-
ment called "logocentricity" woven continuously through the
fabric of Western philosophy, we still have to look at particular
ideological *conjunctures*—to examine the complex interplay of
determinants in any concrete historical context, and to assess
how far logocentricity is a significantly dominant level within
such a formation. One is tempted to speculate that, well, sometimes it will be and sometimes it won't. There is certainly no
a priori reason to believe that it is the pivot on which all else
will hinge—no reason to lapse back into some essentialism of the
ideological that will seek to hunt down its hidden secret, again
and again, to one isolable device. One feels about such a project
rather as one feels about Althusser's grand assertion that "ideology
has no history"[1] —meaning, presumably, that although the "contents" of ideology are of course historically mutable, the fundamental mechanisms whereby it constitutes "individuals" as "subjects" remain, like those of the Freudian unconscious, invariable.
It is an interesting claim; but we just do not know enough at
present about the ruses of ideology to be able to verify it or not,
and it is hard to see how Althusser himself knows any more. (It
is, moreover, difficult not to be a little skeptical about such a
pronouncement when Althusser also assumes that the primary

task of ideology, always and everywhere, is the constitution of subjects, and when his account of such a process contains a fairly drastic misreading of Jacques Lacan.)

Logocentricity is, then, as logocentricity does: sometimes it may have a good deal of ideological work to perform, sometimes not. But it will always in any case be a question of particular conjunctures—a matter, not of some prejudice called "presence" or "logocentricity" lording over coexistent ideological elements, subduing them inexorably to its requirements, but of a logocentricity that is always *overdetermined* by other features of the ideological formation in which it occurs. Even if we take two flagrantly logocentristic practices—say, seventeenth-century preaching and nineteenth-century opera—we shall surely be a good deal more struck by the differences rather than similarities between them, to the point where a simple demonstration of their shared logocentric assumptions may say very little indeed. In claiming that the Western lineage illusorily grounds itself upon some essence, we should be careful not to reproduce such essentialism in our own critique of it. There is no single structure known as "logocentricity" that we can point to as the secret of ideology, any more than we can point to social class, in the manner of certain Marxist traditions, as providing us with such a secret. For there is, strictly speaking, no such thing as a "class-ideology": one does not "explain" an ideology by viewing it as the "expression" of a particular class, so that society can then be seen as composed of a number of discrete social classes each equipped with its own indigenous ideology. It is only because the Diltheyan conception of "world view" has been damagingly assimilated to the notion of ideology by a whole Hegelian-Marxist tradition that such a mistake can be made. The ideology of a class is not a coherent "expression" of its life conditions but articulates its *lived relations to other classes*; and ideology is always, in this sense, "impure." What, after all, is "petty bourgeois ideology" but a profoundly contradictory, decentered assemblage of elements drawn from both the proletariat and the *haute bourgeoisie*? (Not to mention other possible sources: the peasantry, the techno-cratic-managerial class, and so on.) How could a dominant ideol-ogy hope to survive if it were no more than the cunning impress on other classes of a ruling class's self-experience? And how would this come about in the first place? The problem of class hegemony can only be resolved if we recognize that any dominant ideology incorporates within itself (not without ceaseless struggle) the codes and forms whereby subordinate classes "practice" their relations to the social formation as a whole. A dominant ideology in which the proletariat or peasantry or petty bourgeoisie cannot find itself to some extent mirrored and confirmed, and which does not catch up and transform certain vital themes of their experience, is unlikely to survive long.

Particular ideological components, then, are not instantly class-assignable. To what class does feminist ideology belong? Or populism? Ernesto Laclau, indeed, has selected populism as an exemplary case of this *class ambivalence* of ideological features.[2] There is simply no way the ideology of populism can be tied to a particular class: on the contrary, we may speak of an "aristo-cratic populism" just as easily as we may speak of a peasant or petty-bourgeois or proletarian variety. Populism is not an already-assigned phenomenon but, precisely, one to be *fought for*—a bone of contention in the class struggle, as each class seeks to identify its own historical mission with the "national-democratic" or "revolutionary-democratic" rights of the "people." The specific weight and character of populism, then, can only be evaluated within an active historical conjuncture; and the same is true of logocentricity, or indeed of any other ideological constituent. To believe otherwise is simply to produce an ideological account of ideology; and it is not obvious that some "deconstructionist" criticism has not fallen into this trap.

That it may sometimes have done so is in part because of its assumption that the ideological is primarily an effect of discourse.

Now the ideological is certainly that; but there is no discourse not embedded in non-discursive practices. And once you take the force of Althusser's insistence that ideology is always a matter of material practices, then your critique can hardly help but be conjunctural—it cannot avoid scrutinizing historically particular institutions, in a way that questions the idealism of regarding ideology simply as a disembodied textual effect. (It will not do either, though it has been tried often enough, to counter the charge of idealism by pointing out, rightly, that discourse is every bit as "material" as work.) There is no textual effect that is not produced and consumed within an articulated set of social practices, and we should perhaps be wary of claiming to recognize the "same" textual effect across two such historically divergent sets. To do so is to fall back, once again, into a familiar essentialism. It is the lack of such caution that is most marked in some "deconstructionist" criticism—the improper assumption, for example, that what counts as "discursive closure" for one set of historical readers necessarily does so for another.

But there is a danger also that a simple opposition of "ideology" and "textuality" will overlook the *cunning* of the ideological. On this version, the ideological is distinguished by its apparent "innocence," as against the sophistications of the textual: it clings childishly to that naïve belief in the transparency of the signifier and instant accessibility of the signified that a mature textuality has long ago left behind. It is then up to textuality, by virtue of its own stratagems, to confront ideology with what it represses, laying bare the wily feints and dodges of meaning it contains but cannot countenance. In this sense, what ideology is being confronted with is "other" to it—that inevitable surplus of signification it generates but must then alienate. It is difficult, however, to see that this is an adequate view of how ideology works. For it is surely the case that the devices of textuality—displacement, condensation, substitution, redoubling, and so on—are themselves precisely part of ideology's very armory. Ideology is not simply a matter of plenitude but also of elision, not just a question of "representation" but also of slippage; if it works to some extent "frontally," it also operates by indirection. It is not, then, merely a matter of prying open the ideological husk to grasp the textual kernel, for the husk was in some sense textual all along. It is rather a question of seeing how ideology at once *refuses and reproduces* textual strategies. It is here, it seems to me, that its true duplicity lies. This duplicity could no doubt be illustrated in a number of different ways; in what follows I want merely to consider one of them.

What is the meaning of a proposition? If I say to you: "Remove your lazy cabbage from my excessive symmetry," you understand the meaning of my *words* but you don't understand the *meaning* of my words. It should be evident from this simple fact that any semiotic theory of meaning as pure diacritical value within *langue* is therefore inadequate. Meaning is practice as well as structure, conjunctural as well as "given" in language, "performative" (in J. L. Austin's parlance) as well as "constative." It is well known that Saussure, with his excessively *langue*-centered linguistic theory, refuses to explicate meaning in terms of *parole*— a task that was left to the "discourse theory" of Bakhtin and Voloshinov.[3] Saussure is right, of course, to assert that linguistic meaning is diacritical, a matter of pure differences within language; but Wittengenstein is surely also right in his way when he claims that the meaning of a word is its use in a form of life. The first is a necessary, but not always sufficient, condition for the second—for understanding to take place. If I say to you, "Close the door!", then the meaning of my words is not identical with my psychological intentions, nor with the psychological effects it produces in you—a position that, when translated to the realm of literary critical theory, perhaps approaches that of Stanley Fish. "Close the door!" simply means what it means whatever you or I might think it means. But you would of course be perfectly entitled to reply "What do you mean?" if the door were closed already, and I could not cap your response by replying irritably: "You speak English, don't you?" or by handing you a dictionary. Meaning, in short, is practical and contextual; but the interpretation of such conjunctural meaning depends upon our prior access to the *langue* within which the *parole* or speech act occurs. Meaning is an effect of discourses that are governed by, but not reducible to, *langue*; it is the taking up of a particular "site of signification" within *langue* itself. Our need, then, is to avoid at once some pure formalism or structuralism of meaning or the kind that semiotics too frequently offers us, and some "humanistic" speech-act theory that fails to take the inevitable governedness of *parole* into account. It may well be the case that there are certain propositions whose meaning would be clear to any speaker of the appropriate language in any situation, but this is not true, for example, of the meaning of literary texts. For such texts are specific articulations of *langue*, self-constructing conjunctures, so to speak, that enable the dissemination of sense. It is only because they are not *literally* speech acts—rather, perhaps, "virtual" speech acts—that we may be tempted to overlook this fact. We cannot understand the enoncé that a literary text is outside the context of its act of *enonciation*. Grasping a literary convention is not grasping a literary message: it is grasping the conjunctural terms that allow for the construction of such a message.

If I may add here an aside: in one interesting sense, literary texts never "mean what they say" because they are fiction. They do not, in other words, mean what they say in the sense that you may ask me "Do you mean that?" when I tell you that I trust you. They are neither sincere nor insincere, and in this sense resemble goldfish more than clergymen. To say "I didn't really mean that" is to say that my intentions were at odds with the effects produced: I had "true" intentions over above what I actually did or said. A literary text, however, may well not produce in us the effects it "intended," since it is, in Austin's terms, "illocutionary" rather than "perlocutionary," but this cannot be because it somehow has "true" intentions over and above what it says. Its "intentions" just are the way its discourse constructs itself to mobilize certain responses. There are no "intentions" the text conceals, even if, like *Tristram Shandy,* it spends most of its time leading the reader up the garden path; such a strategy is precisely part of the text's "intentionality." This is not to say that a text may not make its "intentions" clear enough, with consequent bemusement for the reader; but this is not because it is being deceptive, hypocritical or insincere. And this is one sense in which literary texts, whatever else they are, are certainly not subjects.

I spoke above of the need for a "prior access" to *langue,* within which *parole* is then the taking up of a specific signifying place—an idiom I use because I want to draw a parallel between what has been said so far and the work of Jacques Lacan.[4] For Lacan, I am able to attain my own signifying place as a subject only by having access to that Other that is the whole field of language, or to the Unconscious. It is an Other on which I am dependent for my emergence into being as a positioned subject, but which I can in no sense appropriate—an Other whose absence or otherness allows me to speak in the first place (since how could I say anything if the whole language was constantly present to my consciousness?), but which subordinates me to itself. The Other is what allows me to address myself to it by evading me; I speak from where I am not, from the place of the Other (the entire network of significations) that—most obviously in the verbal slip or *parapraxis*—decenters my utterance at the very moment of articulation. It is only by virtue of repression that I am able to designate myself as a signifying subject at all, as the use of the personal pronoun most graphically illustrates. For the subject designated by that pronoun, when I use the word "I," can be no more than a stand-in for the "true" subject that cannot represent itself in that deceptively stable verbal index—a subject that is scattered along the chains of unconscious signification, and that is indeed for Lacan no more than an effect flashed from one signifier to another.

If it is true, then, that my own signifying position as subject is being constantly outstripped and subverted by that whole field of signification that is the Unconscious, something similar might be claimed of the literary text. In the text also, *langue* and *parole* are never quite at one, and this is at once a source of embarrassment and effectivity. For clearly, however a text attempts to get its words to mean "conjuncturally," those words always already have meaning by virtue of their positions within *langue*—which is to say, by virtue of the whole network of past and coexistent discursive practices. This is also true of our normal speech acts, but there we can put things right by having a second or third try; the text, however, cannot. Conjunctural meaning constantly is trying to captivate *langue*-meaning and constantly is being captivated by it. And this ceaseless reciprocity could be said to happen in two main ways. On the one hand, it may happen that conjunctural meaning attempts to effect a "closure" that is unfixed, decentered, differentiated by the plurality of *langue*-meaning: the specificity of *parole* is displaced by the heterogeneity of *langue*. A word in a poem may try to achieve its effect by limiting the polyvalence of that word as it appears in the dictionary. On the other hand, we can have the reverse situation: conjunctural meaning may try to unfix and disturb the stability of *langue*-meaning by virtue of the context in which it sets it. The fact that poems are commonly regarded as both unusually precise and unusually ambiguous in their uses of language may be a dim perception of this paradoxical state of affairs.

Now it seems to me that both of these mechanisms may be related to the ideological effectivity of the literary text. For the "ideological effect" can consist *both* in a fixing and arresting of the ceaseless heterogeneity of *langue, and* in a constant gliding away from determinate meaning into various displacements of or substitutions for it. The "semantic saturation" of poetry, as Yury Lotman calls it, no doubt arises from both sources—from the poem trying at once to limit by overdetermination and to pry loose by plurality. This is an important emphasis, because much current semiotic thinking with claims to "political" relevance would locate the ideological effect entirely in discursive *closure*, in that tendentious "buttoning" of language upon certain privileged signifiers that thereby represses its subversive, endlessly heterogeneous productivity. (The work of Julia Kristeva would seem relevant here.) But this merely ignores those ideological effects gained precisely by slippage, substitution, and condensation—the ideological effectivity of Orwell's *Animal Farm*, for example, which by choosing an essentially substitutional, metaphorical form (animals for humans) has built into itself a whole battery of ideological significations from the outset. This, if you like, is certainly a form of discursive closure; but it is one that is only made possible by the insidious, unstable stratagems of language itself. Indeed one might be tempted to say that such a contradictory unity, of simultaneously fixing and displacing, is intrinsic to the whole structure of metaphor. I would hazard a rough definition of metaphor as a figure in which one signifier substitutes itself for another signifier such that the second falls to the rank of a signified and condenses with the signified of the first. Now this is clearly in one sense a "fixing" of signification, in that an "imaginary" relation (in Lacan's sense) now exists between the signifier and the one it has stood in for—a matter of equivalence and identity, rather than difference and opposition. But in another sense the operation involves an unfixing, in that the resultant signifier is peculiarly plural. This paradox may help to resolve a recent debate between Francis Mulhern and myself in the pages of *New Left Review*.[5] I had argued that what occurs in poetic discourse is an "excess" of the signifier over the signified: when Keats describes an urn as a "still unravished bride of quietness," we know that the usual ratio between signifier and signified involved in the act of reference has been peculiarly disrupted. Mulhern responded that, on the contrary, what comes about in poetic language is a *contraction* of the signifier and a consequent expansion of the signified—a pun, for example. I think that we both would now probably agree that this is a pseudo-argument because it really says the same thing in two different ways. Insofar as a signifier condenses two or more signifieds, then it can be described as "excessive" in contrast to a signifier with merely one signified; but insofar as it has two or more signifieds, then it is contracted in relation to them. Condensing means, precisely, enriching by contracting. The signifier in metaphor is "excessive" in comparison with a "normal" signifier but contracted in comparison with its signifieds. A millionaire is richer than a dock worker but poorer than his money. So the ideological effectivity of metaphor is a question of both arresting and pluralizing—producing an "imaginary" equivalence, but doing so in a way that heterogenizes the signifier (since the signifier carries within itself, so to speak, the one for which it is a substitute). Meaning has become more full and fixed, but has also glided off somewhat; and metaphor, like the psychoanalytic symptom, has precisely this structure of presence-and-absence, one signifier making its presence more richly felt by absenting another. If the relation between the two signifiers in question is one of "imaginary" identification, and thus a stabilizing that may be ideologically efficacious, it is nevertheless an identification caught up within a single term, rather than an explicit duality, and so produces an ambiguity, a "hesitation" between literal and figurative meanings. The point is that both devices may have ideological effects—*may*, because whether they do or not depends upon a good deal more than what we can abstractly say about the intrinsic structure of metaphor. Something similar may perhaps be claimed of metonymy, which certainly entails a gliding off or displacement of meaning, but which may be said to unfix meaning from one point only to button it upon another. (The paradigm of which is, precisely, narrative.) The difference, however, is that here the element of "imaginary" identification is not so dominant. "Concorde"/"sky" are not, like "Concorde"/"bird," mutually substitutable—a point about metonymy that might be better appreciated if the examples of it were not so frequently of the synecdochic sub-class. (Although even in synecdoche the substitution is not reciprocal: "sail" may stand in for "ship" but not *vice versa.*)

The dual movement I am trying to identify may help to illuminate what at first sight seems a contradiction in the early work of Pierre Macherey.[6] For Macherey seems to be saying at once that literary form involves a "fixing" of ideology and a disarraying of it—that form, by arresting and distancing the ideological, begins to refuse complicity with it by rendering it perceptible, but that this movement is at the same time one that embarrasses ideology into betraying the gaps and silences within its apparently replete, coherent presence. What Macherey means, I think, is that the literary text throws ideology into disarray *by* fixing it. By endowing the ideological with a precise, specific configuration, it gives it a certain "foregrounding," but thereby also begins to foreground its limits and lacunae, that of which it cannot at any cost speak, those significations that necessarily evade (but also covertly *invade*) it. By "formalizing" ideology, the text begins to highlight its absences, expose its essential incompleteness, articulate the ghostly penumbra of absent signs that lurk within its pronouncements. There are, I believe, real difficulties with these formulations—they belong to the earlier "formalist," rather than later "sociologistic," Macherey and it is not clear by what miracle "form" in itself is able to effect such a significant operation. But I want to draw a somewhat improbable parallel between this case and what I have said already about Lacan—a parallel facilitated by the fact that Macherey himself recognizes that ideology is, so to speak, the "Unconscious" of the text. Macherey too, in short, is speaking of the Other; but for him, unlike Lacan, it is always a specifically *ideological* Other, a network of signs inescapably caught up in specific social practices. To cast Macherey's argument (no doubt to his grave disapproval) in Lacan's idiom: the text comes into being at the point where it separates itself from the Other—it is its differential *relations* to ideology that are in question—but it remains dependent for its "speech" upon it and addresses its messages to that which constantly threatens to subvert them from within. What is thus revealed is the fact that what the work speaks of is never quite what it says; we are examining, as critics, the ways it never quite says what it speaks of. Submitted to the dominion of the Other, the text can never quite be identical with itself: like Lacan's subject, it is continually "fading" in the play of signifiers it attempts to "suture." (I should stress that this comparison of text and subject is merely an analogy, lest it be thought to contradict a point made earlier.) Like the subject, the text emerges into existence precisely by the repression of certain (ideological) determinants it *consequently*, at certain "symptomatic" points, begins to betray.

If a dominant ideology may reproduce itself by various complex permutations of both of the operations (fixing and displacing) that I have been describing (and there are surely many more mechanisms at issue than that), what light might this throw upon the workings of oppositional ideologies? Should such ideologies aim for a ceaseless practice of displacement—of overturning the enshrined representations of the dominant culture—or is there any sense in which they, too, may involve a certain "closure"? The immediate occasion for this debate is the argument over realism; for realism certainly involves the (at least provisional) "fixing" of representation, and there are those who argue that such a signifying practice is therefore inherently regressive.

Part of the problem, of course, concerns the definition of "realism" itself. It can be seen as the ontological basis of all valid art (Lukács); it can mean a specific historical-cultural period that is now, some would claim, on the way to being superseded; it can denote a particular range of aesthetic devices that may be used by various cultural forms without necessarily providing the dominant code; it can suggest a certain kind of politico-aesthetic effectivity, and so on. Some of these usages are descriptive, others normative, and this is surely one of the major sources of confusion. Take the *Tel Quel* case on realism, for example. This is at one level straightforwardly descriptive: realism is, essentially, representationalism. But of course it involves a good deal more than that. Such representationalism effaces the heterogeneity of textual production, insidiously naturalizes the sign, produces discursive closure, homogenizes narrative space and so voids it of contradiction, ranks its codes in a stabilizing hierarchy rather than permitting them to interrogate and contradict one another. And the effect of all this is a fixing of the specular reading or viewing subject in the "imaginary" plenitude of his or her ideological position. So it seems clear that we are dealing here with an account of realism that is at once descriptive and normative, although the relations between the two elements may vary. You can claim, for example, that if this is what realism does then it is inherently reactionary in its effects, and everything from Defoe to Dostoevsky was a ghastly mistake. More plausibly, you can historicize the normative element and argue that such realism was all very well in its day, but its day is now over.

One name with which any such case will have to come to terms is that of Brecht. For Brecht is certainly a revolutionary writer, and yet there are clear enough senses in which he holds to "representationalism." I say "clear *enough*," because the issue of representation in Brecht is not a straightforward one. You can find in Brecht, in fact, more or less what you are looking for: there are plenty of convenient quotations to support a representationalist position, just as there are a good many others that point in the opposite direction. Within a single text—the *Short Organum for the Theatre*—Brecht can be found delivering judgments that would

make the semioticians and "production" aestheticians wince—
"our representations must take second place to what is represented, men's life together in society"[7]; but he can also be found
dismissing any *naïve* representationalism: "we must always remember that the pleasure given by the representation . . . hardly
ever depend[s] on the representation's likeness to the thing
portrayed."[8] There seems no doubt that by "realism" Brecht
sometimes means straight verisimilitude: in his theatrical pedagogy
he trains his actors, among other things, to represent the object
precisely as it is, and for this purpose drills them in meticulous
observation. Yet he also insists that representing a factory on
stage won't tell you anything about capitalism. It is not surprising
that there are such inconsistencies in Brecht's theory: quite apart
from his complex, contradictory inheritance of both "reflection"
and "production" aesthetics, his theoretical work is notably
geared to the rapidly changing nature of his theatrical practice.
And that practice is indeed often more conservative than the
theory, which leads to additional unevennesses. It therefore seems
as plausible to annex Brecht to representationalism as it does to
produce an entire issue of a journal on his work that edits out
such elements in the interests of presenting him as an *avant-
gardist*.[9]

   The truth, I think, is that Brecht was not opposed to representation in itself; he was opposed to *non-contradictory* representation.
Now that, for some, is itself a contradiction. For one meaning of
"representation" merely cancels the notion of contradiction: to
fix the object in an "imaginary" relation with the subject is precisely to repress the contradictions in which both object and
subject are caught up. But it all depends, of course, on what you
mean by "representation." You can argue that since Brechtian
representations involve contradictions, then they are not, in the
classical sense, representations at all; or you can claim, alternatively, that there is indeed such a phenomenon as "contradictory
representation" and that one of its names is Bertolt Brecht.

Either way it is hard to see whether one is doing more than play-ing with words, in ways that Brecht's own residual philistine pragmatism would have found particularly objectionable. But it seems to me that some light may be shed on this problem by looking briefly at the nature of the Brechtian alienation effect. The alienation effect would certainly seem to preserve within its structure a moment of representation, in that the object must be recognized "as it is" for it to be grasped in its non-self-identity. "Deviation" and "norm" are mutually constitutive; and Brecht speaks accordingly of a "return of alienation," glancing sideways at the alienation-for-its-own-sake aesthetic of other *avant-gardisms*. What would seem at issue here is some dialectic between estranged and automated perception, which would certainly seem to involve the "imaginary" relationship to the object as one of its compo-nents. (It is, incidentally, a curious feature of much current discussion of the "imaginary" that its absolutely indispensable role in human practice and perception is at once notionally acknowledged and surreptitiously refused; and indeed one might tentatively claim that there is a certain license for this double-think in the work of Lacan himself. It is a double-think somewhat akin to that of those Althusserians who grudgingly admit that the concept of "everyday life" has its place, while implying with every inflection that they would rather be shut of the whole thing.) In any case, it is surely obvious that the alienation effect, like the metaphor or symptom, has a structure of presence-and-absence. The object is indeed represented, but represented in the context of its non-self-identity, shot through with those contra-dictory possibilities it habitually absents.

In this sense, perhaps, it is possible to speak of "representing contradiction." But one must speak cautiously, because one cannot represent a contradiction as one can represent a *thing*. Contradictions are not objects to be reflected, any more than differences are; one cannot observe a contradiction as one can observe a factory gate. The contradiction between labor and capital, or colonized and imperialist, is a matter of *interests*, and thus belongs to the realm of discourse—without, of course, being any the less "real" or "objective" for that. To mount a shot of a dining bourgeois upon one of a hungry worker will no more "represent a contradiction" than will a shot of a cat mounted upon one of a dog, unless it occurs within a particular kind of discursive practice. Contradiction implies difference, but it is, so to speak, difference doubly articulated, difference differentiated, set in a context where its terms can be grasped as antagonistic, as well as diacritical. Difference is itself already an articulation, an effect of discursive practice; but this articulation is then displaced and re-articulated within a "higher" discourse that transcodes its terms as mutually oppositional. (Not, of course, that the process is in reality as sequential as that.) If difference is already a dislocation of the object's ideological self-identity, contradiction redivides that initial dislocation by rearticulating it in a signifying context that reveals how certain differences will be indissociable from *struggle*. It is precisely the mark of the *ideological* project of Saussure that this, within his system, becomes impossible to reveal. For Saussure's linguistic differences are purely innocent: their *necessity* is to be accounted for entirely within the formal structures of language itself. It cannot be, for him, that such a formal structure is in part determined by the threatening presence upon its margin of significations that must be at all costs banished and repressed, yet that continue to haunt and hollow its securely present signs with their minatory absence. Which is no more than to say that language cannot be for Saussure, as it can be for Voloshinov and Bakhtin, a terrain of ideological struggle. Such a recognition would involve, precisely, the displacement and rearticulation of formal linguistic difference at the level of other theoretical practices. If the dictionary informs us that the opposite of capitalism is totalitarianism, we will need more than the *Course of General Linguistics* to illuminate that particular diacritical formulation.

The problem Brecht poses for us most graphically, however, is that of a double articulation in a rather different sense: the relation between "contradictions of form" and "contradictions of content." It is precisely because Brecht's work raises both questions that one or the other can always be repressed, and Brecht can be appropriated accordingly as a formalist or reflectionist. The first thing to get clear is that "contradictions of content" cannot mean, in the manner of empiricism, contradictions "in" the real, although Brecht himself may well have thought that it did. It can refer only to the "real" as constructed/articulated by the discourse of Marxism; and the question then becomes one of the relations between the contradictions produced by such a discourse, and those of the dramatic forms themselves. It is a question, in other words, of the articulations between two internally articulated discourses: the discourse of dramatic form, which we might term the level of the signifier; and the discourse of historical material-ism, which we might call the level of the signified. The nature of the articulations between these two discourses is obviously variable within Brecht's work. Sometimes it would seem that formal contradictions are directly "reflective" or social ones—that a particular montage of scenes or *gests* stands in fairly direct relation to a particular complex of social contradictions, as in the simple case of the dining bourgeois/hungry worker syntagm I mentioned earlier. At other times, however, the articulations are considerably more complex: formal torsions may be less "re-flective" of social conflicts than strategies for decentering the unitary subject and unleashing ideological contradictions within it. Brechtian commentary has focused upon one or the other of these modes, according to its reflectionist or formalist bent; but it surely has to be affirmed that both are present. If there are times when the level of the signifier seems dominant, there are other times when what is foregrounded is the level of the signified. Now we know, of course, that as far as the *productivity* of art goes, the signifier is always dominant, insofar as the signified is its product. But this does not necessarily hold in terms of textual or dramatic *effectivity*, and it is precisely on these grounds, among others, that we distinguish "realism" from "modernism." For the work of the signifier may, of course, be to efface itself, and this is often enough the case with Brecht: "our representations must take second place to what is represented." And this is so even though we know that no text merely "takes" a pre-existent discourse and then "represents" it, that the "reality-effect" is always an effect of the signifier, and that "extra-textual" codes figure in a work precisely as *text*.

To align Brecht between the coordinates of Lukács and Adorno may sharpen our sense of what is going on here. Luckács is concerned with "contradictions of content," but denounces such conflicts when they appear at the level of form. Adorno ends up by staking everything upon formal contradiction, which is itself the very social content of the work. Brecht, by contrast, implicitly rejects both of these positions, and reaches instead for a third method that seems to me authentically materialist. If he shares Adorno's conviction that the very contradictory interplay of signifiers is itself a signified, he also remains faithful to Lukács's crucially important insistence that texts do, after all, "refer" (to "real life," Brecht would no doubt have sometimes simplistically added). Brecht's dramatic work is, precisely, a ceaseless exploration of the varied possible articulations between these two positions, privileged as he was to work at a watershed where formalism and realism contended and commingled. The alienation effect is precisely one such articulation: for here the effect of a formal dislocation is to produce in the audience a recognition of social contradiction. These levels are neither homologous nor mutually expressive: the signifying device has its own specific materiality as a piece of stage action, synchronized with other signifiers, and is in no sense reducible to a "miming" of social contradiction. It is, rather, a mechanism productive of such contradiction, which, in turn, has its own specific, extra-textual temporality and mode of existence. And that that is so must be included, so to speak, within the signifier: the signifiers must maintain within themselves a certain reticence, must obliquely demarcate their own limits, so as to gesture toward that "real" history that always threatens to surpass them, that inexhaustible matrix of potential production, of other material possibilities, that for Brecht will always encircle and interrogate any particular signifying practice. If the signifier, in alienating a conventional signified, throws it into question, the same process works in reverse: what is then signified—historical contradiction—returns to question the boundaries of the signifier itself. It is precisely in this sense that Brecht is a "realist." And this is rather different from (though it has relations with) the fashionable semiotic case that what ceaselessly surpasses any particular momentarily stabilized signifying practice is the heter-ogeneity of *signification*. It is rather, for Brecht, that what founds and surpasses discursive practices are non-discursive practices—practices that (need one add?) are available only in discourse, but that are nonetheless not to be collapsed into some single abstrac-tion known as "signification."

Quite where Brecht leaves the "realism" argument is not easy to see. What he does, as I have argued elsewhere,[10] is essentially to replace aesthetic and ontological definitions of realism with political and philosophical ones. Sometimes, as I have suggested, Brecht uses "realism" in a very simple mimetic sense: "In each individual case the picture of life must be compared . . . with the actual life portrayed."[11] This, in context, is a polemic against the "formalism" of Lukácsian realism, which would measure the individual work against an aesthetically-derived "realist" canon rather than against "life." But as that phrase "actual life" makes clear, Brecht's corrective to Lukács is not without its attendant dangers. In bending the stick against Lukács, Brecht is for one thing in danger of emptying the concept of realism of any sub-stantive content. For if realism is to be measured essentially in terms of its political effects—did the play uncover for the audience the essential historical contradictions?—rather than in terms of any specific aesthetic mode, then it is difficult to see why "realist" cannot simply be replaced by "revolutionary." "Realism" is shifted to the level of the signified, and then the choice of signifier, of aesthetic form, might come to seem arbitrary; but as Brecht well knew in his own theatrical practice, no such mechanical duality is possible. In certain conjunctures, it will be only certain kinds of signifier and not others that will produce the "reality-effect" at the level of the signified; that is why, for Brecht, the methods of a Balzac will no longer suffice. Faced with this situation, one has essentially two choices: either to confine the term "realism" to Balzacian art and give oneself another name, or to extend the term to cover one's own practice. Given the powerful pressure of "socialist realist" orthodoxy, the second alternative was the one Brecht was constrained to take. As a *stragetic* argument against Lukács, the choice was productive: it enabled Brecht to defeat Lukács on his own ground, while in fact transforming that ground into a place where Lukács could not follow him. But it is effective in the same way that it might be effective to explain to someone who thought there was only one daily newspaper in Britain that in fact we have a "choice"—a salutary widening of his perspectives, but hardly the fundamental point. Brecht's tactic somewhat resembles that of those liberal churchmen who, confronted with the embarrassing existence of doomed pagans, charitably dub them "anonymous Christians." Such an accusation would in fact be better leveled against Ernst Fischer and Roger Garaudy, with their blandly ecumenical concept of *réalisme sans rivages*—the aesthetic inflection of a brand of Communist ideology against which Louis Althusser had to intervene. Brecht's overall position should be sharply distinguished from such soggy humanism: it is, after all, in terms of their *political* effects that he assesses the "realism" of artefacts, their location within the class-struggle, which is hardly a matter of weighty import to Fischer and Garaudy. Brecht's concept of realism certainly has bounds: unlike Fischer and Garaudy, he is astute enough to realize that a concept without bounds is no concept at all, just as a river without banks may be a lake or an ocean but certainly isn't a river.

My own view, however, is that the strategically valuable extension of the meaning of "realism" into which Brecht was effectively forced is, in the end, theoretically counterproductive. The term becomes as much a ritual incantation as the word "material" in much current Marxist-semiotic discussion. What Brecht is getting at, of course, is that certain artefacts are "realistic" in effect even if they are not, in the classical sense, representational. This means, then, that you can have realistic realism, non-realistic realism, realistic non-realism, and non-realistic non-realism. How far that typology helps is surely dubious; it looks as though we need to find another term altogether for "realistic" if we are not to be plunged in hopeless confusion. For Lukács, "realism" is at once a descriptive literary category and, inseparably, evaluative; and this is so because he does not, of course, equate realism with representationalism *tout court*, but rather with a particular epistemological and ontological form of representationalism, one dependent upon "typicality," "totality" and the rest. I do not see any reason why we should confine realism to this particular variant: "typical" characters are sometimes (in Brecht's sense) "realistic" but sometimes not. You could have a very "realistically" effective character who was not historically typical in the least. So there are problems if, like Lukács, we try to build these evaluative elements into the definition of realism, for then we end up with a highly selective version of realism within what is an absurdly selective view of literary history in the first place. But if it is dangerous to conflate descriptive and normative categories in this way, it is equally confusing to pursue the logic of Brecht's approach and make "realism" essentially evaluative. If the Lukács case is a good deal too restrictive, this alternative seems perilously over-expansive, retaining, perhaps unconsciously, the traditional force and authority of the term "realism" but then projecting it into non-representational works and ending up with an unsatisfactorily amorphous case. My own position would be to accept the descriptive aspects of Lukács's position—that is to say, that "realism" refers to a specific literary-historical mode—but to join Brecht in evacuating this description of its built-in normative elements and refusing the privileged status Lukács assigns to it. I would again side with Brecht in recognizing that the realism of which Lukács speaks has been a particular, limited form, but I reject his attempt to carry over the authority of the word to plainly non-representational art forms. Perhaps I am really just reproducing what Brecht means to say; all I am quibbling with is his apparent readiness to use the noun "realism" to cover something that for him is really adjectival. And if that is so, then perhaps we need a different adjective. It would seem simpler to reserve the term "realism" for representational art; although deciding whether a text is representational or not is, of course, not always an easy matter. (If we were to come across a text in which all of the figures were characterized primarily by the size of their feet, then no doubt we would believe ourselves to be in the presence of some bizarre modernist work. But if we discovered that the text belonged to a society in which foot size was indeed extremely significant as a code for identifying and discriminating individuals, then we might conclude instead that the text was representational.) And there are always, naturally, "mixed" cases: if one thinks of some surrealist painting or certain types of science fiction, then it seems that you can have non-realist "content" presented in "realist" form—a realism of the signifier and a non-realism of the signified. Or you may have the reverse: non-realist form presenting realist content, as the account of Bloom taking a bath in *Ulysses*. As one would expect, there are always limit cases; but as Wittgenstein remarked, just because a field doesn't have a geometrically precise boundary doesn't mean that it isn't a field at all. I am thinking, then, of paradigmatic cases of representationalism like Dutch interiors or *David Copperfield.* The ideological-aesthetic *effectivity* of such representationalism then seems to me entirely conjunctural; and it would seem wiser not to describe that effectivity as "realist." It may be that reading Defoe today can do no more than arrest the reader in regressive relation to a deceptively "transparent" reality. But imagine a contemporary reader brought up on a diet of sermons stumbling across such pages: how could that dense, remorselessly realist registration of the material world in all its autonomy not be, in *that* conjuncture, "progressive"?

Both dominant and oppositional ideologies, then, may be seen to have at least two faces. Both contain moments of arrest and release, fixing and overturning, representing and displacing. My argument has been that it would be a serious political error to "pair off" such operations with fixed, immutable, ideological effects. There is no telling when an effect of slippage, or of representation, may contribute to securing or transforming the ideological conditions necessary for the reproduction of a dominant set of social relations. Or rather, there is such telling: but it can be done by looking, not at texts, but at historical conjunctures.

NOTES

1. Althusser, *Lenin and Philosophy* (London: New Left Books, 1971), p. 150.

2. Ernesto Laclau, *Politics and Ideology in Marxist Theory* (London: New Left Books, 1977), chap. 4.

3. See M. M. Bakhtin, *Problems of Dostoevsky's Poetics*, trans. R. W. Rotsel (Ann Arbor, Mich.: Ardis Publishers, 1973); and V. N. Voloshinov, *Marxism and the Philosophy of Language*, trans. Ladislav Matejka and I. R. Titunik (New York: Academic Press, 1973).

4. See especially his *Ecrits: A Selection* (London: Tavistock Press, 1977).

5. Mulhern was reviewing my *Criticism and Ideology* (London: New Left Books, 1976) in *New Left Review* 108 (March–April 1978).

6. See *Pour une théorie de la production littéraire* (Paris: Maspéro, 1966), trans. Geoffrey Wale as *A Theory of Literary Production* (London: Routledge and Kegan Paul, 1978).

7. *Brecht on Theatre*, ed. John Willett (London: Methuen, 1964), p. 205.

8. Ibid., p. 182.

9. *Screen*, Spring 1974.

10. "Aesthetics and Politics," *New Left Review* 108 (March–April 1978).

11. Brecht, *Theatre*, ed. Willett, p. 112.

Catharine R. Stimpson

Ad/d Feminam: Women, Literature, and Society

Bacon's idols of the Tribe, the Cave, the Market-place, and the Theater stubbornly dominate our thinking about women, literature, and society. This error offends intellectual propriety and the demands of the issue itself. For contemporary forces are generating both a compelling need to reconstitute our sense of the female subject and a number of women writers, with a maturing tradition, who have begun that task. Among those forces are the development of a class of literate, educated women; the entry of women into modern public life and its labor force; and the formation of feminist ideologies that construe culture as potentially useful and liberating, not as necessarily futile and alienating. Consciously or unconsciously, many critics confuse what they are saying about women and literature, if they are saying anything at all, and what there is to be said.

To help reduce that disorder, I want to offer three questions, a set of co-ordinates, that people can use to place women and literature in a social context. Applying my method of interrogation, as I will briefly do, will not reveal a single definition of women's literature, a woman's book. Rather, women's literature will consist of those texts that my questions may most lucidly reveal. I will distinguish between *female* and *male*, terms that refer to biological classes, and *feminine* and *masculine*, complementary terms that refer to social constructs that have governed and interpreted those biological classes. We write about, not simply from, our bodies.[1] However, my queries may be put to texts that more arduously conflate nature and culture, sex and gender, the flesh and history.

Regulating my interrogation is the conviction that women writers

174

have had to overcome a devaluation of them as producers of public culture. Balancing this, as matter does antimatter, has been the pervasive insistence that women's primary work ought to be that of eros and of reproduction. Obviously, the degree of devaluation has varied from society to society, historical moment to historical moment. Some salons, for example, gathered women, culture, and politics in ways that render "devaluation" too superficial a description.[2] As obviously, certain women, such as George Eliot, have been exempted from those assessments that judge "woman" and "serious writer" an odd coupling. Yet, most women writers have confronted a trivialization of their textual ambitions, whether they attribute this to divine displeasure, constricting social structures, or their own lacks, their own castrating wounds.

If a woman, then, has been literate, she has had to work to be educated. If she is educated, she has had to work to be published and criticized justly; if she has been published, she is more welcome in "empty fields" than in prestigious ones. She has been more able to "move into an area of endeavor when it is not valued. As it becomes more esteemed, the field is increasingly populated by men."[3] If she wishes to extend respected genres, she experiences the skeptical pressure of a patriarchal tradition.[4] She is left with the more despised forms: letters, diaries, children's stories, modern Gothics, or "feminine" texts. In the American tradition, the "feminine" signifies vapidity, gentility, conformity, sentimentality, mawkish morality; in early-twentieth-century France, a lyrical celebration of nature, the body, and tender flights from male brutality and from life's more tragic, existential tests.[5] Because public acts of the imagination are stifled, like fallopian pregnancies, many women writers anxiously inhabit a realm between the to-be-said and the not-said. They are like a Mary Wollstonecraft heroine: "She could not write any more; she wished herself far distant from all human society; a thick gloom spread itself over her mind: but did not make her forget the very beings she wished to fly from."[6]

The responses of women reflect strategies with which people integrate deprivation into their lives, rebel against it, or balance submission and subversion. Some writers, like the Brontë sisters, though not always as modestly as they did, deny a female identity. Pseudonyms have been a helpful device in achieving this. So have been the romantic and modern myths of the artist as a privileged figure who soars beyond the vulgarities of imposed labels and identities. The woman who calls upon these myths trades the recognition of her female birth for the chance to express herself publicly. So doing, she risks indifference to social issues about women. Other women acknowledge the significance of sex and gender, but speak for, to, and from the self. They explore the subjective consequences of female birth, but refuse to project themselves as citizens of a sexually bounded community that society has also helped to structure. They tempt lapses into a lyrical solipsism. Perhaps deceptively, *Aurora Leigh*, that epic about the woman artist, begins:

> Of writing many books there is no end;
> And I who have written much in prose and verse
> For others' uses, will write now for mine,—
> Will write my story for my better self, . . .[7]

To speak, as I have done, about the female writer as a figure separate from the male writer is the inevitable heritage of cultures that have made much of sexual differentiation. Indeed, the first of my questions accepts the necessity of confronting that legacy. It asks what notions of sexual differentiation, which must entail mutually dependent senses of the female and male, a text embodies. If a woman writer replicates an ideology that suspects women as public voices, contradictions will bloody her. She will be saying that she ought to be silent. The status of her text will resemble that of a bastard. Its mere existence challenges hegemonic notions of appropriate birth, but its acceptance of the label of bastard, if done without the ironic self-consciousness of Lear's Edmund, will simultaneously endorse those notions. If, however, a male writer replicates the same ideology, he will have the luxury of being congruent with tradition.

Implicit in every notion of sexual differentiation is a sense of time, an attitude about the permanence of difference. Historical processes may create and then amend differences, except for obvious anatomical ones. If so, difference belongs within the domain of the temporal and of specific societies.[8] Men and women may have dissimilar experiences and histories, which the content of literatures will reflect, even perpetuate. But such diachronic asymmetries and inequalities may dissolve, even disappear. A writer—from a Charlotte Brontë to a Carolyn Keene, from a John Stuart Mill to a Frank O'Hara—may help that process along.

However, others believe that supernatural forces, or psychic and somatic structures, or the overwhelming evolutionary needs of the species, are responsible for sexual differences. They belong, then, within and beyond the domain of the temporal and of specific societies. Female and male subjects will have states of being that persist across time and space. The content and the forms of literature, perhaps even of language itself, will reflect this. Among the markers that distinguish interpretations of women and literature, and the presentation of women in literature, from the interpretations of class and literature, and the presentation of class in literature, is the frequency of the assumption that differences of sex and gender are immutable, asocial, atemporal—a human embodiment of natural law. Ironically, both sexual conservatives and certain radical cultural feminists share an attraction to such assumptions. The former tends to prize the male; the latter certainly celebrates the female, but both seek synchronic securities in dimorphism.

A powerful conceit magically lifts the artist from society and stabilizes the assignment of creativity to an ahistorical realm. Using metaphors from nature, it conflates pen and penis, writing and maleness. Modern technology (the typewriter, electronic voice-processing machines) is pushing the pen, and the pencil, toward obsolescence. As they wither away, the easy jump in English from pen to penis will seem less and less a sanctifying metaphor, more and more a curiosity. Nevertheless, it persists, to compel some women to find substitutes, signs of female creativity that draw on female biology, on blood, ova, genitalia. Such efforts repeat the pattern of using organic language of the body to transform a social role into a transcendent calling.

The belief in difference influences the perception of the audience of a text, the concern of the second of my critical questions. Because a sociology of reading is imperfect; because "uses and gratification" research is incomplete; and because reading, particularly about a subject like sexuality that is both a code and encoded, is indeterminate, no one can fully analyze the patterns of consumption a text might stimulate. This holds true for individuals and groups. Nor, because of the inadequacies of self-consciousness, can any writer say precisely for whom a text came into being. Despite these theoretical and practical strictures, we can tell, roughly, if a text is written for women, and for what kind of women. It suggests if it is meant to be instructive, a command to ego and superego, an exortation of obedience to the reality principle; if it is meant to be gratifying, an appeal to eros and thanatos, a suggestion of cultivation of the pleasure principle; or if, like *Clarissa*, a text claims to be both. To ask about the woman reader ascribes to her the dignity of being a subject and involves the book in an active social relationship, in which the primary bond is that of consciousness.

My third question inquires more specifically about the sense of community a writer establishes with other women, the projection of a shared society or of shared experiences. The male writer, to do so, must deal with a difference rooted in the body.[9] He may translate and inflate a lack of biological identity with the female into the verbal space between subject and object that characterizes scientific discourse; didactic tales; narratives of Oedipal disenchant-

ment; romances of domineering or unrequited love; phenomeno-
logical analyses of the Other; or pornography. Writing to or of
women, he implicitly or explicitly accepts socially maintained
distinctions between feminine and masculine behavior. Other male
writers—a Genet—can appropriate the feminine as a stance for the
male through which to express receptive subordination before God
or a godlike phallus. Self-consciously sacrificial, they speak from
the feminine. Because chosen, this placing of the self is paradoxically confident and assertive. It lacks the nervousness of male
artists in modern capitalist societies that denigrate them as woman-
ish or infantile.[10] Still other male writers, like a Henry James,
write about women, particularly lovely victims. Self-consciously
empathetic, they speak of and for the feminine.

Each of these strategies is limited, if only because of the obvious
anatomical differences I mentioned, perhaps too cursorily, before.
A male writer may speak of, for, to, and from the feminine. He
cannot speak, except fictively, of, for, to, *and* from the female.
This inability hardly has the dignity of a tragic fact, but it does
have the grittiness of simple fact. The woman writer—because she
can speak of, for, to, and from the female; of, for, to, and from
the feminine—has a wider choice of genres in writing about women
in general. She also becomes more existentially plausible if she
chooses to establish any sort of community among them. If she
does so, she can, as Aurora Leigh sometimes does, accept the
gravities of leadership. She serves as vanguard, witness, and chorus.
She constitutes her social responsibility as the naming of a reality
that has been pushed to the edge of invisibility; as the reclaiming
of names that have been obliterated. As Virginia Woolf wrote
bitterly in 1929, "I would venture to guess that Anon, who wrote
so many poems without signing them, was often a woman."[11]

But this posture can become arrogant. A writer can become
cannibalistic, devouring her collective subject. Without much
theoretical fanfare, women writers have devised the strategy of the
synecdochical voice to avoid such difficulties. In "Prologue," for

example, Anne Bradstreet exemplifies this tactful performance. She pictures herself as a woman writer; to forestall charges of preposterous presumption, she cleverly manipulates an ironic self-deprecation. She refers to "my mean pen," to "my obscure lines." She says she is "obnoxious to each carping tongue/Who says my hand a needle better fits." Then, shifting from the first-person singular to the third-person plural, from a private to a collective identity, she generalizes about the sex of which she is a part. "Men can do best," she moralizes, acidly aflutter, "and women know it well."[12] The synecdochical voice is hardly the property of women writing about women. "I, too, dislike it . . ." is a statement of personal and group taste. However, an Anne Bradstreet is special because she negotiates both the hazard of speaking for herself, a violation of social authority, and that of speaking for other women, a reinforcement of the enforced practice of having others speak for them. Her text itself displays the process of those negotiations.

If the woman writer is conscious of Western cultural tradition, she must ask if she wishes to include the Muse—that figure of memory, speech, inspiration, and reward—in a community of women. Women writers—Sappho, Anne Bradstreet—have been called the Tenth Muse. The apposition controls as it flatters. For the Muses, though charming personifications of creativity, are not themselves strenuously creative. If a woman is to be actively aesthetic and intellectual, she may renounce the myth of the Muse and other acculturating myths. If such a stripping away of tradition is impossible, she can practice an imaginative form of sexual inversion and declare the Muse male. She then may inadvertently reincarnate the inhibitions of patriarchal tradition in the Muse himself. If she retains a female Muse, she may shift the sexual metaphor for writing from heterosexuality to homosexuality and drape her text in wisps of social deviancy.

Let us think, then, as if the classes in a taxonomy of a women's literature are attitudes toward sexual differentiation; projections and recognitions of a female audience; and some sense of community or society between author and audience. Women's literature will organize a multiplicity of conventions, forms, and genres. It will include the mass media. Popular novels, women's magazines, and the women's pages of newspapers have provoked critical contempt and the professional jealousy that Hawthorne expressed and James parodied.[13] However, they have given women a profession and a living. Because they depend on sales for survival, they have to be alert to female audiences. Because of this, they provide sensitive, shifting registers of an audience's tastes and beliefs, needs and aspirations, fears and desires. If texts from the mass media are less visionary, imaginative, and strange than those from "literature," they may be more cunning guides to social realities.

I will first apply my questions, then, to a recent copy of the *Ladies Home Journal*. A purpose of the professional men and women who manage, edit, and write for the *Journal* is to help their readers manage their own world in ways profitable to the *Journal*. Producers and consumers apparently both act on the assumption that men and women inhabit the same society, but in ways so dissimilar that each sex needs its own pragmatic counsel. The *Journal* has some ideas about the cause of sexual differentiation. A feminist editor, associating herself with her readers through their common training in appropriate gender roles, blames socialization. "While boys and men were taught to ask themselves, 'Who am I and what do I want to be when I grow up,' girls and women—no matter what our unique talents—were taught that it was enough to grow up to be women, wives, and mothers."[14] However, to explore the origins of sexual differentiation fully demands logical rigor, anthropological zeal, biological awareness, and historical knowledge. Such scholarship might alienate readers. To end the unfairness of institutionalized differentiation demands political commitment—if only to a modestly feminist ideology. Such a program might divide readers whom domestic interests unite.

Shrewdly, the *Journal* avoids too much attention to the beginnings and to the end of differentiation. It concentrates on the energetic administration of its effects.

The title, *Ladies Home Journal*, both evokes a reassuring moral and social status for its readers and reminds them of their proper sphere. The same melding of idealization and bluntness appears in advertisements. They emblazon pictures of competently sleek, physically comfortable, wholesomely healthy women—generally between twenty and forty years of age, almost always white. The ads also iconographically gloss the domestic contents of a reader's world: animals; husbands and father; appliance repairmen; an enormous number of things: items of clothing, toys, food, furniture. They apparently make the home at once attractive and inevitable. So do features. A male writer muses about "What Marriage Means to Men." Sitting next to his wife on a sofa, a setting that evokes intimacy and evades naked passion, he is "stunned by how much [he loves] her." A female model on the cover wears an exotic headdress that is at once alluring helmet and erotic wimple. A line of print counsels, "Crochet this stunning outfit from our do-ahead Christmas boutique."

However, the contemporary *Journal* reader/buyer inhabits a world in which the meaning of sexuality and the demands of gender are irrevocably changing. The *Journal* cannot underwrite any of several competing ideologies of women's nature too rigidly. As a result, a male doctor anoints divorce as an appropriate solution to a bad marriage. A woman professional and her male collaborator discuss incest, a devastating critique of family life. A special section, "The Complete Working Women's Guide," helps women enter the public labor force. Famous working women, such as movie stars or the *Journal*'s editor herself, stress the anxieties of success, the joys of family tradition, but they also remind their audience that they have conquered public domains. For women in the paid labor force, the *Journal* erratically subscribes to a sliding scale of sexual differentiation: more of it at home or between lovers than at work, where equality of opportunity has become a social goal.

The *Journal* publishes its contradictions without comment, without apparent shame.[15] So doing, it becomes a collage of possibilities. If readers are to mediate the contradictions and choose among the possibilities, they must primarily do it themselves. Individual effort, the autodynamic will, not politics, must resolve conflict, strain, and the clash of heterogenous roles. Such sources of authority as magazines provide enlightened guidance— for self-reliant deeds. Yet, the *Journal* reader must exercise only a moderate self-reliance. She must eschew both solitude and excessive solicitations of subjectivity. She must continue to serve others and an ego ideal. The *Journal* is also chary about publishing flagrantly emotional material, though its poetry and fiction can be sentimental. It is wary of too much Gothic or romantic fantasy, though it dreams of moral and social mobility. Brisk, jauntily productive readers are to consume the *Journal* and to honor the home without excluding the world beyond the home; to improve family and society without disrupting them; to applaud the female and the feminine without obvious masochism. From time to time, the *Journal* will soothe and console them as they do so, but a more primary pact is to be reliable.

That assurance of trustworthiness links the *Journal* to more seriously regarded mimetic texts that promise to describe women's lives as honestly as possible. If the *Journal* helps women to do things, these texts help readers to see situations. At one extreme, that of Colette, they may be lyrical. At the other extreme, that of Mary McCarthy, they may be ironic. Between them is Doris Lessing's *The Golden Notebook*. Firm, compassionate, judgmental, it is a noncommercial commodity that asks to be read for the enhancement of consciousness and conscience. Lessing also tests herself against an ideal text: "a book powered with an intellectual or moral passion strong enough to create order, to create a new way of looking at life."[16]

The Golden Notebook names aspects of sexual discrimination that make women second-class citizens. The modern woman feels "emotions of aggression, hostility, resentment." In theory, a woman writer ought to express them; if she can, she will speak for her contemporaries as well as for herself. Lessing believes in a literary adaptation of theories of an organic relationship between microcosm and macrocosm. However, the inferiority of women means that their thoughts and perceptions will be disregarded. Aware of this, the woman writer, an Anna Wulf, fears using language publicly. Though the author of one novel, she now "stammers," an act that lacks the mystery of silence and the power of confident speech.

Yet, in *The Golden Notebook*, sexual discrimination fails to explain all of sexual differentiation. Women bear children; men do not. Women have intuitive, emotional, vaginal orgasms; men do not. Sexuality binds women with entangling cords of familial and personal dependency men escape. Reformers may dismantle inequities, but they cannot abolish all difference. An Anna may eventually write a second novel, but both Anna and Saul will retain some elements of self that the other can perceive in intersubjective transactions but never fully experience subjectively.

Curiously, in 1971, nine years after its publication, Lessing repudiated *The Golden Notebook* as a woman's text. Declaring that people had misread it, she said its central concern was not sex and gender, but fragmentation and reintegration. She admitted that she was chary about issuing such a public denial, because she did not wish to reject women. With her usual dogged candor, she said:

> . . . nobody so much as noticed this central theme, because the book was instantly belittled, by friendly reviewers as well as by hostile ones, as being about the sex war, or was claimed by women as a useful weapon in the sex war.
>
> I have been in a false position ever since, for the last thing I have wanted to do was to refuse to support women.

(p. viii)

Yet, Lessing did not stop there and leave a double text: the public *Golden Notebook* and her private interpretation. She consistently endorses a morality of generosity. For example, in *The Golden Notebook*, Saul and Anna give each other the first sentence of the book each will write. Lessing extends to her readers the enabling charity Saul and Anna have shown toward each other. She alters her charge of misreading to the more benign one of multiple re-readings. If women wish to use the novel as a document in the sex war, they may. If an "old Red" wishes to use it as a political memoir, he may. Lessing gives up a community organized on the principle of sex or a shared interpretation of sex and gender to accept one based on the values of perceptiveness, thought, and discussion.

The Virginia Woolf of *A Room of One's Own* speaks for women, of women, to women far more unequivocally. She refuses to separate herself from them as Anna and Molly part from each other at the end of the *Free Women* portions of *The Golden Notebook*. The actual audience for the first version of her text were women at Cambridge University. Her implied audience consists of persons interested in women and fiction. Woolf and both audiences are meant to share an affection that history has repressed; a "common life" history has ignored; and a hierarchal structure of sexual differentiation that history has enforced. Following John Stuart Mill, preceding Simone de Beauvoir, Woolf explores men's apparent psychic need to dominate women. Longing for self-esteem, they construct women as the Other, "by nature" inferior. "Women," she notes sardonically, "have served all these centuries as looking-glasses possessing the magic and delicious power of reflecting the figure of man at twice its natural size."[17] Dramatizing her sexual protest, Woolf offers the parable of Judith, Shakespeare's sister, an extraordinary fiction of grievance, a compressed historical novel about the tension between social structures and the aspiring woman artist. She pictures as well the forms the language of the frustrated woman writer might take: witchcraft, the laments of the mad, folk songs, lullabies.

However, Woolf's community of women shares a tradition of resistance and triumph as well as one of suffering. The members have appropriated whatever cultural and economic opportunities their days have given to them. Having claimed their right to public language, they now need privacy, economic independence, and a self-determined isolation in order to exercise it. An exemplary synecdochical voice, Woolf urges women further into language, into the imagining of the possibility that this exploration will end in the articulation of women's forms, perhaps even of a women's syntax, "a women's sentence."

Even as *A Room of One's Own* exhorts women to adventure—as recorders, architects, and prophets—into a woman's world, it contains a second, strangely inconsistent message as well. For Woolf also advocates androgyny as an ahistorical description of the artist's state of mind. Her comments about androgyny are tentative, perhaps playful. It is unclear whether she believes that artists are neurologically wired as both "male" and "female" or if she believes artists perceive and balance contradictions, a feat of consciousness that androgyny metaphorically represents. Nor are the motives for her flight from a society of women into a theory of androgyny wholly deciphered. Elaine Showalter, Adrienne Rich, and others have argued persuasively that if Woolf were to have investigated a woman's world too deeply, be it that of the devalued past or of the to-be-transvalued future, she would have been forced to encounter feelings of anger that would prove too threatening. In addition, I believe, such investigations might have pulled her too close to other difficult regions: to public discussions of female homosexuality, which, in Woolf's fiction, rarely goes beyond a kiss; to memories of grief and of the loss of women, her mother, her half-sister; and to sustained thought about an intimate unit that might replace marriage and the family. Significantly, in *To the Lighthouse*, published only two years before *A Room of One's Own*, a married couple with children, Mr. and Mrs. Ramsay, form an androgynous whole.

Whatever her reasons, Woolf, who writes so eloquently about male social control of women and the woman artist, who claims the female subject as the great subject for that woman artist, also asks that she integrate the male for the sake of that art. Lily Briscoe cannot finish her painting until she incorporates Mr. Ramsay into her vision. As Woolf instructs other women artists in *A Room of One's Own*, the "I," the controlling voice, sinuously advances, and then withdraws. It alternates between assertion and qualification.

More than thirty years after *A Room of One's Own*, Adrienne Rich's poems, in *Diving into the Wreck*, explicitly continue its feminist analysis of sexual differentiation as a heirarchy that men dominate.[18] Women must succor them psychically, protect them from the "abyss," keep their houses, bear their children, and provide the substance of their dreams. For men to be free, women must be constrained. For men to "see," women must be blinded. Like Woolf, Rich offers women her text as a weapon in the struggle for consciousness, in their review of patriarchal culture that serves as a life-saving prelude to abandoning it. Words "are purposes./The words are maps." Like Woolf, Rich also plays with the androgyne as a redeemed, redemptive figure. In "The Stranger," a speaker serves as a synecdochical voice for both sexes. The woman writer who accurately weighs sexual iniquities becomes capable of transfiguring differentiation. The androgyne becomes "the living mind you fail to describe/in your dead language."

However, *Diving into the Wreck* reverses Woolf's flight from a woman's world into the myth of androgyny. A text from a period of transition in which definitions of sex and gender are increasingly unstable, it moves closer and closer toward a woman's world. The androgyne is less an endgame than a midpoint between an attempt to live with men and the need to be with women. There principles of differentiation are not sex and power; but experience, politics, and personality. One major poem suggests,

"I would have loved to live in a world/of women and men gaily/in collusion with green leaves," but men have rendered nature barren, civilization a technological monstrosity, paternity possessive, and the male principle suspect. The first poem in *Diving into the Wreck* is "Trying to Talk with a Man," but the next is "When We Dead Awaken," spoken to a "fellow-creature," a "sister." Rich borrows from Ibsen, neither to mimic nor to serve, but to show how some cultural remnants may serve women. The growing community of women has several modes of discourse available: dialogue, song, prophecy, open protest. Unlike Woolf, Rich, through precept and percept, encourages her readers to express their rage against male outrages. "Fire" signifies the anger that will purge anger's cause. Rich's text is to prove as contagious as flame for a reader who will consume language to escape from the present.

Like Rich, Hélène Cixous allies herself with a public women's movement, for Cixous *écriture féminine*, the extraordinary attempt to discover what community of discourse women, freely writing "as women," might build.[19] "The Laugh of the Medusa" expands the revisionary demands of *Diving into the Wreck* into deconstructive explosions. Her text pulsates with the rhetoric of rebellion, insurgency, militancy, rupture, demolition. She then stretches beyond anger at the male to celebrate the female. Feminizing the ideology of the avant-garde, she proclaims the joyous primacy of a future in which women, singly and collectively, will discover, through writing, their previously repressed bodies; psyches; memories. *Diving into the Wreck* tells of women as mothers. The female world embraces children through bearing them, through raising them, and through a shared status as patriarchal possessions. "The Laugh of the Medusa" also promises that language will reveal the female's own creative response to the presence of the primordial, the maternal.

Obviously, "The Laugh of the Medusa" exuberantly proclaims the ahistorical strength of sexual differentiation and of feminine

and masculine writing. "In the beginning are our differences."
The historical repression of the female has simply blurred our
vision of differentiation and blocked feminine writing. After
women have flown from men; after they have reveled in their love
for each other; after they have seized language; an authentic,
dynamnic bisexuality will be available to us. Moreover, Cixous
asserts, the release of the female will be of such bounty, such
fluent plentitude, that it will spontaneously revolutionize all
structures and movements. "The Laugh of the Medusa" lacks the
detail of the Utopian narratives of Ursula LeGuin or Marge Piercy,
but it states that the praxis of the boldly linguistic woman will
mutate politics: "Because the 'economy' of her drives is prodi-
gious, she cannot fail, in seizing the occasion to speak, to transform directly and indirectly *all* systems of exchange based on
masculine thrift. Her libido will produce far more radical effects
of political and social change than some might like to think"
(p. 882).

Casually Cixous assumes that men might read her lyrical, lin-
guistically complex polemic. A footnote warns with some indifference that men, too, will have everything to write about
themselves if phallogocentric laws are deregulated. As women
transform what men have said about them, men must transform
what they have said about themselves. However, her primary
audience is female. Passionately, charismatically Cixous is writing
from herself to other women to bring them to self-revelatory
writing. She urges them to inscribe themselves. She is a singular
participant, witness, and synecdochical voice in the process of
recognizing the vibrant grammar of self and differentiation. Like
those of Wittig, Cixous's own text is a kinetic sculpture. Its
rhythms replicate the flight from repression toward the expression
of an atemporal female that will live itself out in history. As Cixous
constitutes herself through her language, that language summons
other women to follow her, without being followers. Cixous
and her reader/writers will form a community that neither psycho-

analysis, nor literature, nor sociology, nor philosophy has yet discerned.

Cultural history demonstrates that the genderized ways in which men and women have construed themselves as writers has been a social product. History in general shows that the human body has natural elements, but that "woman" has been a socially produced concept, role, metaphor, fantasy, and set of statistics as well. I have suggested a critical method that assumes the validity of such instruction. Yet, texts that represent "women's literature" often deny the primacy of social forces. Some rebel magnificently against their society, anathematizing it as destructive to women. Others submit that society alone cannot explain the sexual differentiation that has required a separate category of women's literature. Too often, such a conviction sustains powerful, discriminatory ideologies, but it may also valorize the female as women attempt in clear and coded ways to overthrow their place.

To mediate among hypotheses about the origins and perpetuation of differentiation, of the feminine and the masculine, may not lie in the province of literary criticism. That task may be claimed by the biological and neurological sciences, history, anthropology, or even, as some believe, by cosmology. However, literary criticism, when ambitious, has proposed that the study of texts and languages will reveal the structure of human nature and the meaning of our social patterns. If that is true, a fresh, scrupulous attention to "women's literature" will tell us if our dimorphic bodies have pertinently, permanently generated our culture, or if, as I believe, our vast social capacities have done so, too often unscrupulously assigning a permanent significance to human physical forms.

NOTES

A version of this essay was given at Princeton University in November 1978 at a seminar sponsored by the Council of the Humanities.

1. A coherent defense of such a position is Joan Kelly-Gadol, "The Social Relation of the Sexes: Methodological Implications of Women's History," *Signs: Journal of Women in Culture and Society* 1, no. 4 (Summer 1976): 809–23. A cogent assessment of the positions from which the permanence of "feminine" and "masculine" traits have been argued is Anne Dickason, "The Feminine As a Universal," in *Feminism and Philosophy*, ed. Mary Vetterling-Braggin, Frederick A. Elliston, and Jane English (Totowa, N.J.: Littlefield, Adams, 1977), pp. 79–100. Texts that give historical solidity to some of my concerns include Alison Adburgham, *Women in Print* (London: George Allen and Unwin, 1972); Germaine Brée, *Women Writers in France* (New Brunswick, N.J.: Rutgers University Press, 1973); Ellen Moers, *Literary Women: The Great Writers* (Garden City, N.Y.: Doubleday, 1976); Ann Douglas, *The Feminization of American Culture* (New York: Alfred A. Knopf, 1977); Elaine Showalter, *A Literature of Their Own* (Princeton, N.J.: Princeton University Press, 1977).

2. Carolyn C. Lougee, in *Le Paradis des Femmes: Women, Salons, and Social Stratification in Seventeenth-Century France* (Princeton, N.J.: Princeton University Press, 1976), persuasively points out relationships among women as writers; women as cultural arbiters; the argument about the nature of women; and a revision of the French social structure.

3. Gaye Tuchman and Nina Fortin, Department of Sociology, Graduate School and University Center, City University of New York, "Men, Women and the Novel: Submissions to Macmillan and Company, 1866–1887," p. 4. Tuchman and Fortin have analyzed the submissions of men and women to the English publishers. They are careful not to conclude too much from their material, but their findings have parallels elsewhere.

4. A brilliant interpretation of that tradition is Sandra M. Gilbert, "Patriarchal Poetry and Women Readers: Reflections on Milton's Bogey," *PMLA* 93, no. 3 (May 1978): 368–82. I have also discussed this problem in "Sex, Gender, and American Culture," in *Women and Men: Changing Roles,* ed. Libby A. Cater, Anne Firor Scott, Wendy Martyna (New York: Aspen Institute for Humanistic Studies, 1976), pp. 201–44. Praeger reprinted the book in 1977.

5. My thanks to Robert D. Cottrell for his succinct labeling of that tradition in "Colette's Literary Reputation in the Twenties," a paper read at the Rutgers Conference on "Women, the Arts, and the 1920s in Paris and New York," April 1978.

6. *Mary, A Fiction*, ed. Gary Kelly (London: Oxford University Press, 1976), p. 52.

7. *Aurora Leigh and Other Poems*, intro. by Cora Kaplan (London: The Women's Press, 1978), p. 38. As they have done for subversive and avant-garde movements in general, small presses now transmit much of the contemporary women's writing and reprint valuable, out-of-print books.

8. For a recent defense of women's literature as historical, see Lillian S. Robinson, *Sex, Class, and Culture* (Bloomington: Indiana University Press, 1978). Robinson argues that the proper female text calls for both gender and class revolution.

9. In terms of comprehensiveness, no one has probably yet surpassed Simone de Beauvoir's analysis of men's writing about women in *The Second Sex*. Among the more valuable recent explorations are Froma I. Zeitlin, "The Dynamics of Misogyny: Myth and Mythmaking in the *Oresteia,*" *Arethusa II*, nos. 1–2 (Spring–Fall 1978): 149–84; John Goode, "Women and the Literary Text," *Rights and Wrongs of Women*, ed. Juliet Mitchell and Ann Oakley (Harmondsworth, Middlesex, England: Penguin, 1976), pp. 217–55; Annette Kolodny, *The Lay of the Land* (Chapel Hill: University of North Carolina Press, 1975).

10. Though good critics no longer repeat that slur, it persists informally and in some academic circles. See, for example, an article assessing children in day care centers that had male teachers: Bryan E. Robinson and Helen Canaday, "Sex-Role Behaviors and Personality Traits of Male Day Care Teachers," *Sex Roles: A Journal of Research* 4, no. 6 (December 1978): 857. Robinson and Canaday list under "masculine behaviors" such actions as "ride trikes" and "build blocks, build structures, set up farms and villages." Under "feminine behavior" they have, among other things, "paint," and "artwork, cutting, pasting, drawing with crayons or chalk."

11. *A Room of One's Own* (New York: Harcourt Brace and World, Harbinger Book, 1957), p. 51. To interpret the lack of an author's name as a sign of deprivation is, of course, historically conditioned, not a necessary act.

12. Anne Bradstreet, "The Prologue," in *The Works of Anne Bradstreet,* ed. Jeannine Hensley, foreword by Adrienne Rich (Cambridge: Belknap Press of Harvard University Press, 1967), pp. 15-16. Unfortunately, the question of a special female poetics is beyond the scope of this essay, but such a poetics, when codified, could easily be compatible with my suggestions about women's literature here.

13. In *The Bostonians*, Matthias Pardon tells Olive Chancellor that he suffers "from the competition of the 'lady-writers.' . . . They certainly made lovely correspondents . . . you had to be lively if you wanted to get there first. Of course, they were naturally more chatty; and that was the style of literature that seemed to take most today." (London: John Lehmann, 1952), p. 116.

14. *Ladies Home Journal* 95, no. 11 (November 1978): 197. All quotes are from this number. An excellent collection of essays about women and the mass media is Gaye Tuchman, Arlene Kaplan Daniels, and James Benét, *Hearth and Home: Images of Women in the Mass Media* (New York: Oxford University Press, 1978), esp. pp. 93-221. For a reanalysis of some of its points, see Tuchman's "Review Essay: Women's Depiction in the Mass Media," *Signs: Journal of Women in Culture and Society* 4, no. 3 (Spring 1979): 528-42.

15. Commentators on such contradictions are indebted to Roland Barthes, *Mythologies,* trans. Annette Lavers (New York: Hill and Wang, 1972), pp. 50-52.

16. Doris Lessing, *The Golden Notebook* (New York: Bantam Books, 1977), p. 61.

17. *A Room of One's Own,* p. 35. The mirror image is shifting in current women's writing, from the polished surface in which men reflect themselves or women their putative narcissism, to a speculum with which women explore their bodies and themselves.

18. *Diving into the Wreck: Poems, 1971-1972* (New York: W. W. Norton, 1973). In 1971, Rich gave the lecture "When We Dead Awaken: Writing as Re-Vision," a prose equivalent of many of these poems. Published in 1972, it was republished in *Adrienne Rich's Poetry*, selected and edited by Barbara Charlesworth Gelpi and Albert Gelpi (New York: W. W. Norton, Norton Critical Edition, 1975), pp. 90-98. Rich's work after *Diving into the Wreck* has explored a female world in far more radical ways.

19. I am using the Keith Cohen and Paula Cohen translation of "Le Rire de la Méduse," *Signs* 1, no. 4 (Summer 1976): 875-93. For Cixous's place in the movement, *écriture féminine*, see Elaine Marks, "Women and Literature in France," *Signs* 3, no. 4 (Summer 1978): 832-42; Carolyn Greenstein Burke, "Report from Paris: Women's Writing and the Women's Movement," *Signs* 3, no. 4 (Summer 1978): 843-55; and Georgiana Colvile, "The Future of Ecriture: Cixous," given at the meeting of Section 472, "Theories of 'Feminine Writing' among French Writers," Modern Language Association, 29 December 1978.